Admiral Tōgō: Nelson of the East

ALSO BY JONATHAN CLEMENTS
AND AVAILABLE FROM HAUS PUBLISHING

IN THE *MAKERS OF THE MODERN WORLD* SERIES
Wellington Koo: China
Prince Saionji: Japan

IN THE *LIFE & TIMES* SERIES
Marco Polo
Mao
Mannerheim: President, Soldier, Spy

Admiral Tōgō:
Nelson of the East

Jonathan Clements

Haus Publishing
London

First published in Great Britain in 2010 by
Haus Publishing Ltd
70 Cadogan Place
London SW1X 9AH
www.hauspublishing.com

A CIP catalogue record for this book is available from the British Library

ISBN 978-1-906598-62-4

Typeset in Warnock by MacGuru Ltd
Printed in the UK by
CPI Antony Rowe, Chippenham, Wiltshire
Beccles NR34 7TL

Contents

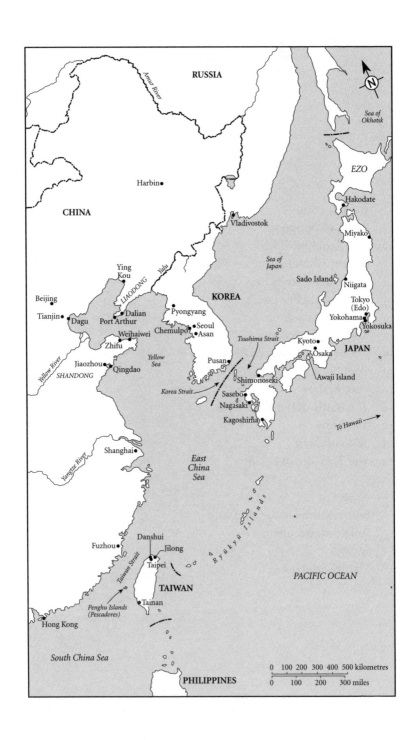

For Stephen Jones

Introduction

In 1996, during a British parliamentary debate on the selling of naval assets to a Japanese consortium, an MP alluded to the awful prospect that a road on former Admiralty property might be renamed Admiral Tōgō Avenue.[1] It was assumed by both speaker and audience that this would be a bad thing – a strange and inadvertent reversal of fortune for a naval commander who had once been so feted by the British establishment. Nobody pointed out the irony that the same Admiral Tōgō had been trained by the British, that he had held that rank for a 20-year period when Japan and Britain were allies, or that his presence was already stamped on British road maps, in the form of Mikasa Street in Barrow-in-Furness, named after his flagship. Once hailed as a world-class hero, Admiral Tōgō's reputation was sunk in the afterlife, consumed in the maelstrom of war crimes by others. Six decades after his death, he was simply assumed to have been Britain's enemy.

Tōgō Heihachirō's military career began in the last days of the samurai, when Japan's self-imposed exclusion was smashed apart by Western powers in search of trade concessions. He became a member of what would become the Japanese navy during the brief civil war that constituted the Meiji Restoration, in which he was a low-ranking samurai in just one of several factions, all claiming to be 'loyalists'. Luckily for Tōgō, his faction was victorious, and thereby able to impose its concept of loyalty on the rest of Japan – a loyalty that favoured the abolition of the Shōgunate, the restoration of power to the Emperor himself and the modernisation of Japan to meet the challenge from the West. It was as part of this modernisation that Tōgō was sent to learn from the British – he studied for seven years in England, to the extent that his later victories were often misleadingly claimed by British newspapers to be the accomplishments of a local hero, in imitation of a British icon.

It is considered condescending today to attach associations of one culture to that of another. Calling Tōgō the 'Nelson of the East' implies by some token that he is merely a mimic of a European predecessor, a pale shadow of a true hero. However, Tōgō's interest in Horatio Nelson was a much-recorded feature of his own time, and so I have retained the sobriquet that was so often heaped upon him in the early 20th century, including: 'Nelson of Japan' (*Western Mail*), 'Nelson of the East' (*Glasgow Herald*), 'Nelson of Japan' (*New York Truth*), 'Nelson of the East' (*Newcastle Chronicle*), 'Nelson of the East' (*South Mail*), 'best compared with Nelson' (*New York Tribune*), and 'modern naval officers should find it more helpful ... to study tactics of Tōgō than those of Nelson' (*New York Sun*). Indeed, the concept was soon embraced by the Japanese themselves, who never seemed to tire of styling themselves as the 'British of Asia', or comparing Tōgō to the victorious admiral of Trafalgar. Nelson was Tōgō's hero, a figure who inspired him during his student days in England, and whose Trafalgar tactics he adapted at Tsushima. In the *Song of Condolence* composed to mark Tōgō's funeral, the poet Doi Bansui defiantly reversed the cliché, instead referring to Nelson as the 'Tōgō of England'.

Tōgō was witness to the bloody birth-pangs of modern Japan, and one of the victors in the conflict that toppled the short-lived breakaway Republic of Ezo. While some of his countrymen, and even family-members, clung to the old order, Tōgō embraced the new, abandoning his clan allegiances to become one of the first officers of the national navy. He was, fortunately for him, posted abroad in the 1870s, and hence was not dragged into the counter-revolutionary Satsuma Rebellion, which saw the death of his brother and many of his old clan colleagues in a protest against the end of samurai traditions. He is remembered chiefly for his command of Japanese fleets as a high-ranking officer approaching retirement, but the groundwork for his achievements was undoubtedly laid during the long years of peace, when a younger Tōgō gained a reputation as an expert, or even something of a stickler, on the subject of maritime law. His grasp of naval etiquette and protocol was no idle occupation, but allowed him to maintain 'active' service even during long stretches bedridden with illness. It also kept the young captain from making hot-headed decisions during tense stand-offs that could have ruined a less careful sailor's career. Crucially, it gave him the incisive intellectual tools to deal with the thorniest problem he ever faced: the no-win situation in the Yellow Sea in 1894, when he was confronted by mutinous Chinese soldiers aboard the British-registered transport ship *Kowshing*.

Tōgō was closely associated with the transformation of Japanese sea power and its first relations with the Western world. As a teenager, he saw samurai standing waist-deep in water, angrily brandishing their swords at distant British warships. He witnessed the last gasp of old-school *abordage*, as sword-wielding marines braved a deck-mounted machine gun to leap aboard one of the first ironclads. After decades with barely a shot fired in naval combat, or overwhelming broadsides by European ships against hopelessly outclassed native boats, Tōgō was a participant in the first battle to pit modern naval technology against itself. The Battle of the Yalu set the German-built battleships of the Chinese navy against the British-built cruisers of Japan, a generation before the First World War. Most famously, Tōgō was the admiral who led the Japanese navy to a resounding, crushing victory against two fleets from the Tsar's Russia, the first time that an Asian nation had bested a modern European power.

In later life he was a reluctant celebrity, embraced by the Japanese as a man whose sense of duty placed him above party politics, and feted by the wider world as an invincible admiral. His fame seems odd today because he was far from charismatic. His nickname among his men, *Oni* ('The Devil'), may even have been a facetious, sarcastic sass – a terrifying name for a commander who was actually rather quiet and unassuming. Throughout his life his associates described him as quiet, dedicated and stubborn, but also as workmanlike. Tōgō's genius lay in training, in operational ideas, in strategic thinking. His great victory at Tsushima was arguably won not at sea in 1905, but in the drills and intelligence-gathering of the preceding two years. He is certainly not the kind of man who would become a celebrity today: he was not a creature of soundbites, nor did he cut a conspicuous figure in a crowd. And yet, Tōgō was the first Japanese subject to grace the cover of *Time* magazine, which described him in 1926 as 'short even for a Japanese, shy even for a hero'.[2]

Tōgō was at the forefront of the 20th-century rise of Japan, the poster boy for a generation of Japanese that expected to be taken seriously by the Great Powers, and whose hopes were dashed by the First World War and the Peace Conferences that followed. In old age Admiral Tōgō was an example to both his naval inheritors and to the future head of state – he was placed in personal charge of the education of the teenage Hirohito, the Shōwa Emperor. Seven years after Tōgō's death, his successors in the Japanese navy re-enacted his textbook assault on Port Arthur and shocked the world by making Pearl Harbor their target. But it seems strange, almost suspicious in the hindsight of history, that naval analysts in the USA did *not* expect the Japanese to try something akin to Tōgō's Port Arthur strategy in the infamous 1941 surprise attack.

The life of Tōgō Heihachirō is also, by necessity, an oriental tragedy: the story of the insistence of Western powers that the isolated, mysterious Empire of Japan join the international community, and the hellish uproar that ensued when that genie was let out of its bottle. Tōgō was one of the engines of Japan's dramatic rise and response, instrumental in the winning of new conquests on Taiwan, in China and Korea. He died in 1934, in a Japan drunk on militarism, determined to build its empire even further and doomed to lose it all within a decade in a cataclysmic fall.

The naval hero of Japan and the battleships under his command; the *Mikasa* his flagship, the *Shikishima*, *Fuji* and *Hatsuse* in an illustration of 1904

1

The Last Samurai

The domain of Satsuma was as far to the south as it was possible to go and still be in mainland Japan. It sat at the furthest south-western tip of Japan's southernmost main island of Kyūshū – beyond, there were only the scattered islands of the Ryūkyū chain; to the east, the open Pacific stretched thousands of miles, all the way to Mexico.

The ruling clan, House Shimazu, had its headquarters in the castle town of Kagoshima, a picturesque huddle of fishing villages partway up the long north-south inlet of Kagoshima Bay. In June, warm rain poured from the skies. Fierce summer sun sparkled off the waves, and the same semi-tropical light beat down on the verdant hills. Spring came to Kagoshima many weeks ahead of more northern parts of Japan. The temperature rarely fell below freezing in winter, and the grass grew all year round. Only half a mile to the east of Kagoshima sat the huge, smouldering bulk of Sakurajima, a triple-peaked volcanic island that almost entirely blocked the mid-point of the bay, and loomed ominously above the daily life of Satsuma samurai.

Satsuma and the nearby enclave of Chōshū were still paying the price for a civil war some centuries earlier, when their ruling lords had been slow to pledge allegiance to the first victorious Shōgun of House Tokugawa. The lord of Satsuma had to make regular pilgrimages to the Shōgun's headquarters in Edo, involving weeks of slow litter-borne transit along half the length of Japan, attended by platoons of soldiers. But for as long as he paid lip-service to his Shōgunal master, the Satsuma domain remained his – a prosperous coastal fief that had been in the hands of House Shimazu since the Middle Ages.

When House Shimazu had first gained control of the region in the 13th century, Kagoshima had been five townships, granted to a loyal retainer of a samurai master. Each was initially ruled by a son of the original lord, with their descendants taking their surnames from their new areas of responsibility. In particular, we might note the domains of *Saigō*, literally 'West Village', whose leading men would become famous in the time of the Meiji Restoration, and *Tōgō*, the East Village, whose scions were often depicted in local legend as driven and dedicated.

The founder of the Tōgō family was a retainer of House Shimazu from Japan's medieval civil war, rewarded with the administration of one of the local hamlets for his prowess in battle. But the Tōgō family seemed unable to stay out of trouble. The most famous pre-modern Tōgō was one Shigechika, a samurai frustrated by a three-generation feud with nearby rivals, who donned full armour and rode his horse off a cliff. Although such an act initially baffled his enemies, Shigechika had claimed he was dying in order to enlist supernatural aid. When his enemy perished soon after, it became a matter of local superstition that Shigechika had returned from the grave to win a supernatural victory. Such was the legendary, bloody-minded stubbornness of the Satsuma men, and the Tōgō family in particular.

Politically and geographically on the edge, the lords of Satsuma looked to illicit foreign trade. Even before the upheavals of the 19th century, the men of Satsuma belonged to the sea. They maintained ties with the Ryūkyū Islands, allowing for a discreet two-way trade in Chinese and Japanese goods and information. It was at a trading post on Tanegashima, a small island just off the Satsuma coast, that the Japanese saw their first Europeans in 1543, and hence became the first to meet with Christianity and musketry. The matchlock arquebus, or *tanegashima* as it was then known after its place of 'discovery', thrust Satsuma men to the forefront of Japan's 16th-century civil war, briefly carrying them to the position of rulers of almost all Kyūshū, before they were beaten back to the south by the overwhelming forces of the warlord Toyotomi Hideyoshi.

Cowed but still proud, men of the Tōgō and Saigō families accompanied House Shimazu and thousands of other samurai in an ill-fated invasion of Korea in 1592, organised, at least in part, as an exercise to export idle warriors out of the newly pacified Japan. The invasion of Korea raged for a decade before the troops pulled out, but the Satsuma men did not leave empty-handed. Along with the spoils of war, they returned to their domain with a number of skilled Korean artisans. It was these prisoners of war, forced to revive their craft in their new home, who created the polychrome dishes still known around the world as Satsuma ware. Such exotic 'imports' gained greater value during the period of seclusion that followed, as a Japan fearful of foreign intrigues walled itself off from all but a handful of approved merchant contacts.

For two centuries the Japanese islands maintained a strict policy of exclusion. No foreigners were permitted to set foot in Japan, except for a few Chinese sailors and a tiny coterie of quarantined 'Dutchmen' in Nagasaki harbour. The Shōgun, the supreme general who ruled Japan in the Emperor's name, had been most specific about the dangers presented by foreign contacts.

For the future, let none, so long as the Sun illuminates the world, presume to sail to Japan, not even in quality of ambassadors, and this declaration never to be revoked on pain of death.

Despite such a clear admonition, ships continued to arrive, with entreaties for trade, for coaling facilities, for simple repairs. On all reported occasions, the authorities shooed the foreigners away. In 1808, the British naval vessel *Phaeton* was refused entry to Nagasaki after a tense stand-off – several Japanese officials were obliged to commit suicide as an act of contrition, simply for letting matters go so far. In the same year, the Shōgun felt obliged to dispatch an expeditionary force to the lawless island of Ezo in the north, to thwart Russian attempts to build a base. In 1837, the American vessel *Morrison* arrived off the Satsuma headquarters, Kagoshima, ostensibly to return some Japanese sailors who had been shipwrecked in America. Its captain had already been turned away from the Shōgun's city, but hoped to conclude a separate deal with the local samurai of the Shimazu clan. Despite the temptations he offered, the Shimazu still feared the Shōgun's wrath, and after some tense negotiations, opened fire on the *Morrison* with land-based artillery.

The incident spoke volumes about the troubles that were to come. The cannonballs of the Shimazu clan fell short of the *Morrison*, plunging harmlessly into the waters of Kagoshima Bay. The captain of the *Morrison* took the hint, raised anchor, and sailed lazily back out to sea, entirely untroubled by the coastal defences.

Tōgō Heihachirō's father Kichizaemon had been one of the witnesses of the *Morrison*'s dawn departure. He was thirty-two at the time, and a minor officer in the military hierarchy of House Shimazu. Kichizaemon's wife, Masuko, was also the child of a samurai family. She bore her husband five boys and a girl, although the girl and the second son died in infancy. Her fourth son, born in 1848 and called first Nakagoro and then Heihachirō, would make the Tōgō family famous all over the world.[1] As a result, Masuko was destined to become one of the last of the legendary samurai wives, with several memorable episodes of stoicism or martial intractability entering 20th-century Japanese folklore as the recollections of her most famous son. According to later stories of Tōgō's youth, Masuko insisted on strict rules of propriety in her house, even to the extent of refusing to pass her sleeping sons except by the foot of their futons, it being considered ill-mannered to pass at the head.

However, such stern parenting does not seem to have been much help. Surviving stories of Tōgō's childhood paint him as a boisterous, unpleasant child, constantly vying with his brothers. Once, up to no good in the family stables, he teased one of his father's horses and the beast responded by biting him on the top of the head. The young Tōgō retaliated by striking the horse with a stick, but was found out later in the day when Masuko noticed the wound on her son's head. Confessing immediately, Tōgō was punished for his misbehaviour, only to return to the stables to beat the horse again for causing him such inconvenience.[2]

In 1856, the eight-year-old Tōgō took full advantage of a day off school for the Feast of Lanterns. Instead of joining in local festivities, he was found in a nearby stream, slashing at passing fish with a short sword. In the space of only a few minutes, Tōgō managed to slay over fifty fish, although the story seems to lack context. How would Tōgō find so many carp in such close concentration? Were they really just swimming past, or did the young Tōgō go on a killing spree in a nearby pond? If so, there is no record of any punishment he may have received. Nor is he known to have been chastised for another incident, in which he stole and ate an entire jar of candies from his mother's kitchen. Tōgō had asked his mother if he could have some of the sweets, and Masuko had replied with a parental deception: that all the candies were gone. Tōgō then reportedly waited until his mother was out of the house, climbed up to the cupboard and ate the contents of the entire jar. Berated by an angry Masuko on her return, Tōgō replied with an icy rationalisation, calculated to strike at his mother's sense of fair play: 'What wasn't there can't have disappeared.'[3]

At around the age of ten, Tōgō argued with his brother Sokuro about an unknown point of contention. Later in the day, his brother came out of an inn's communal bath parched with thirst and ordered Tōgō to bring him a drink. Quarrels or not, Tōgō was obliged by custom to obey his elders and he dutifully fetched some water. However, he added a liberal seasoning of raw pepper. Sokuro drank deeply from the cup, only realising his mistake as the hot pepper caused him to choke and splutter.

The errant Tōgō was dragged before the family and ordered to apologise. He refused to do so, immediately elevating fraternal high spirits to a matter of honour – he was not now teasing his brother, he was disobeying his father, a far more serious offence. With Tōgō refusing to budge, he was sentenced to ten days 'exile' from the family, confined under house arrest at the home of one of Kichizaemon's subordinates. He returned to the family when his sentence had passed, unrepentant.[4]

Tōgō's education followed traditional lines, even in progressive Satsuma. He would wake before dawn each day, leaving at sunrise for the house of Saigō Kichijirō, a local dignitary who taught the boys calligraphy. In this capacity, Tōgō also met Saigō's elder brother Takamori, who would become a famous military hero. Two hours later, the boys would return home for their ablutions, the 'tying-up of hair' before heading out for a second home school where they studied the Confucian Classics – long regarded as the only education worth having. In the afternoons, Tōgō would practise for an hour each day with a sword, and any energy that may have remained after such exhausting studies would be dissipated in afternoon play by the banks of the River Kotsuki. Among Tōgō's childhood playmates were at least two men who would go on to military careers, Kuroki Tamesada, who would become a general in the Russo-Japanese War, and Ijichi Hiroichi, who would be Tōgō's companion in his early naval days.

History and Japanese literature were added to Tōgō's curriculum at the age of eleven, and by 1860, when he was twelve by Western reckoning, he was officially recognised as an adult. The teenaged Tōgō was put to work for his clan as a minor clerk in one of the Shimazu clan offices. As with all samurai, his salary was paid in rice, half a bushel a month. But it would be inaccurate to describe Tōgō as a mere clerk – he was also a sometime farmer, tending the family's vegetable patch and studying gunnery.

The samurai expected trouble, and largely expected it from foreigners. While there were still ample quarrels among the various noble houses, the Japanese were united in their mistrust of the Europeans and Americans and their constant agitations for trade. Even progressive Japanese, keen to learn from the new arrivals, often couched their rhetoric in terms of knowing one's enemy. The Japanese may have been isolated, but they were well aware of the behaviour of the Westerners in China, where they had ignored Imperial edicts, peddled drugs to the populace, and carved enclaves for themselves out of Chinese territory. The Westerners constantly spoke of 'trade' as if buying and selling might solve all the world's ills. The Japanese, whose social system placed merchants at the very bottom of the hierarchy, below bold warriors and honest farmers, preferred to keep foreign trade corralled into specially delineated ghettos, and opened new ports to foreigners only with great reluctance.

The other favourite subject of the foreigners was religion, which the Europeans and Americans were keen to force upon the Japanese. Christianity had been one of the most unwelcome foreign imports in the samurai era and its practice was still an offence punishable by death. This would only add to the unease of the government in years to come, as the foreign visitors began to insist on freedom to worship and, eventually, to proselytise.

The peculiar rules of Japanese diplomacy made it difficult to mount a concerted defence. It was, supposedly, the Shōgun's job to keep out foreigners. With every indignity or incursion, the Shōgun's competence was called into question. The Emperor would order him to deal with the foreign problem, and he would promise to do so. Meanwhile, the Shōgun's rivals would fume that they could do a better job themselves, and in some cases took matters into their own hands.

The southern domains of Satsuma and Chōshū were particularly notorious. Chōshū even commenced firing upon foreign shipping in the Straits of Shimonoseki, leading to the arrival of a punitive multinational task force. Not to be outdone, Satsuma soon manufactured an incident of its own in 1862. The catalyst was outrageously disproportionate to the response, amounting to a scuffle on the road in the small village of Namamugi, near Yokohama. Shimazu Hisamitsu, father and regent to the young ruler of House Shimazu, had completed his most recent period of mandatory attendance in the capital, and was returning to Satsuma. As was usual for samurai potentates, he travelled in a long caravan of horsemen, retainers and palanquins. Outriders galloped ahead announcing the approach of a feudal lord, ordering all in the Satsuma lord's path to avert their eyes, bow low to the ground and above all, to stand aside.

At Namamugi, the Satsuma group ran into a small party of mounted foreigners, who refused to give way. Charles Lennox Richardson, a British merchant with a bullish reputation, was accompanied by his associates Mr Marshal and Mr Clarke, and by a lady, Miss Borodaille. Reputedly proclaiming, 'I know how to deal with these people', Richardson deliberately rode into the path of the Shimazu lord, intent on forcing his way through.

Neither side can be relied upon for an unbiased account. The British survivors would claim that they had simply refused to dismount – which would have been rude, but was still legal under the extraterritorial agreements that allowed British subjects to disregard Japanese law. The samurai saw things differently, and interpreted their behaviour as a direct challenge. Even if Richardson had merely crossed in front of the baggage train, that would have been tantamount to an assault in the eyes of jumpy henchmen – the Satsuma finances were being carried in the foremost boxes.

In the melee that followed, the Satsuma retainers drew their swords, killed Richardson and seriously wounded the other two men. Miss Borodaille escaped with 'only the loss of her hair', implying perhaps that a samurai had hacked off her braid before she fled. One of the foreigners pelted off back to the safety of the foreign concession in Yokohama, while the Satsuma party continued on its way.[5]

The samurai knew that there would be trouble. On the advice of Ōkubo Toshimichi, a young tax administrator in the group, they did not spend the night in nearby Kanagawa as originally planned, but ran for the more distant Hodogaya instead. It was a deliberate attempt to get away from the scene of the crime, but *whose* crime remained a matter of some dispute.

When the news reached Britain, the blame was immediately laid at the feet of the Japanese. An angry diplomatic communiqué ordered that the lord of Satsuma was to pay substantial damages in atonement for his regent's misdeeds. Furthermore, an even more substantial sum was to be handed over by the Shōgun himself. The incident was an awful loss of face for the Shōgun, who had been embarrassed enough by the requirement of dealing with foreigners at all, and was now obliged to pay damages on account of his inability to guarantee the safety of foreigners within his own domain.

Vice Admiral Augustus Kuper, commander of the British fleet in China, was ordered to send ships to Yokohama. Lieutenant Colonel Edward Neale arrived in August 1863 with seven ships and a total of 121 guns.[6] Shōgunate officials had little choice but to pay their share of the indemnity. But with the Satsuma samurai refusing to acknowledge their supposed crime, Neale was ordered to sail south to Kagoshima. This was, pleaded the Shōgun's envoys, a matter of great embarrassment to the Shōgun. The Shōgunate even offered to send one of its own ships to accompany the British to Shimazu, although the promised support never arrived. Nor did it seem likely, since in actively resisting 'barbarians', the samurai of Shimazu were effectively showing greater obedience to the Emperor than the more accommodating Shōgun.

The imposing British ships dropped anchor in the deep water between the harbour town of Kagoshima and the nearby island of Sakurajima on 11 August 1863. Tōgō, it is said, watched them as they arrived, his fists clenched in frustration. Satsuma envoys rowed out to the ships, where they were presented with a 24-hour ultimatum to pay up. Instead, as the weather turned stormy in poetic sympathy, the guns of the Satsuma forces fired a series of blank charges. It was a signal to the samurai of Kagoshima to prepare for battle.[7]

The 15-year-old Tōgō reported for duty, along with his father and two elder brothers. Kichizaemon was posted to the Yamaguchi Fort, which sat at the entrance to the bay. The boys served at the headquarters, Kagoshima Castle, set back from the coastal batteries. The boys donned their long coats and their broad *hakama* trousers, before placing lacquered helmets on their heads, each decorated with the family crest: five ivy leaves. At his waist, Tōgō wore the two swords of a samurai, but at his shoulder he carried a matchlock musket. The boys stood to attention outside their home, waiting for their mother Masuko's word. She waved them off with the laconic command of a samurai mother: 'Do not lose.'[8]

The Shimazu samurai were more prepared than the British had assumed. The small bay was guarded by a total of ten gun batteries, mainly armed with Dutch-made cannons, fifty-four siege guns, thirteen field guns and fifteen mortars. Twelve boats, each mounted with a single gun, were intended as suicide rams for use against the British. There were even three mines in the water, each attached to a long copper wire awaiting an electrical charge to detonate them.[9]

Out in the bay, the envoys continued to stall, claiming that the Lord Shimazu was away at distant Kirishima and there was nobody in port with sufficient authority. They asked if Neale could wait a while. Used to Japanese delaying tactics, Neale curtly told them that he was waiting twenty-four hours and no longer. His orders from

Vice Admiral Kuper were to deliver Richardson's murderers and a £25,000 indemnity, otherwise there would be dire consequences.

Meanwhile, the dozen suicide boats attempted to put men aboard the British vessels by posing as merchants and hawkers. They were given short shrift by the British, who refused to let them approach. A second espionage mission also foundered, when an envoy approached the flagship HMS *Euryalus* and asked to be permitted onboard with his entourage to deliver the Satsuma samurai's answer. This 'answer' was intended to be a suicidal attack, in which the members of the entourage would draw their swords, hack at the British sailors and either scuttle the *Euryalus* or die trying. This, too, was a damp squib, when Captain John Josling of the *Euryalus* sternly noted that it only took one man to deliver a message.

His bluff called, the commander of the samurai was allowed aboard the *Euryalus* by Vice Admiral Kuper and Lieutenant Colonel Neale, where he offered the entirely pointless suggestion that the British might consult instead with the Shōgun. Neale's ominous and angry reply was that negotiations were at an end, and the Japanese officer was sent back to the shore.[10]

The streets of Kagoshima were quiet. In many of the temples, the womenfolk had gathered to pray to Buddha for a supernatural intercession. The last time Japan had been threatened by foreign invasion, at the time of the Mongol Armada in the 13th century, the prayers of the Japanese had, they believed, successfully summoned not one, but two fierce storms to destroy their enemies. It was hoped that the prayers of the people of Kagoshima would rustle up a similar Divine Wind, or in Japanese, *Kamikaze*. Miraculously, the weather seemed to be obliging. The skies darkened noticeably after noon; and aboard the British ships, the barometers fell with alarming speed. As the waters of the bay grew choppier, the British changed their anchorage, moving closer to the volcano of Sakurajima in order to shield themselves from the worst of the oncoming storm.

The following morning, determined to fulfil his orders to the letter, Vice Admiral Kuper decided that three foreign-built steam vessels, merchant ships owned by House Shimazu, had a value roughly equivalent to the money that was owed for the Satsuma indemnity. Accordingly, he ordered a group of his men to sail closer to the shore and commandeer the ships. The drizzle rendered visibility so poor that many of the Japanese could not see what was going on. By the time riders had relayed the news to headquarters, the British had already seized the three vessels and moved them over to their own part of the harbour.

Finally, the samurai opened fire. As the Japanese guns began to boom, Kuper ordered his men to take out their aggression first on the three newly captured steamers. It was only as the column of flames and smoke began to twist up from the captured Satsuma ships that the British vessels returned fire. The Japanese were using old-fashioned cannon, employing the antiquated method of 'red-hot shot' – cannonballs pre-heated in a furnace. It was hoped that these would start fires within the enemy ships, but they also added extra dangers for their gunners. Mere contact with the hot shot would be enough to set off gunpowder, forcing the Satsuma gunners to wad their powder down with a divot of earth before gingerly dropping the glowing cannon ball from their tongs into the gun's mouth.

The British, however, had modern weapons, with shaped, tapered shells. The long line of British ships erupted in a series of bright flashes, milliseconds behind the roar of the explosions and dozens of simultaneous impacts on the shore. Amid the British bombardment, the samurai raced to reload their cannon and return fire. The fires that broke out in Kagoshima town were largely left to rage, while the samurai womenfolk scurried from battery to battery with pots of Satsuma-jiru, a pork and vegetable stew.

At one moment in the bombardment, Tōgō caught sight of his own mother, down by the shoreline, calmly combing her hair. A British shell landed perilously close to her, throwing up a massive cloud of dust and rock shards, but Masuko seemed undaunted. She rose to her feet, continuing to run her comb through her hair, staring out at the enemy ships in silent contemplation.[11]

Despite their military strength, the British were taken by surprise – it seems that they had genuinely been expecting the Satsuma resistance to collapse as soon as faced with the threat of force.

The ships chugged into action, brashly sailing along the coastline into the path of the Satsuma guns, firing their guns into the town of Kagoshima. The shells were devastating the wood and paper houses of the town, but the population had been largely evacuated in anticipation of hostilities. HMS *Havoc*, a small gunboat, directed her fire at a cluster of trading junks from the Ryūkyū Islands, sinking five ships. Other British vessels did not fare so well. HMS *Racehorse* briefly ran aground in the mud right in front of the fort, while the captain and first officer of the flagship, HMS *Euryalus*, were both decapitated by the same enemy cannonball. The *Racehorse* was soon retrieved, towed out of danger after a tense hour in which the grounded ship maintained a constant barrage of shellfire against the shore batteries, while her sister-ships attached cables and dragged her out of the shallows.

Time after time, the flotilla of British ships sailed along the Kagoshima shoreline, pounding the forts into rubble and lobbing explosive shells into the combustible streets of the town. The British only gave up when night fell once more and another storm threatened. With Kagoshima in flames, the British pulled back to their starting position beneath Sakurajima, and whiled away the night celebrating and listening to their bandsmen play a series of martial toe-tappers. The sound of their party drifted in snatches across the water, where it could occasionally be heard through the roar of the fires in Kagoshima.

Tōgō and his fellow warriors had been led to expect that the British bombardment was merely the opening phase of an attack. Samurai leaders were sure that once the Satsuma defences had been sufficiently softened up, the British would land in force. The samurai had assured each other that a land battle would be the great equaliser, and that the British would be no match for samurai when they came out from hiding behind their modern guns. The British, however, considered their mission to have been largely accomplished. The following morning the ships weighed anchor and steamed out of the bay and back to sea. Quite literally as a parting shot, they trained their guns on a couple of small forts they had previously missed and shelled them as they passed. Out on the shoreline, Tōgō and his fellow young samurai stared in disbelief. Some of their number even ran into the water, hurling abuse from the shallows or making futile efforts to swim after the departing ships.

The differing priorities of the opposing forces live on to this day. British history books usually refer to the incident simply as the Bombardment of Kagoshima, in which a group of ships arrived, punitively scuttled a trio of merchantmen, shelled Kagoshima and then set off again, the fractious samurai of Satsuma having been taught a lesson they would not forget. Japanese sources, however, refer to the exchange of fire as the Anglo-Satsuma War, and regard it as a Japanese victory. After all, the British ran without attempting a landing, no Satsuma cannon fell into enemy hands and the murderers of Charles Richardson remained at large. Moreover, just as a *true* battle – the clash of swordsmen – was due to commence, the cowardly British had turned tail and fled.

Moreover, although the Shimazu clan did supposedly agree to pay an indemnity in the end, the amount was eventually reduced, paid for with a loan from the Shōgun (which Satsuma never repaid) and used, ironically, to buy several ships from the British.[12]

Tōgō, like his superiors, had been impressed with the performance of the British. In years to come, he would cite the appearance of the Royal Navy as a turning-point in his life, when he realised that the only way to fight a sea power was on the sea. The British ships had also been a revelation to Tōgō – until hostilities broke out, he and many of his associates had believed that the technology possessed by the foreigners would be little different to that possessed by the Japanese. It was time, believed the Satsuma leaders, for their clan to learn from their enemies.

Within a year, Kagoshima was home to a school of modern skills. The likes of Tōgō, who had learned old-fashioned artillery methods, were now instructed in naval gunnery, fortification against modern aggressors, astronomy, mathematics and navigation, ship-building, physics and even medical science. By 1866, the school had been renamed the Naval Institute, and Tōgō and two of his brothers had signed up as pupils.

In 1867, the 19-year-old Tōgō was a star pupil, chosen for minor duties on a Satsuma mission to the Imperial capital of Kyoto. His duties did not extent far beyond guarding the Kyoto residence of the Shimazu envoy, but it gave him a window on momentous changes in the Japanese government. The white lies that had preserved harmony in Japan for centuries were unravelling. The Shōgun, charged with keeping barbarians out, had failed in his duties. The Emperor, although powerless, continued to chastise the Shōgun for his failures. Among the Japanese nobility, factions sprang up among local rulers who hoped to replace the errant Shōgun. Strangely, however, House Shimazu was not among them. Having experienced 'barbarian' aggression first-hand, the men of Satsuma were fully aware that the Shōgun was helpless, and that nobody could stand up to foreigners without first adopting foreign technology. Consequently, House Shimazu now advocated closer contacts with the outside world, so that Japan could learn from its enemies.

The former Emperor, who had ruled Japan for two decades, died in February 1867, leaving the throne to his teenage son, the Meiji Emperor. The last Shōgun, Tokugawa Yoshinobu, pointedly requested that the new Emperor define the parameters of his job on 9 November. Ten days later, the Shōgun officially resigned. These seemingly innocuous events would set off a chain reaction in the Japanese government. The Shōgun had expected his resignation to shame the Emperor into begging him to return, or perhaps even offer to reinstate him under more realistic terms, but the Shōgun's enemies within the noble houses greeted his departure with glee and began manoeuvring to replace him.

The result was a brief and violent civil war, usually known as the Meiji Restoration. A baffling array of combatants duelled over who was the most loyal. The question of 'loyal to what?' would be answered with the deaths of thousands. Some clung to the notion that Japanese spirit would oust the foreigners, just as soon as the right man was put in charge as Shōgun. Others argued that Japan should invite foreign contact, all the better to learn how to defeat the new enemy. The factions were broadly divided into those who supported the old Shōgun, and those who nominally supported the Emperor. These groups were further divided into those who wanted to use their 'loyalty' as an excuse to overthrow the old order and those who wished to cling to it.

Satsuma nominally supported the Emperor, as one of the fiefs that offered military support and modern weaponry to the Emperor's faction. Buried somewhere within Satsuma's rhetoric was a replay of the wars of centuries before, a long-awaited chance for revenge against House Tokugawa in the Emperor's name. As a sea-faring domain, it was perhaps unsurprising that Satsuma soon constituted a large part of the nascent Imperial navy. At the time of the outbreak of the conflict, the young Tōgō was just old enough to qualify for service.

Tōgō was ordered to report to his first naval posting as a gunner on the Satsuma clan vessel *Kasuga*. The *Kasuga* was a fully-rigged paddle frigate, originally built by a British firm to meet an order from the Chinese navy. When the Chinese had reneged on their contract, the vessel instead found a ready buyer in Satsuma. She had barely arrived at Kagoshima before she was dispatched north to bolster Satsuma's bargaining power against Shōgunate forces.[13]

Unfortunately, the Shōgunate forces had the upper hand and blockaded Hyōgo harbour, damaging the Satsuma steamship *Heiun*. The *Heiun* and her fellow vessel, the *Shoho*, were now stuck in port, along with the *Kasuga*, the pride of the Satsuma fleet – and, if truth be told, its sole warship. An official protested to Enomoto Takeaki, leader of the Shōgunate naval forces, and got an unambiguous reply.

'The Tokugawa and your clan have already fought in Edo,' said Enomoto. 'From this fact, I can safely conclude that your clan is our enemy. How could one suffer an enemy's vessel to leave port? You may give this message of mine to every vessel of your clan.'[14]

The *Kasuga*'s new captain, Akatsuka Genroku, was with Tōgō when the news arrived of his appointment at New Year. The group of samurai immediately left their quarters at Fushimi near Kyoto and made the short trip downriver to Osaka. The *Kasuga*, however, was down the coast at the port of Hyōgo (now a district of modern Kobe), which was already blockaded by Shōgunate forces. Nor was there any marine transport available from Osaka, as all boatmen had been ordered to stay off the water.

With no time to lose, Tōgō and his fellow officer Ijichi were ordered to requisition a boat at all costs. This Tōgō managed by bodily seizing crewmen by their collars and threatening to kill them unless they followed his orders. With a sulking but compliant crew, the Satsuma officers were able to make the relatively short distance to Kobe, where they sneaked aboard the *Kasuga* during the night.

There, they heard of Admiral Enomoto's threats and of the *Kasuga*'s response, which was to stoke up her boilers ready for action. Captain Akatsuka ordered that at dawn the ships would run the blockade of Tokugawa vessels. The *Kasuga*, towing the slower *Shoho*, would engage the enemy, while the *Heiun* ran for Kagoshima to report developments.

However, before Captain Akatsuka's plan could be put into action, the Satsuma ships received some unexpected assistance. Late that night, Admiral Enomoto's lookouts reported the flashes and orange glows of fires, and the distant rumble of explosions on the horizon. Believing that Shōgunate forces were under attack elsewhere, the blockading Enomoto gave the order for his fleet to weigh anchor and head back towards Osaka.

At dawn on 28 January 1868, Captain Akatsuka could not believe his luck. While the crew of the *Kasuga*, Tōgō among them, sulked that they had missed the chance for battle, Akatsuka ordered his ships out of port before Enomoto could return. All three ships successfully made it out of the harbour, and the *Heiun* steamed at full speed for the west, out of harm's way.

The *Kasuga* and *Shoho* continued towards the south in the winter mist, until a lookout reported the news that Akatsuka had been dreading. There was a column of black smoke on the horizon growing steadily nearer – one of the Shōgunate vessels was in pursuit. It was the *Kaiyō*, the majestic triple-masted flagship of the Tokugawa fleet, a state-of-the-art propeller-driven cruiser, whose construction Admiral Enomoto had personally overseen in the Netherlands. Her coal-fired engines topped out at 400 horsepower and her guns were European-standard, manufactured by Krupp.

The *Kasuga*'s guns were no match for those on the *Kaiyō*, but Enomoto trusted in blind luck. When the distance between hunter and hunted closed to 2,800 metres, the *Kaiyō* let loose one of her 100-pound rounds. It splashed harmlessly into the sea, but the battle was on.[15] The smoke columns of two more Shōgunate ships were now closing in. Captain Akatsuka was forced to give up on towing the *Shoho*, and ordered for the hawser attached to the slower ship to be cut. The *Shoho* peeled away from the battle and steamed after the *Heiun*. Had Enomoto been interested, he could have easily caught the *Shoho*, but his eyes were on the biggest prize, the *Kasuga* herself.

The gunners on both ships opened up, with little success at long-range. As the range dropped to 1,200 metres, Tōgō's piece scored a direct hit, as did two of his fellow gunners. Another of Tōgō's shots carried off part of the *Kaiyō*'s rigging. The *Kaiyō* wheeled to the side, letting off a broadside of thirteen guns. All, however, missed, although one glanced off the outer cowling of the *Kasuga*'s paddle wheel. Had the *Kaiyō*'s cannonball hit squarely, the *Kasuga* would have been crippled, but now she was pulling steadily ahead. The *Kaiyō* might have had superior guns, but the *Kasuga* had superior speed and she steadily began to leave her pursuer behind.

The Battle of Awa, as this exchange of fire became known, was the first occasion that Japanese ships had fought with European technology. It showed that the Japanese still had much to learn – of the 138 shots fired, only three, including Tōgō's own, hit their targets. The *Kasuga* successfully evaded pursuit, and the *Heiun* made it safely back to Kagoshima. The *Shoho*, however, barely made it more than a few miles before she ran aground and was burned by her crew to avoid falling into enemy hands.

Mutsuhito, the Meiji Emperor is restored to power after 250 years of rule by the Tokugawa Shōgunate

2

The Republic of Ezo

The smoke and fires on the horizon that had lured Admiral Enomoto away during the blockade had been the Battle of Toba-Fushimi, a four-day conflict between Shōgunate samurai and forces proclaiming themselves to be loyal to the young Meiji Emperor. It was a chilling presentiment of the differences between the old and new orders. The Shōgunate forces were armed with swords and pikes, charging a line of soldiers from Satsuma and Chōshū who were armed with machine guns and artillery. The Shōgun, Tokugawa Yoshinobu, was greatly troubled by the appearance of the Meiji Emperor's brocade banner among the hostile forces of Satsuma and Chōshū, which was sure to cost him support from some of the less sure samurai. He got a taste of his diminishing power-base when he sought refuge in nearby Yodo castle, only to be curtly refused entry. The lord of the castle, a noble who knew which way the wind was blowing, announced he could not be seen to be offering support to a man who had opposed the Emperor's own flag, regardless of the Tokugawa claim to be doing so out of 'loyalty' to what he thought the Emperor ought to be commanding. Although Tokugawa did not know it at the time, the influential Imperial banner was actually a Satsuma forgery – but it had the desired effect.

Running out of options in the Kyoto/Osaka region, Tokugawa Yoshinobu fled for the coast, where he passed an uneasy night aboard the sloop USS *Iroquois*. The *Iroquois* was one of several American vessels that had been sent to the area, ironically to protect the interests of the self-same foreigners that the Shōgun had been ordered to expel. Instead, Tokugawa was obliged to sleep on a 'barbarian' vessel until the tardy arrival of Admiral Enomoto the following day. Fresh from chasing the *Kasuga*, and still missing part of her rigging thanks to Tōgō's gunnery, the *Kaiyō* arrived off the coast in time to pick up the fuming Shōgun, along with as much gold as he could pilfer from the local treasure houses. The *Kaiyō* and her important passenger then sailed for Edo, where he hoped to fight another day. His refusal to accept the new order led to the next phase in the upheavals of the Meiji Restoration, the Boshin War – the War of the Year of the Dragon.

The *Kasuga* was only back in port in Kagoshima for a few days before she was ordered north once more as an escort for a troop transport. Tōgō and his fellow officers passed a tense few days sailing back through the Inland Sea, towards the site of their recent chase off Awaji Island. However, in the aftermath of Toba-Fushimi, forces hostile to Satsuma had quit the Inland Sea, and the *Kasuga*'s trip was uneventful.

Tōgō returned home in February 1868, granted shore leave while the *Kasuga* sailed on without him to Shanghai for a four-month refit. He went to see his mother, who tried to put a brave face on her solitude. A mother who had given birth to six children, she had already seen two, a boy and a girl, die in infancy. Now, in the space of twelve months, her husband had died and all her surviving sons had marched off to war. Tōgō passed the spring dividing his time between Masuko and his duties in Kagoshima, which now included teaching at the Naval Institute.

Tōgō and Captain Akatsuka rejoined the *Kasuga* in Shanghai in midsummer and sailed her back to Kagoshima. News drifted down from the north that Edo, too, had surrendered without a fight to the Imperial forces, and was now renamed Tokyo. The Shōgun had surrendered to the Meiji Emperor and had been ushered into a quiet retirement.

However, merely because the Shōgun had given in did not mean that the other samurai clans would do so. Many in the north of Japan regarded the Meiji 'Restoration' with some justification as little more than a power-grab by the clans of Satsuma and Chōshū, and refused to back down. They argued that merely because the former Shōgun had failed in his duties, that was no reason to abolish all the old institutions. Furthermore, whether Japan was to be 'modernised' or not was largely moot if the decisions were all being taken by Satsuma and Chōshū. Northern noblemen, such as Lord Matsudaira of Aizu, protested that they were not being asked to submit to the Meiji Emperor, but to the Emperor as a figurehead for usurpers. With that in mind, out of 'loyalty' to what the Emperor might have otherwise wanted, they refused to submit, and the civil war continued to rage in the north.

Tōgō now had new orders to sail for the north, and waved his mother goodbye once more. Soon after he left, Masuko would receive more unwelcome news. Tōgō's youngest brother Shirozaemon had succumbed to an unspecified illness while serving with the Satsuma forces, and died in September 1868, aged seventeen.

The *Kasuga* steamed up the western coast of Japan, accompanied by two other Satsuma vessels. On the coast opposite Sado Island, she took another VIP onboard. Saigō Takamori, a hefty Satsuma military leader, boarded the *Kasuga* with some of his men in order to be transported further north to new battlegrounds. Remembering the young Tōgō from his brother's childhood calligraphy classes, Saigō playfully referred to him as a 'dunce'. Despite the implied insult, the sharp words had the reverse effect on Tōgō's shipmates, establishing that he was on first-name terms with the Satsuma clan's best-known military leader, a man renowned for his gruff, belligerent nature.[1]

The typhoon season was looming and the seas were becoming increasingly rough, but Saigō was full of praise for the sailors, whose efforts allowed him and his men to leapfrog ahead of the Shōgunate dissenters. The *Kasuga* shuttled back and forth on Japan's west coast for over a fortnight, forced on nine separate occasions to seek shelter from the frequent storms in the waters off Sado Island.

On the other coast of Japan, Admiral Enomoto was suffering the same storms, but without any convenient shelter. Enomoto's flagship *Kaiyō* and her fellow warships, the *Kaiten* and *Chiyoda*,[2] were escorting four troop transports north, hoping to reach a stronghold at Hakodate, on the coast of Ezo. There, Enomoto hoped to regroup with the remnants of the land forces and make a stand on the northernmost island. The storm cost him two of his transports and caused substantial damage, but after repairs made on the run in several harbours, Enomoto reached Ezo and put his men ashore.

Enomoto's resolve paid off. While the Imperial forces were still huddling out of the rain further down the coast, his men were able to land and reinforce the troops already there. A dual land and sea action saw the Shōgunate forces snatch three important towns in south Ezo, ending with the occupation of Goryōkaku ('The Pentagon'), a massive modern fortress in the shape of a five-pointed star. The victory, however, was tainted by a great loss – Enomoto's beloved *Kaiyō* ran aground and sank in one of the autumn storms. The Admiral, who had personally supervised the *Kaiyō*'s construction, sailed her all the way from Europe, and commanded her in countless battles, was inconsolable.

Despite their losses, the Shōgunate forces had a secure base on Ezo, where they rightly believed that they would be left unmolested until the passing of the winter. With the Shōgun's surrender, however, they no longer regarded themselves as Shōgunate forces. Indeed, the bulk of Japan was lost to them, with only Ezo in their hands. Consequently, the rebels ended the Year of the Dragon by taking a bold step. They proclaimed that Ezo was no longer part of the Japanese Empire proper, but a newly independent nation.

The Republic of Ezo, with Admiral Enomoto as its president, would be a place where traditional values still held, where samurai would be free to live as they had in the old days and, most importantly, where the usurpers from Satsuma and Chōshū would not enjoy any authority. Even in proclaiming a Republic, the rebels maintained a sense of loyalty – their flag retained the chrysanthemum symbol of the Japanese Empire. As far as Enomoto could see, Ezo was still an outlying region of the Japanese Empire and not part of the Japanese 'homeland'. The Tokugawa clan, which had ruled Japan in the Emperor's name for two centuries, could not simply be struck off and cast out. Surely, it was better to give the Tokugawa a parcel of land on the borders, Ezo itself? This would save honour on all sides, prevent the many loyal Tokugawa retainers from destitution, and help firm up Imperial control over Ezo. So sure was Enomoto that this suggestion would work that he even formally presented it to the Emperor. The Imperial faction, however, was not prepared to let its bitterest enemies set up a semi-independent state at the edge of the Empire. That was, after all, how Satsuma and Chōshū had come to power in the first place.

Enomoto's Republic was funded with the 180,000 gold coins he had managed to snatch from the south. It was supported by his own troops and conditionally recognised by both the British and the French, whose consuls on Ezo saw new opportunities for treaties and concessions. The French were particularly keen on the Republic of Ezo. The second-in-command of Enomoto's land forces was Jules Brunet, a former military adviser to the Shōgun, who had 'resigned' his commission after the Shōgun's surrender in order to stay with the rebels. Brunet led eight samurai brigades, each commanded by a French lieutenant, and was instrumental in the incorporation of French military discipline into the nascent Republic.

Tōgō would get new orders in the spring. He and the rest of the crew of the *Kasuga* were to head north once more, to rendezvous with a fleet of four armoured transports and three other battleships to prepare for an assault on Ezo. The *Kasuga*, however, was no longer the star of the Imperial fleet. In February 1869, the Emperor's faction had taken delivery of a new vessel, bought from the American government. The new flagship was an ugly metal beast, two-masted but with a tall funnel amidships as an exhaust for her twin steam engines and a prow dominated by an ominous ram. She was armour-plated all over. Built in France, she had been purchased by the Confederate States during the American Civil War, which was all but over by the time she arrived. The USA had been all too happy to offload the unwanted vessel on the Japanese, who renamed her from css *Stonewall Jackson* to the altogether more descriptive *Kōtetsu*: 'Ironclad'.[3]

The name alone was enough to worry the Republic's officers. The French hatched a plan to deal a double blow to the Imperial forces, planning to steal her and turn her against her Imperial masters. Henri Nicol, a native of Bordeaux, revealed that he had actually seen the *Kōtetsu* being built. He felt that he knew the ship's lines rather well, and found it ludicrous that the Japanese were discussing her as if she were a doomsday device, when to him she had been yet another vessel in a dry dock. The *Kōtetsu*, argued Nicol, was merely a military tool, and one that the Republic of Ezo could regain for its own uses.

'After many reports,' wrote his fellow plotter Eugène Collache, 'and considering what we know of the usual negligence of the Japanese, we could hope that our enemies would drop their guard. We discussed the fact that if we did not maintain the element of surprise – that is to say, to go on the offensive – then all that would be left to us would be a defensive role.'[4]

Nicol told the assembled officers about the ironclad, which was something of a sore point with the Tokugawa men, as the *Kōtetsu* had originally been ordered and paid for by the Shōgun, but had fallen into Imperial hands on her delivery. Fellow Frenchmen Jean Marlin and Arthur Fortant also agreed that the time to strike was now, before the Imperial vessels reached Hakodate. The most vital support, however, had come from Arai Ikunosuke, the Navy Minister of the Republic, who was eager for action and had found willing accomplices in the form of the Shinsengumi, a body of hardline samurai who had left many dead on the battlefields of 1868.

'It was decided,' wrote Collache, 'to embark upon each ship a certain number of soldiers from the land army, who, with their terrible sabres, would make excellent boarders. We were counting largely on boarding, for which our men had been actively practising, in the hope that we could acquire enemy vessels.'[5]

Jules Brunet enthusiastically gave his blessing to the enterprise, 'but we had not counted on the immense arrogance of the Admiral [Enomoto]. Affronted at not having been consulted, he searched for every sort of pretext to delay our departure,' and was only talked around by a grave conference with Brunet himself.[6]

If the French had their way, they would have attacked the Imperial vessels a day earlier, but bad weather and broken machinery delayed their progress. Collache's vessel, the *Takao*, developed engine trouble *en route* and the Ezo flotilla was forced to drop anchor for repairs. It was there, in a secluded bay north of Miyako, that the Ezo men first used a false flag, running up American and Russian colours in an attempt to hide their true identity from observers. Instead, the sight of 'barbarian' vessels soon attracted a number of local Japanese, keen to get their first sight of white men.

The locals were open-mouthed with surprise when they neared the Ezo vessels and realised what they really were. Believing themselves to have found kindred spirits, the Ezo crew explained their mission. Collache was already nervous at the risk of discovery, and demanded hostages be put aboard the *Kaiten* in order to prevent the locals selling news of his plans to his enemies.

The Ezo fleet got underway again, armed with new intelligence that the Imperial fleet was indeed in nearby Miyako Bay. However, the *Takao*'s engines continued to give trouble, causing Collache to drop further behind the *Kaiten* until the lead vessel was barely a speck on the horizon. Reduced to a crawl of three knots, Collache was forced to chug slowly towards Miyako, even as the first signs of battle erupted in the distance.

It was daybreak on the morning of 6 May 1869. Some of the Imperial sailors were ashore at Miyako, but not Tōgō, who was aboard the *Kasuga* with his gun crew. He was, therefore, awake in time to see the approach of two unknown ships. The foremost was flying the Stars and Stripes. Some distance behind her, a second warship was flying the Russian ensign. The 'American' ship was actually the *Kaiten*, whose complement included Henri Nicol and the suicidally heroic samurai of the Shinsengumi. However, the *Kaiten* was not immediately recognisable, even to those such as Tōgō who had seen her before, as two of her three masts had been lost in a storm, radically changing the shape she presented to observers. After the choppy waters of the previous night, the sea was once again calm, and a bright spring sun turned the polished steel and brass of swords and machinery into dazzling sparkles of light.

As the 'American' ship came perilously close to the *Kōtetsu*, she ran down her US flag and replaced it with the chrysanthemum and star of the Republic of Ezo. Before any of the Imperial sailors had time to register the implications, the *Kaiten* rammed into the *Kōtetsu* and discharged her guns right into the unsuspecting sailors on deck.

Now was the time for the Shinsengumi to board the ship, swords in hand. However, Henri Nicol's role as adviser and expert, while well intentioned, had failed to inform the would-be hijackers of the relative height differences between the two ships. The squat, low *Kōtetsu* only had a forecastle and stern at a height that matched that of the decks of the *Kaiten*. As a paddle steamer with bulky wheels at her sides, the *Kaiten* could not come directly alongside, but was instead forced to ram the *Kōtetsu* at an angle. At the single place where the prow of the *Kaiten* touched the hull of the *Kōtetsu*, the *Kaiten* loomed over her prey by a difference of three metres.

This was a major flaw in Nicol's plan, which required the samurai of the Shinsengumi to leap over the gunwhales like a swarm of old-fashioned pirates. Instead, their approach was considerably slowed. They had to queue to get into the limited platform afforded by the prow, and even then were only able to drop, roll and swing onto the ironclad in ones and twos.[7]

This delay proved fatal. Crewmen on the *Kōtetsu* swiftly manned the ironclad's deck-mounted Gatling gun, and opened fire on the samurai. Meanwhile, the other Imperial ships began to draw close, threatening to block off the *Kaiten*'s escape. Tōgō and his fellow sailors on the *Kasuga* did not dare fire the ship's main guns. Instead, they snatched up rifles and pistols, taking aim at specific enemy officers on the *Kaiten*. Uniformed officers were particularly obvious targets, and the *Kaiten*'s Captain Kōga Kengo was hit in the right arm and left leg. Even as he tried to rally his men, a third bullet hit him in the throat, and he fell silent to the deck. The onslaught made similarly swift work of the swordsmen, leaving the *Kōtetsu*'s crewmen free to turn their machine gun on the *Kaiten* itself. Taking charge, Arai Ikunosuke successfully steered the *Kaiten* out of direct contact and steamed for safety.

Out in the open sea, Eugène Collache was entirely in the dark. The smoke from the initial exchange had swiftly obscured his view of developments, and he was forced to listen to the booms and bangs for twenty minutes, with no clue of who was winning.

'My men and I,' he wrote, 'were in a state of over-excitement that was easy to understand. The battle was on, barely a few hundred metres away, and we could not see a thing. The battle was on, and we were not even there!'[8]

The first indication that Collache had of events came with the sudden appearance of the *Kaiten*, powering out of the smoke and running for the north at full speed. Collache frantically signalled for information, but the only clue he had was the thick, black cloud vomiting from the *Kaiten*'s smokestack. The *Kaiten*'s boilers were at full power, and she was running away. When even a cannon shot failed to attract the *Kaiten*'s attention, Collache swung his ship to starboard and began to slowly steam after her, although the *Kaiten* was already travelling four times as fast as the jury-rigged *Takao*.

The confused Collache had only just completed his turn when he saw why the *Kaiten* was running. Barely a minute behind the fleeing ship came the Imperial fleet, in full battle array, with the ironclad *Kōtetsu* in the lead. The *Kasuga*, with Tōgō aboard, was right behind her. The *Kōtetsu* rammed into Collache's ship without even stopping, shoving the *Takao* aside in her pursuit of the *Kaiten*. While Collache frantically tried to regain control of his ship and stay on his feet, the Imperial vessels disdainfully ignored him in their eagerness to run down the great prize.

The *Kaiten*, however, her boilers at full power, successfully made it out to sea and out of range. With her fires fully stoked, she was easily able to reach her top speed, while the Imperial ships, who seem to have had to raise steam while under attack, were still relatively slow. Within half an hour, it was clear that the *Kaiten* would get away. The Imperial ships broke off pursuit and turned back towards Miyako, intent on dealing with the *Takao*.

Realising that he had no chance of getting away, Collache resolved to run his ship aground and blow her up. He beached the *Takao* in shallow waters and tried to organise an orderly abandonment that moved essential supplies off the ship. 'Unfortunately,' he observed, 'the Japanese didn't have any biscuits.'[9] This bizarre comment, in the midst of a chaotic evacuation, was based on the realisation that the only food aboard ship came in the form of large sacks of rice, which were nowhere near as portable as standard naval provisions. In the midst of unloading, the beached *Takao* suddenly listed dangerously to one side, pitching men and materials into the water and causing Collache's inexperienced men to panic.

It took Collache 30 minutes to evacuate the *Takao*. Collache himself was the last to leave, and lit a fuse that ran into all the remaining powder in the ship's magazine. As he and his men picked their way across the rocks towards the shore, they suddenly heard the sound of guns. The *Kasuga* and the *Kōtetsu* had returned. As Collache and his seventy men scrambled for safety under fire, the *Takao* exploded in a massive column of fire and smoke.

The Battle of Miyako Bay was a relatively minor incident in the Boshin War, but left a deep impression on its participants. 'The fight at Miyako,' observed one sailor from the *Kaiten*, 'deserved special mention in the history of naval warfare on account of the fine *abordage*, by which the two forces fought at close quarters as if they were on land. Such fighting was resorted to in Nelson's time; but nowadays with the navies so highly developed, such fighting never takes place, and this fight at Miyako has probably never since had a parallel.'[10]

Tōgō himself was left in awe at the audacity of his enemies, in the pragmatism that led them to attack a vessel with swords instead of cannon and the suicidal bravery of the samurai on the decks of the ironclad. However, he regarded swordsmanship as a doomed art; he remained sure that gunnery was the future. 'The days of boarding are over,' he observed, 'and in the future naval actions must be fought at distant ranges.'[11] None of the sixteen enemy swordsmen who reached the deck of the *Kōtetsu* left it alive, but were it not for the Gatling gun and the bad luck that kept Collache out of action, the battle might have swiftly turned in the Republic's favour. Collache later voiced his suspicion that news of his plot had already reached the Imperial vessels and that they were effectively planning a surprise attack of their own. But surely the Imperial vessels would not have allowed the *Kaiten* to get close enough to ram the *Kōtetsu* if they already knew of the plot. Instead, it seems more likely that the Imperial forces gained the upper hand through a simpler means. Whereas Collache had scoffed days earlier at the 'usual negligence of the Japanese', the men of the Imperial fleet had remained calm under fire and had been diligently able to repel boarders and initiate a counter-attack, despite the surprise assault. Collache would later speculate that the Imperial forces had been forewarned, but if that were the case, surely the *Kōtetsu* and *Kasuga* could have easily matched speeds with the fleeing *Kaiten*. Instead, it seems that the Imperial forces had staved off disaster through the priceless virtue of remaining calm under fire. Such an achievement makes the Battle of Miyako Bay another first for the Japanese navy – a skirmish won by discipline and training.

Tōgō next saw action in late May.[12] The war was now taken to the Republic of Ezo itself, and the main function of the Imperial fleet was to guard and transport the soldiers required for a land-based assault. The *Kasuga* and *Kōtetsu* were charged with testing the resolve of the coastal forts at the southern tip of Ezo. After supervising the landing of several thousand Imperial troops, the *Kasuga* experimentally fired upon the coastal fort at Esashi, but found it to be deserted. Instead, the rebels had fled to the nearby town of Matsumae, upon which the Imperial forces closed from two sides. Tōgō played an active part in the battle that ensued, ordered by Captain Akatsuka to fire upon the rebel forces as they came out of Matsumae Castle and during their eventual retreat. As the light faded, Captain Akatsuka peered through his binoculars and announced that he was unable to tell whose troops were where. Accordingly, he called off the bombardment, unwilling to order the *Kasuga*'s gunners to fire on what might be friendly forces.

On the night of 28 May, Tōgō was given his first brief and rather humble independent command, sent in a rowing boat with his friend Ijichi to assess the progress of the land battle. Tōgō and Ijichi stealthily approached the shoreline in the twilight, wary of any Ezo soldiers that might be lurking in the trees near the shoreline. Instead, they found the coastal road deserted, and the first men they encountered were fellow Imperial troops. Tōgō returned to the *Kasuga* and reported that the quiet ashore was not a sign of trouble, but a sign of victory. Matsumae was in Imperial hands and the Ezo rebels had fled further up the coast.[13]

With 7,000 Imperial troops safely landed near Hakodate, the Emperor's forces were closing in on the Republic of Ezo. The last battle would be fought, as both sides had known all along, over the town of Hakodate and its massive star-shaped fortress of Goryōkaku – 'The Pentagon'. The *Kasuga* was one of four Imperial ships that approached Hakodate harbour. Before the harbour was even clearly in view, Tōgō saw the columns of smoke from vessels sent to hold them off. The Republic's fleet had once comprised more ships, but the steady attrition of fighting had worn them down. Several had been sunk by storms and enemy action, and others had fallen into enemy hands. The 'fleet' of the Republic, such as it was, now comprised three ships. The lead vessel was the same *Kaiten* that had rammed the Imperial ironclad at Miyako. She immediately opened fire, perhaps in the hope of a lucky shot. Tōgō was ordered to reply in kind, and the ships' guns were soon booming across Hakodate bay, with little obvious success. Suddenly, the three Ezo ships turned and ran back for the harbour. Presuming that they feared to engage any closer with forces that clearly outnumbered them, the Imperial ships chased after them, into the harbour of Hakodate itself.

But the Republicans' apparent retreat was a trap. Older maps of the Hakodate area would have shown a shrine to Benten, the goddess of fortune, on top of the hill that guarded the entrance to Hakodate harbour. However, the shrine had been repurposed in 1866, and was now Benten *Fort*. The fort's soldiers had obediently bided their time while the three Republic vessels lured the Imperial ships towards Hakodate harbour. As soon as the Imperial ships were bunched together at the harbour entrance, the guns of Benten Fort opened up. Only luck saved the Imperial forces, which were forced to turn and run out of harm's way. In successive days, however, the Imperial fleet wore away at the Republic's last remaining ships. The *Chiyoda* ran aground and was captured. The *Kaiten* was heavily damaged by Imperial gunners and put out of action. The last stand came from the *Banryū*, 'Restrained Dragon', which charged directly into the fray in a doomed assault. A lucky shot from the *Banryū* blew up the magazine of one of the Imperial ships, sinking her with the loss of seventy-six lives. But the *Banryū* was so badly damaged by her efforts that she, too, was sinking.[14]

With the last remnants of the fleet gone, both land and sea belonged to the Imperial forces. Goryōkaku held out for a few more days, but was cut off from all supplies. Even the Shinsengumi fanatics in Benten Fort, sworn to commit suicide rather than face surrender, largely submitted to the Imperial forces. Jules Brunet, the Frenchman who had enjoyed such a high position, found a way out of trouble by surrendering not to the Imperial forces, but to the crew of a foreign ship that had been observing the action. His 'surrender', such as it was, was hence accepted onboard the French warship *Coëtlogon*, which spirited him home.

The fall of Hakodate spelled the end of the short-lived Republic of Ezo and the final destruction of the old order. A handful of the Republic's men, including its president Admiral Enomoto, would be co-opted into the new Imperial order. But most were marginalised and forgotten, stripped of their status and left to fend for themselves as commoners in the new, modernised Japanese state. With the Meiji Emperor now the head of state, his supporters got the rewards for which they had been waiting. The Shōgun's old alliances and favourites were swept away, and the new government was dominated by cliques of men from the southern domains that had resisted the Shōgun all along. Men of Chōshū gained a head start in the new Imperial Army. As for the Navy, it was staffed chiefly with Satsuma men, including Tōgō Heihachirō.

Early accounts of Saigō Takamori's suicide, such as this 1877 woodblock triptych by Yoshitoshi Tsukioka, claimed that he had died at sea. In fact, he killed himself on a hill near Kagoshima, accompanied in death by Tōgō's elder brother Sokuro

3

Johnny Chinaman

In the wake of the Meiji Restoration, Japan sought even stronger ties abroad. Students were sent to learn from the major powers of the era, regardless of the sides they may or may not have taken in the Boshin War. France, still the pre-eminent military nation in the world, was a major destination for servants of the new order, as were Prussia and the United States. In an age when one in every four ships on the sea flew the British flag, however, the United Kingdom was the favoured destination of the navally-minded men of Satsuma.

Tōgō returned to Kagoshima for the summer, but by the autumn of 1869 he was sent by the Shimazu clan to Yokohama to study English. His lessons began with Shibata Daisuke, a native of Nagasaki who was supposedly an expert in barbarian tongues. Before long, he was taking extra tuition with the Englishman Charles Wirgman, the Yokohama-based expatriate better remembered as the correspondent of the *Illustrated London News* and publisher of the satirical magazine *Japan Punch*.[1] After lessons with his English tutor, Tōgō moved on to a language institute where the 21-year-old military man was obliged to sit at desks with boys half his age. Learning from the West was the new craze and Tōgō was determined not to let it pass him by.

'Several of us,' Tōgō recounted, 'who were anxious to get selected for study in England met one day and exchanged views regarding our chances of selection. One of the party proposed that we should go to Sekiryushi, a noted fortune-teller who lived in Shiba district in Tokyo. Then we went at once and consulted him. He told all but one of us that our wish would be fulfilled, but to the one excepted he said that he would be left out and advised him to give up all hope. Upon hearing this, the unlucky student became angry and went away in a huff. And, strange to say, he was the only one of us who was not selected.'[2]

Tōgō's return to school paid off in late 1870. He was ordered to report for duty aboard the corvette *Ryūjō*,[3] then at anchor in Yokohama harbour. Until that day, Tōgō had been an employee of the fief of Satsuma and its ruling Shimazu clan. But with his admission aboard the *Ryūjō* he was now a sailor in the direct employ of the Emperor rather than aboard clan ships on loan.

In 1871, Tōgō was one of twelve young officers selected to study abroad, in Britain itself. With both hair and clothes cut in Western style, Tōgō was put aboard a British steamer in Hong Kong, which took him and his fellow students across the Indian Ocean to the Red Sea. Although the Suez Canal was open by this time, Tōgō and the other Japanese crossed into the Mediterranean by a land route, riding on camels across the isthmus and boarding another British steamer at Alexandria. On 24 May, he left instructions that he was to be woken when the passenger ship on which he was travelling came within sight of Cape Trafalgar. He was paged in the grey dawn of the 25th and eagerly ran on deck with his fellow travellers to see the famous cape in the distance.

Once the Japanese students reached Portsmouth, they were taken on a trip to London by members of the Japanese Legation. They were taken to see the guards on parade at St James's Palace, and treated to a trip to the theatre to see an unknown play. Kitted out in English fashions, the Japanese students were then sent their separate ways, in order to prevent them from leaning on their countrymen instead of learning English. Tōgō was quartered with a British family, in a homestay that was hoped to teach him the rudiments of British etiquette, and to hone his language skills still further. He was packed off to Cambridge to stay with the Reverend A D Capel, a kindly Methodist minister who was both Togo's landlord and instructor in higher mathematics.

The Capel family had been excitedly awaiting Tōgō's arrival, largely because one of the young sons had become convinced that all Japanese people were accomplished acrobats. He seems to have picked up this assumption after witnessing a performance by the Imperial Japanese Troupe a couple of years previously: a group of 'jugglers', one of whom went by the name 'All Right'. Young Master Capel eagerly questioned the new arrival as to whether he knew them. A baffled Tōgō stoically explained that 'jugglers and public entertainers belonged to a different class of society, and that therefore he knew nothing about little "All Right" or any of his companions'.[4]

Despite this crushing blow to the young Capels' expectations, Tōgō soon proved to be a hit with the minister's children. He caused a great stir with the minister's daughter Ella, by taking a hair from her head and knotting it carefully to a captured fly. He then tied the other end of the hair to a piece of paper identifying the fly as Ella Capel's property, perplexing the near-sighted father of the house with the sight of what appeared to be a piece of paper floating around the drawing room in mid-air.

Reverend Capel noticed that Tōgō demonstrated extreme patience with childish ways. Apart from the acrobat interrogation, the closest he came to losing his temper during the months he lodged with Capel was another prank. One of Capel's other pupils, a young boy, had found some text which he presumed to be Japanese and had carefully copied it out onto a postcard. Tōgō was entirely flummoxed, either by the amateurish calligraphy or by the appearance of words from an unknown context on a postcard addressed to him, and puzzled over the note for some time before he realised that he was being strung along. He then threw away the card with the curt dismissal 'Silly!'

Capel was deeply impressed by Tōgō. 'He ... came to learn Western manners,' noted the minister, '[but] whilst he was in my house I was constantly urging my pupils and others to learn Eastern manners. He had, I thought ... more consideration for the feelings of his fellows than anyone I have ever had much to do with.'

Tōgō's education with the Capels comprised total immersion. He eagerly accompanied Capel to the church, where he followed the services in a prayer book, although he made sure to state that he was no Christian – Christianity was still illegal in Japan, and Tōgō was a loyal subject of the Emperor. He spent much of his time accompanied by two huge quarto dictionaries, which he even kept by his side at mealtimes, so as to better understand the things that the Capels said. Curiously, considering Tōgō's future career and his biographers' habit of presenting him as a driven, dedicated seaman, Capel noted that his lodger seemed lukewarm at best about the prospect of a naval career.

'When he was with me,' wrote Capel, 'he had, so far as I could understand, no intention of becoming a sailor. One day I asked him what he was thinking of being, when he said he was going to be a sailor on dry land, which after many questionings, to say nothing of references to the big dictionaries, we discovered to mean that he hoped to go into the office which would correspond with our Admiralty.'

Tōgō lived at Capel's house for several months as his studies continued, but began to suffer from a worrying deterioration of his eyesight. Although no contemporary account of Tōgō is able to explain his condition, he came to believe that he was genuinely going blind. Consultations with a number of Cambridge specialists led him to try several painful courses of treatment. For some time, Tōgō kept his difficulties secret from his tutor, hoping to deal with the problem before it attracted the notice of the Japanese legation – his very real fear would have been that his many years of study would prove to be for nothing if he was unfit for military service. Eventually, however, Tōgō informed Capel, who forced him to tell the legation. This act may have saved Tōgō's sight, as the young officer was swiftly put on a train to London's Harley Street, where Tōgō finally received the treatment he required for the mysterious and unspecified condition.

Many years later, at the time of the Russo-Japanese War, Capel was asked for his views on the character of his former lodger. He observed: 'His patience and quiet endurance of all this suffering were quite a revelation to us. Had I not had this personal acquaintance with the way in which Japanese can endure and bear, I should have almost doubted the truth of many of the stories told of them during this present war, whereas with the remembrance of Tōgō so indelibly printed on my memory I could believe them all.'

Tōgō also attended classes at a preparatory school for naval service, and had plainly hoped to study at the Royal Naval College.[5] However, the British government informed the Japanese that the Royal Naval College was apparently (and suspiciously) 'full'. Consequently, after some time spent in Portsmouth, and after possibly attending a handful of classes without actually gaining entry, Tōgō was forced to enrol elsewhere. Eventually, Tōgō was accepted to the Thames Nautical Training School, not quite the highbrow institution he might have hoped for. In years to come, both the Japanese and British press would refer to Tōgō's 'training' in England, but both would conveniently forget that his studies were almost entirely undertaken in a school for merchant mariners.

The Nautical Training School was based on an antiquated Royal Navy vessel, the *Worcester*, which had spent several years moored off the shore of Southend-on-Sea in the Thames Estuary. The *Worcester*, later incorporated within the Thames Nautical Training College, seemed happy to take Tōgō, quite possibly because enrolment numbers were down – the school's Southend mooring had proved deeply unpopular with the students, who were often cut off from supply by the estuary's rolling waters and rendered seasick by the pitching waves. In an effort to keep things calmer, the *Worcester* had recently been moved upriver to Greenhithe, near Dartford in Kent, where Tōgō came aboard.

At that time the school was run by one Captain John Henderson-Smith, described by one of his class as 'a most magnificent figure in his Cocked Hat and Epaulettes, usually sported on a prize day or some other equally important occasion; a genial man when the wind was fair, but a fearsome person to go before if you had been guilty of some wicked but boyish prank'.[6]

Tōgō remembered Captain Henderson-Smith as 'the kindest of masters and most generous of captains', would keep a picture of the Captain in his office for the rest of his life, and corresponded regularly with his former mentor throughout his naval career.[7] Smith himself, in later years, would damn the young Tōgō with faint praise.

'Tōgō was an excellent fellow,' recalled his teacher. 'He was not what you would call brilliant, but a great plodder, slow to learn, but very sure when he had learnt; and he wanted to learn everything! He was a quiet, good-tempered young fellow, and as brave as a lion ... The English boys used to tease him by calling him Johnny Chinaman and when they went too far, he would quietly face them and declare, "I'm not a Chinaman! Say it once more and I'll break your bones!"'[8] Whereas most graduates of the Nautical Training School's went into civilian shipping, Tōgō's military career ensured that he would become one of the institution's most famous alumni, and he was remembered as such in the School's commemorative history, in an account that similarly emphasised his resistance to taunts:

> The short, strongly-built little Japanese had to fight hard to achieve popularity as a foreigner among British boys, but his alert mind and his physical abilities, together with his unfailing good humour, carried him through. Tōgō endured the chaff without resentment, except when any would-be humorist called him a Chinaman. At that, the young Japanese would turn upon his tormentor with flashing eyes.
>
> 'I'm not a Chinaman!' he would cry. 'If you call me that, you wait! When I am the admiral I'll hang you on the yard arm!'[9]

For the other cadets, there was no difference between China and Japan. As far as they were concerned Chinese and Japanese were yellow-skinned men with black hair, and that was all that mattered. Tōgō's fellow cadets were similarly unkind about his unfamiliar name, which they consistently mispronounced. It became something of a joke on the *Worcester* to refer to him as 'One-Go, Two-Go, Three-Go,' as demonstrated by an incident when the young Tōgō was confined to the ship for an unspecified minor offence. At the sound of the pipe that signalled shore leave for those who had merited it, someone inevitably turned to the Japanese cadet and asked: 'Are you to go?'

'No,' answered Tōgō, sadly.

Then a dozen or so cadets gathered around him chanting: 'Don't tell lies, you are To-go!' It was all good fun as a rule, and what was meant in jest was always taken in the spirit in which it was offered.[10]

Tōgō stoically endured such puerile larks, as well as the return to a school life for two long years of drills and backbreaking exercises – a strange reversal for the veteran of several battles. Tōgō's shipmate for much of his *Worcester* term was a boy called Ernest Vanderstegen, who remembered the Japanese cadet as 'silent and thoughtful, his main desire was to hear, and emulate'. Vanderstegen and Tōgō were both short in stature, and quite possibly the put-upon runts of their squad. They unfailingly drew the short straw for an unwelcome duty, raising the Blue Ensign on the 'eighth bell' on Sundays – a responsibility which required them to get an early night on Saturday and clamber from their hammocks in the small hours of the morning. It was thus, perhaps to Tōgō's great fortune, that he found little to distract him ashore in England.

As Vanderstegen recalled, Tōgō 'like Horatio Nelson would prefer a ramble among the country lanes round Greenhithe to walking about the town'. His sole recorded complaint about his time on the *Worcester* related to the meagre food supply. 'The English do not seem to eat as much as we Japanese do,' Tōgō confessed. 'What I suffered most from on the *Worcester* was the shortness of rations, which I ate up in a moment. I used then to soak bread in tea and eat it in large quantities, while the English students watched me in great surprise.'[11]

HMS *Victory* herself, flagship of Nelson at the Battle of Trafalgar, was preserved at Portsmouth, and the *Worcester* students were given the opportunity to see her for themselves on the 68th anniversary of Trafalgar. The boys were escorted aboard the famous ship, and asked to read the signal flags fluttering from her masts. It did not take Tōgō long to puzzle it out, but the message was one he might have guessed; the ageing *Victory* was flying her most famous captain's famous signal: 'England expects that every man will do his duty.'

Captain Henderson-Smith addressed the boys on the deck of

the *Victory* with a speech intended for the British, but favourably received by the lone Japanese: 'The great Nelson is not dead,' Henderson-Smith said. 'His glorious spirit defies time. It will ever live to defend this country.'[12]

While Tōgō carried on with his studies, Japan's modernisation continued to cause friction in the Far East. Nor was everyone in Tōgō's faction entirely happy with the change in affairs. Just as the Republic of Ezo had tried to create an enclave where samurai could continue their old way of life, some of the Satsuma men had begun to wish for somewhere to put their samurai skills to good use. Saigō Takamori, who Tōgō had once ferried to battles in the Boshin War, had even begun agitating for the Japanese to invade somewhere close by in order to put the soldiery to work.

Japanese territory touched foreign powers at three points. The first, and hardest to define, was in the far north, where both Japanese and Russians had settled on the frozen island of Sakhalin. Negotiations proceeded over the desolate land, part of which was so close to the Russian mainland that it was often possible to walk from one to the other across the winter ice.

The furthest point of contact was far to the south, where the waters around the Ryūkyū Islands met those off the shore of the Chinese possession of Taiwan. The closest was in the Straits of Tsushima, where Japanese waters met those of Korea. Both were points where Japan's centuries of isolation had been secretly permeable – the Ryūkyū Islands were supposedly a Chinese tributary, and hence had natives who could pass with relative ease between the shores of China and the 'Chinese' enclaves in the Japanese ports of Hirado and Nagasaki. Similarly, the sailors of Tsushima were welcomed as traders in the 'Japanese' enclaves of certain south Korean ports, even though Korea itself remained resolutely closed to the outside world.

The *de facto* ruler of Korea, the King's father and regent, known as the Daewongun, protested about the change in the character of Japanese traders. There were, he noted, significantly more of them all of a sudden; and many appeared not to come from Tsushima at all, but were merely using Tsushima as a base of convenience to gain access to a closed market. Moreover, to the resolutely conservative

Koreans, the new arrivals' 'European' hairstyles and clothes were deeply unwelcome, and indeed offensive to Korea's centuries-long adherence to old-fashioned Confucian values and costumes.

A notice in a south-western Korean port unwisely echoed the Daewongun's protest, but went so far as to describe the new Japan as 'a country without laws'. What had begun as a discreet point about unlicensed traders soon escalated into a national insult, with some in the Japanese government even contemplating the sending of troops. True enough, this was exactly the sort of foreign campaign that Saigō Takamori was hoping for. However, he surprised many of his colleagues by opposing such a move. Instead, he suggested, it would be much better for Japan to send an envoy to Korea to talk matters over. When the Koreans inevitably offended the envoy, the Japanese would have a much better reason to invade. As if he needed to, Saigō nominated himself as a prime candidate to elicit offence from the Koreans, even if it cost him his own life. The arguments led to the resignation of a Prime Minister, and ended, at least for the time being, with Saigō and many members of his clique resigning from the government in disgust. Japan backed away from invading Korea, at least for now.

Tōgō continued his studies, unaware of what personal implications such distant developments would have. In the early grey days of March 1874, the boys of the *Worcester* were drafted in to form an honour guard at the Gravesend docks, ready to welcome Queen Victoria's second son Albert, Duke of Edinburgh, and his new bride, the Russian Grand Duchess Maria Alexandrovna. The couple had been married at the Tsar's Winter Palace in St Petersburg and escorted to England by a Russian warship. The *Worcester* boys formed part of the welcoming committee, and Tōgō was reportedly standing at Ernest Vanderstegen's side when Maria Alexandrovna's ship arrived at the jetty. Out in the Thames Estuary, the escorting warship let off an artillery salute. It was, believed Vanderstegen, the first time that the young Tōgō had heard a Russian warship fire a gun. The *Worcester* boys subsequently got a day-trip out of the festivities, under the pretext of presenting a wedding gift at Buckingham Palace.[13]

The final order for Tōgō and his fellow students was a round-the-world cruise in 1875, aboard the training vessel *Hampshire*. The

Hampshire sailed out of the Thames in February and rounded the Cape of Good Hope on 19 April. The object of the mission was to put the cadets' training fully to the test, but also to inure them to life on a long sea voyage – the *Hampshire* did not put ashore until ten weeks after she left London, when she reached Melbourne, Australia. There, Tōgō and the other cadets had two months of relative freedom, sightseeing and travel, before the *Hampshire* weighed anchor again for the long journey home via Cape Horn.

It was while Tōgō was in Australia that news arrived of Japan's latest great naval undertaking, a punitive expedition against Taiwan. For a Satsuma man like Tōgō, it would have been the worst of missed opportunities, an extension of Satsuma's sphere of influence deep into the southern seas and an early test of Japan's young navy.

The first Japanese ambassador to China began his assignment by protesting about the massacre of some shipwrecked Okinawan fishermen by Taiwanese aboriginal tribesmen. The protest had two powerful implications, the first being that Okinawa and, by association, the entire chain of the Ryūkyū Islands, was Japanese territory and had no business claiming to be a Chinese tributary any more. Moreover, the eastern coast of Taiwan was notoriously lawless, and the Chinese would eventually admit to being unable to exercise much control over it. Some interest groups within Japan thought that this was the ideal opportunity for Japan to seize eastern Taiwan, with the tacit assumption that since the Chinese could not control it, they could not lay claim to it.

Amid Chinese protestations that eastern Taiwan, albeit danger-ous, was still under their jurisdiction, 3,600 Japanese troops landed on the Taiwanese coast for a punitive expedition in 1874. The soldiers were largely from southern Japan, particularly Saga (the Nagasaki area) and Tōgō's home domain of Satsuma. The expedi-tion was led by Saigō Takamori's younger brother Tsugumichi and had Tōgō's former vessel, the *Ryūjō*, as its flagship. Tempting fate, the younger Saigō sent word to the Chinese that his mission was underway, hoping to establish that he was not 'invading' Chinese territory at all, but helping the Chinese deal with unruly elements on their own borders.

The Chinese begged to differ, and sent two warships across the Taiwan Strait. Busy shooting at aborigines, Saigō met with the Chinese envoys, and assured them that matters of jurisdiction were not his concern, but that a Japanese envoy was sure to be sorting matters out with the Chinese even as they spoke. In fact, diplomatic wrangles stretched out for more than six months. Saigō's men killed a couple of dozen Taiwanese on arrival, and spent the rest of the long, hot summer succumbing to a variety of tropical diseases. By the time the Chinese unhappily paid out an indemnity to make the Japanese leave, Saigō had lost over 500 men. The Japanese withdrew from Taiwan, satisfied that, in paying damages to the murdered fishermen's families, the Chinese had inadvertently conceded that the Ryūkyū Islands were part of Japan and not part of China. While the 'Taiwan' Expedition achieved nothing in Taiwan itself, its indirect outcome was the annexation of a lengthy strip of islands and their attendant seas, the whole Ryūkyū chain, stretching from the edge of Satsuma for 400 miles to the south-west.[14]

A similar incident threatened to unfold in Korea, where a Japanese navy survey vessel was fired upon by Korean shore batteries. The incident led to the dispatch of several hundred Japanese marines; and by 1876, Korea had been forced to sign a treaty of friendship with Japan. In a single generation, the Japanese had transformed themselves from the victims of imperialism to its agents – the 'Opening of Korea' seemed almost designed as a re-enactment of the way that the American 'Black Ships' had first opened Japan.

Throughout these machinations, Tōgō was stuck in Australia or aboard the *Hampshire*, while news drifted in of his elders' successes – Saigō Tsugumichi was only a few years his senior. However, the after-effects of the Taiwan Expedition and the Korean treaty of friendship would continue to affect Tōgō, even upon his return to distant England.

Tōgō graduated second in his class on the *Worcester*, a fine achievement, although he was appreciably older than most of his classmates and had significantly more experience than many of them. With the end of their studies, the boys scattered to their homes or to their first postings aboard merchant ships. But while his fellow students were now only beginning their careers, Tōgō was returned to the middle of his; the Japanese legation ordered him to a new posting in London, caused, at least in part, by the way that the distant Taiwan Expedition had played out.

The Taiwan Expedition had succeeded, in part, because of the sluggish Chinese response. While Saigō and his men had been succumbing to malaria and dysentery on the east coast, the Chinese commander Shen Baochen slowly shipped 10,000 Chinese soldiers across the strait, ready to fight for Taiwan if necessary. With the Japanese departure, he had then shipped them all back again. The Japanese invasion 'fleet' had only had three ships, and the *Ryūjō* was a museum piece. Had Shen been able to rustle up enough of the Chinese Navy's twenty-one available steam ships, he might have been able to sink the invasion force before it could even reach Taiwan. With a bit of luck, he might even have been able to manage it with just the two vessels whose impotent late arrival led to little more than unreliable assurances from Saigō.[15]

Even if this had not occurred to the Chinese, it certainly occurred to the Japanese. The Admiralty in Tokyo ordered three new warships for the navy – the *Hiei*, *Fusō* and *Kongō* – to be built in Britain to even the odds in the future. The instructions reached London as Tōgō neared the end of his studies, and he found himself reassigned by the Legation to the role of 'inspector'. Tōgō was charged with observing the construction of the *Fusō* at the Samuda Brothers shipyard among the docks of the Isle of Dogs on the River Thames.[16]

Tōgō found lodgings at the Royal Naval Hospital at Greenwich, just across the river from the docks. Each day, he made the short ferry crossing to see the armoured, steel-hulled frigate *Fusō* taking shape at the Samuda shipyard. Tōgō and eight of his fellow trainees were now expected to remain in Britain until the ships were completed, and to then make their way home on board. This simple delay may have saved Tōgō's life. In the years he had been away, some of his fellow Satsuma men had embraced the new order, particularly in naval service – there were many Satsuma men in the Japanese navy. However, many others considered themselves to have been betrayed by the Meiji Restoration. They had overthrown the Shōgun because he had failed in his duty to preserve the purity of Japan and expected the new order would be different. There remained considerable debate over precisely what 'different' meant. For Saigō Takamori, alongside whom Tōgō had fought during the Meiji Restoration, the new order was supposed to represent a return to old values, a resurgence of the prominence of the samurai spirit. And that, inevitably, would mean war.

Since resigning from office in 1873, Saigō Takamori had set up a series of schools in the old Satsuma domain. Although the curriculum included the Chinese classics, Saigō's academies were samurai training grounds in all but name, concentrating on the martial arts and military drills. The schools reflected a general anti-government attitude among the former samurai families of Satsuma, whose position had been gradually undermined and, as of 1877, would no longer receive their rice stipends from the former feudal lord. Government agents sent into Satsuma to spy on the schools were captured, tortured, and made to 'confess' that they were assassins sent to kill Saigō. A steamship sent to confiscate arms in Kagoshima was approached by seven or eight hostile boats, and forced to cut her anchor cable and run for safer waters. In February 1877, while Tōgō was still supervising the construction of the *Fusō*, the Satsuma Rebellion broke out in earnest, with Saigō's army marching on Kumamoto Castle.

Saigō's bid to reassert the old samurai ways was doomed to failure. Kumamoto Castle held out until Government forces came to its rescue in April. Saigō's army fell back in a series of defeats, until by September, it had been reduced to its leader and fifty diehard rebels. Severely wounded, Saigō either committed suicide or bled to death (modern myth prefers the former) on Shiroyama, a hill outside Kagoshima, close to the original location of his first academy. One of the men to die with him was Tōgō's brother Sokuro, who had once been duped in childhood into drinking a draught of peppered water. Another of Tōgō's surviving brothers had joined the rebellion, but had escaped with serious wounds.

Tōgō Sokuro had fallen in the chaotic last stand on Shiroyama. He had been hurriedly buried in a mass grave by his comrades-in-arms, and would have remained there were it not for his mother, Masuko. After government forces restored peace to Satsuma and proclaimed the reign of the samurai truly over, Masuko walked up to the burial site on Shiroyama and dug up her son's body. Out of a superstitious desire not to allow any metal object to touch Sokuro's corpse, Masuko used her bare hands, dragging Sokuro up from the ground and then arranging for his remains to be carried downhill to the Tōgō family cemetery. The news of the grim journey only reached Tōgō himself second-hand, long after his brother's remains had been re-interred. 'Had I not been in England,' Tōgō commented, 'I would have expired as the smoke on Shiroyama, sharing the fate of Saigō Takamori.'[17]

By serving as a naval officer thousands of miles from home, Tōgō had inadvertently avoided the pressures that doubtless would have been brought to bear on him as a loyal son of the Satsuma regime. Almost everything that he had once stood for had now been wiped out by the new order; nothing remained for Tōgō but to stay on the path that had been chosen for him ever since he boarded a ship. There was no such thing as a Satsuma man any more, only Navy men.

The French naval bombardment of Fuzhou by Vice-Admiral Amédée
Courbet in 1894

4

Delicate
Diplomacies

'A ship's commander,' Tōgō commented to younger officers in later life, 'is not infrequently placed in such a position that he must make important decisions unconnected with tactics or strategy. If, therefore, he has allowed his mind to concentrate only on naval problems, he will be apt to commit some gross error when he suddenly comes face to face with a delicate diplomatic situation, and his action will be detrimental to his country. I do not, of course, suggest that you should neglect your study of matters appertaining to your profession, but to diplomacy also you must give a great deal of attention. The man untrained in these questions will often be deceived by apparently insignificant details behind which lie motives which may lead to serious consequences. The naval officer who can detect such things will be of the utmost value to his country.'[1]

For sixteen years, Tōgō would learn this maxim the hard way, when placed in several situations where he was obliged to think less as a naval officer and more as a diplomat. For a generation, Tōgō's battles were fought with flags and signals, his victories won by lateral thinking and careful planning, his potential foes often dissuaded from fighting at all.

Tōgō returned to Japan in 1878, as one of only three Japanese officers among the largely British shakedown crew of the *Hiei*. The *Hiei* returned along the course Tōgō had followed many years before, stopping off for coal in Malta and Port Said, sailing through the Suez Canal, and putting ashore at Aden and Singapore on the long cruise home. For the next sixteen years, Tōgō made a continued, steady progress through the ranks of the Japanese navy, rising in rank, often transferred between vessels, as he embarked upon the standard practises of a navy in peacetime – cruises and inspections designed to familiarise officers with the waters and harbours of any area likely to become the scene of conflict. But although Tōgō spent a generation without any full-scale wars, his experiences were anything but uneventful. In the behaviour of Tōgō the junior officer, we see much of the making of the man who would find international fame in the early days of the 20th century.

Tōgō remained on the *Hiei* for several months, before being transferred to the *Fusō*, that same vessel he had watched take shape in London's Docklands. Now Lieutenant Tōgō, he experienced a curious reversal of the taunting he had endured in England, as younger officers trained in the Japanese home islands reacted with barely suppressed amusement to Tōgō's curious use of foreign terminology. Less than two years after returning to Japan, now promoted to Lieutenant Commander, Tōgō was transferred again for two years of service on *Jingei*, the Imperial yacht and the last paddle-steamer built for the Japanese navy.[2]

The *Jingei* had taken almost as long as her new Executive Officer to get into service. Locally built at Yokosuka, her active service had been repeatedly delayed by design considerations and the march of progress. Although officially 'launched' in 1873, the *Jingei* was still undergoing refits and fine-tuning when Tōgō arrived onboard in early 1880, and was barely pronounced complete by the time Tōgō left her in December 1881. While the *Jingei* looked impressive when under full sail, her armament was light, and her propulsion system was an outmoded paddle wheel – the last time such a one was used in the Japanese navy.

Tōgō's service on the *Jingei* was not characterised by any moments of naval brilliance. The vessel performed its Imperial duties and ferried Japanese attachés in local waters; but its Executive Officer was remembered by his shipmates only for his dependability and his reticence. 'In the *Jingei*,' one remembered many years later, 'he was always quiet and never talked very much.'[3]

Despite the *Jingei*'s apparent unsuitability for full and proper service for much of his time aboard, Tōgō still kept her crew busy. True to his duty, he was found every morning supervising the scrubbing of the decks, his feet bare and his trousers rolled up, whatever the weather. Tōgō was also reported to be a stickler for the correct protocols, which, for a man in his position, required him to supervise every action by the seamen. It became something of a respectful joke on the *Jingei* that Tōgō could be found on deck in all weathers, all but anonymous underneath a tent-like raincoat if necessary, waiting for his men to gather the sails.

In February 1881,[4] partway through his service on the Imperial yacht, Tōgō got married. His bride, whom he had not seen before the day of the ceremony, was the 19-year-old Kaieda Tetsu, the daughter of a prominent Kagoshima man, agreed by both Kaieda and Tōgō family elders to be a reasonable match for a naval officer in his thirties. Mrs Tōgō was doomed to a life without her husband's presence. Shortly after their perfunctory marriage ceremony, she moved in with her mother-in-law Masuko and spent a year at the Tōgō family's Kagoshima home, where she occupied herself with a small but lucrative home business making decorative matchboxes. Tetsu brought with her a substantial dowry, likely to be of great use to an impoverished widow's son with little to his name but his uniform. Tōgō wasted little time putting his wife's wealth to use, purchasing a modest house on a hill in Tokyo, which would remain the family home for the rest of his days.

Mrs Tōgō was a traditional Japanese wife, given complete authority in the home. Her husband appeared to pay her little heed, and maintained his notorious silences even when off-duty in his own house. He busied himself, if he busied himself at all, in his garden, and left all household matters to his wife, except one. In matters of wall decorations, Tōgō asked and was granted permission to put up pictures of naval subjects. He seemed oblivious to the effect the pictures had, as they only served to remind Tetsu of the distances and dangers between herself and her often absent spouse.[5]

Three days before the end of 1881, Lieutenant Commander Tōgō was made the Vice Captain of the *Amagi*, a small wooden despatch vessel that might be better described as a gunboat.[6] Like the *Jingei*, the *Amagi* was locally built and hence a little behind the times. Unlike the Imperial yacht, which was for show only, the *Amagi* was expected to participate in naval actions, both in Japanese waters and beyond.

It was not long before Lieutenant Commander Tōgō had his chance. Ironically, considering his recent move to Tokyo, his ship was sent back down south, dispatched with several other vessels to the port of Shimonoseki to await further instructions. The Japanese authorities already assumed that trouble was brewing in the country's closest neighbour. It was, after all, but a short hop to the north-west to the offshore Japanese island of Tsushima. From Tsushima, it was only another sixty miles or so to the coast of Korea.

Like Japan in decades past, Korea had attempted to block out the outside world. Nominally, the peninsula was a tributary state to the Chinese Empire. Abroad, Korea had gained the sobriquet of 'the Hermit Kingdom', and continued to fend off foreign incursions by force. In 1866, the refusal of the trading vessel *General Sherman* to leave when commanded led to the burning of the ship and the slaughter of her crew by Korean forces. The Koreans similarly scared away two French warships in the same year. Soon after, a group of European opportunists hired a crew of Chinese outlaws and sailed into Korean waters. Their mind-boggling plot was to raid the tomb of the infant Korean king's late grandfather, steal the corpse and hold it to ransom pending the signature of foreign trade agreements. Although their plan failed, they were not the last to attempt to force the Koreans to trade with the outside world. American warships arrived looking for evidence of the fate of the lost *General Sherman*, and vessels from other powers were soon sniffing around.

Japan had learned its lesson well from the foreign powers. A mere generation after the humiliations enforced by the Black Ships, and by foreign attacks on Shimonoseki and Kagoshima, the Japanese now tried to force similar ignominies on their Korean neighbours. The means of access, however, remained resolutely friendly. Japanese agents sought to exploit the factional rivalry within the Korean court between those loyal to the king, those loyal to his father and former regent, and those loyal to his wife, the scion of a powerful noble family.

Shortly after Tōgō was appointed to the *Amagi*, Korea concluded its first trade agreements with the United States of America. When the news reached Britain's minister in Japan, a British ship was sent to secure similar protocols. The Germans and the French soon secured access of their own. Just as in Japan a generation earlier, Korean court circles were preoccupied with the best course of action to take – what would be most loyal, to stand up to the new arrivals, to learn from them and turn on them, or to seek help from elsewhere? Some in Korea might have expected help from the Chinese Emperor, but China had problems of its own with external pressures and internal revolts. Instead, one faction in Korea turned to the Japanese, who were all too ready to offer advice and assistance in dealing with the challenges of the age. Supposedly at Korean invitation, the Japanese soldier Horimoto Reizō arrived in Seoul to train and drill a new, modernised fighting force. However, the employment of Japanese officers to train Korean troops was regarded by Korean conservatives as yet another foreign imposition on an order that had lasted for centuries.

1882 was also a very warm year. In Tōgō's native Kagoshima, and in his new anchorage at Shimonoseki, the heat bordered on the tropical. Conditions were similar across the strait in Korea, where an early summer threatened to dry up the rice paddies. The unseasonal warmth killed the Korean rice crop, piling a risk of famine onto the local government's concerns. Since Korea was a Confucian country with conspicuous strife at court, it was soon suggested by conservatives that the country's troubles were divine punishment for the government's failure to keep out unwelcome foreign influences.

As the summer dragged on, and no clouds could be seen in the sky, the Korean king was sent to renew his efforts to intercede with the gods and bring rain. This was his sovereign duty, but also presented the ideal opportunity for his opponents to fight back. A force of starving soldiers, secretly loyal to the King's father, attacked the royal procession in the midst of the rain-bringing ceremonies on 23 July. The attack escalated into a city-wide battle in Seoul between the supporters of the King and Queen, and 'dissident' factions with allegiances to arch-conservatives, most particularly the former regent.

Leaving a suicidally loyal lady-in-waiting in her stead to delay the mob, Queen Min fled her palace. Some of her relatives were not so lucky, and were lynched by the mob. Lieutenant Horimoto, whose appointment had been one of the catalysts for the protests, died in the palace fighting along with seven of his Japanese officers, his notorious modern weapons and training overwhelmed by the vastly greater numbers of his adversaries.

From the palace, the mob turned on the Japanese legation, rumoured to be Queen Min's refuge.[7] The Japanese officials present seized guns and fought their way out of Seoul (against what appears to have been an angry but largely unarmed crowd) to the nearby port of Chemulpo (modern Incheon). In this manner, the Japanese Minister in Korea, Hanabusa Yoshimoto, was able to clamber aboard a tiny Korean boat, which got him and his men as far as a small offshore island, where they were later picked up by the British survey vessel HMS *Flying Fish*. In an unpleasant irony that must have caused great elation among the victorious conservatives, the retreat of the Japanese was accompanied by a powerful summer storm, bringing the long-awaited rain. The bedraggled Minister Hanabusa barely had time to disembark in Japan before he was sent back with reinforcements. 'The insult,' commented the captain of the *Amagi*, 'is intolerable. We can expect a punitive expedition to start at once.' 'As far as we are concerned,' replied Tōgō, 'the ship is ready.'[8]

However, it was several days before the rest of the ships of the expedition were as ready for action as the *Amagi* was. Tōgō was aboard the *Amagi* on 10 August when she sailed as one of eight ships, with orders to restore the Japanese Minister's affronted honour, by force if necessary.[9] The Japanese flotilla was led by Rear Admiral Nire Kagenori – like Tōgō, a former Satsuma man and a survivor of the British bombardment of Kagoshima. His flotilla reached Korean waters without incident, but was temporarily troubled by the lack of reliable charts for the treacherous coastal waters of Chemulpo Bay. Korea's isolation had served at least one defensive purpose, by preventing foreign shipping from surveying the shoals and reefs of the area. From his flagship, Nire ordered his flotilla to wait for further instructions and weighed the chances of feeling a path through the waters, one oar-length at a time.

It was Tōgō who offered a new and original solution. One did not, he observed, even need a telescope to see the tall masts and dragon flags in Chemulpo harbour that indicated a number of Chinese vessels were already in port. Tōgō suggested that the Japanese simply bided their time until one of the Chinese ships came out.[10] They did not have long to wait. Tōgō and his fellow officers watched the Chinese ship intently, marking every one of her course corrections as she zigzagged slowly past unseen underwater hazards. Entirely oblivious as to the service she was performing, the Chinese vessel continued on her way, while the Japanese flotilla carefully steamed in single-file back along the same precise course.

There were three Chinese warships in Chemulpo harbour, and their commander, Commodore Ding Ruchang, wasted no time in sending across a dispatch boat to explain that he was in Korea to 'restore order'. This was precisely what the Japanese did not want, as it was the pro-Chinese conservatives who hated the Japanese presence in the first place. Ignoring the protests of Commodore Ding, the Japanese put ashore a force of marines and marched the short distance upriver to Seoul itself. As the second in command of the *Amagi*, it was Tōgō's duty to lead his own vessel's shore party.

Tōgō's first sight of the legendary 'Hermit Kingdom' was a shock. The road from Chemulpo to Seoul was little more than a dusty track, passing by ruined and deserted farmsteads. Those few Koreans that Tōgō saw on his journey were emaciated and listless.

In Seoul itself, Hanabusa delivered a stern ultimatum to King Gojong, who had been restored to 'power', but had suffered just as much as the Japanese at the hands of the mob. Regardless, Hanabusa demanded reparations from Gojong for insults against the representative of the Japanese throne. Along with a punitive fine, Hanabusa demanded the right to keep an armed force at the Japanese legation in case of any future uprisings. It was the thin end of a wedge that was sure to lead to extraterritoriality and unequal treaties, much as had been imposed on China by the West, and also on Japan.

While Hanabusa argued with representatives of the King, including the wily Daewongun himself, the Chinese landed their own cargo: a group of dignitaries including the influential military officer Yuan Shikai. Yuan and his party secretly enticed the Daewongun aboard their ship at Chemulpo and promptly set sail for China. The former regent was kept locked in his own palanquin until the ships reached China, where he was confined under house arrest for three years.[11]

Ironically, the removal of the Daewongun's influence removed much of the opposition to the Japanese, and Hanabusa was able to ram through his demand for reparations and the quartering of Japanese troops in Seoul. The parties signed the Treaty of Chemulpo, while the crew of the *Amagi* busied themselves with a mission of crucial importance: sounding the Taedong River 70 miles inland as far as Pyongyang. We should assume that at least one of the other boats in Nire's flotilla performed a similar task on the Han River that connected Seoul to the sea – next time the Japanese arrived uninvited, they would not need to spy on Chinese vessels to navigate their way inland.

It was in the days following the signing of the Treaty of Chemulpo that Tōgō had the occasion to meet the 23-year-old Yuan Shikai, a young military officer who was fated to become the mouthpiece for the Chinese Emperor in Korea. Yuan agreed to meet with Tōgō and the Japanese military attaché in Seoul, and proceeded to harangue them both with his views on the political future of East Asia and the unwelcome presence of 'foreigners', including the Japanese, in the territory of a Chinese vassal state.

While Yuan blustered and harrumphed about the political situation, Tōgō remained impassive and expressionless. His legendary reticence was unknown to Yuan, who came to believe that he enjoyed a captive audience and continued to hold forth with a well-rehearsed speech about what needed to be done in Korea, and how the Chinese and the Japanese needed to conclude a mutually beneficial and respectful alliance. At long last, Yuan's speech ended with a flourish, followed a few moments later by the final utterances of the Japanese interpreter. In the silence that followed, Tōgō rose to his feet. 'I am sorry,' he said. 'I do not understand. Goodbye.'[12] Presuming that Tōgō merely wanted clarification, Yuan launched back into his pontificating on politics. Tōgō, however, shook his head, bowed, and left the room while Yuan was still talking.

The political brinkmanship of the Korean intervention had clearly rubbed off on Tōgō. He had only been back in Japan for a few days in February 1883 when he became the centre of an embarrassing incident that threatened his future career. The *Amagi*'s captain had gone ashore on business, leaving Tōgō in command. During Tōgō's watch, a British warship arrived in the Shimonoseki Straits, a matter that demanded Tōgō's attention. According to naval protocol – a rulebook largely written by the British themselves – it was considered seemly for the commanders of other vessels to acknowledge the presence of the new arrival by firing a salute. The guns were to be loaded with blank charges, which were then discharged out to sea, a relic from the days of slow-loading cannon, when the firing of a ship's guns at nothing would effectively render it unable to repel an assault for several minutes and hence a sign of respect and trust towards an ally or non-combatant. The number of guns required in a salute varied with the rank of the arriving officer. Through his spyglass, Tōgō read the flags on the British ship and determined that a 13-gun salute would be appropriate. The guns on the *Amagi* duly made a satisfactorily large series of bangs in the February air, only for the British commander to complain.

The precise nature of the complaint is unclear – many sources on Tōgō, written years later in the days of the Anglo-Japanese Alliance, refuse to even reveal that the plaintiff was British, in order to save the Royal Navy's blushes. However, it appears, through a technicality concerned with the leadership of not one ship, but several, the British captain believed himself to rate a larger salute. Apologising for the oversight, Tōgō ordered his men to let off two more shots, an oddly facetious decision that was sure to annoy the plaintiff. Sure enough, a message soon arrived from the captain demanding the reason for Tōgō's piffling two-shot postscript. 'If you will add both salutes together,' Tōgō replied, 'you will find the total correct.'[13]

Unused to such insubordination from the Japanese, the British commander protested again. Tōgō, however, proved implacable, displaying every sign of the impish Kagoshima boy who had once stolen his mother's sweets and spiked his brother's drink. The British captain had the greeting that he had demanded, but merely with a very long gap between the opening salvo and the conclusion. This reply was not good enough for the British, who complained through official channels, sending a telegraph message all the way to Tōgō's superior at the Japanese Admiralty. Before long, an order arrived from Tokyo ordering Tōgō to fire the correct number of shots, with a reasonable gap between them. Fuming, Tōgō did as he was told.

It was perhaps no surprise when a second order arrived on 24 February, removing Tōgō from the *Amagi* and commanding him to sail immediately for Tokyo aboard the corvette *Nisshin*. It was less of a revelation for anyone familiar with Japanese etiquette. To any foreign observers at Shimonoseki, the rude Lieutenant Commander Tōgō was being ordered off his ship and packed off to headquarters for a dressing-down. To the Japanese, however, it was nothing of the sort. Instead, Tōgō was called away to a banquet – quite possibly a banquet that had been in the offing for some time, as it seemed intended to honour his activities in Seoul. There, he was presented with a gift from the Meiji Emperor himself and informed that he would be receiving a command of his own.

It seems likely that the decision to reassign Tōgō had been made before any reports reached the Japanese Admiralty of his behaviour at Shimonoseki. Since Tōgō was not officially reprimanded, and indeed, was effectively promoted by being given his own ship, it seemed at first like good news all round. However, his commission was hardly what he might have called active service. His new ship was an ageing wooden gunboat, the *Teibō II*, one of a pair that had been built in Britain for the Chōshū clan, had transported Imperial supporters during the Boshin War, and had been donated to the Imperial Navy in the aftermath. She was at the very end of her service life and only seemed to have survived to reach Tōgō's hands because the Admiralty had a special use for both him and the *Teibō II*.[14]

Tōgō had performed admirably in his sounding of the River Taedong. Now the Admiralty wanted Tōgō to perform a similar task closer to home, surveying the coastal waters near the harbours of Kure and Sasebo. It was work that seemed ideally suited to the plodding, stubborn Lieutenant Commander Tōgō – Kure was a harbour near to Hiroshima, on Japan's Inland Sea, far out of the way of any possible run-ins with short-tempered Britons. Sasebo was out on the western edge of Kyūshū, a fine harbour protected by a fiendish maze of shoals, which the Imperial Navy needed to map precisely, and at greater depths than before, in order to ensure that there was a reasonable approach available to ships of the future with deeper draft. Both ports were earmarked for massive expansion as part of a reform of Japanese waters into five naval districts, and Tōgō's work was hence important, albeit little more than surveys. In years to come, the two ports would indeed become major parts of the Japanese naval machine, with Sasebo functioning as Japan's main staging post for attacks beyond its shores, and the impregnable Kure becoming the nerve centre of Japan's defence, both at sea and, in the 20th century, for the navy's aircraft.

After just over a year surveying on the *Teibō II*, Tōgō returned to the *Amagi*, this time as her captain. He was ordered to proceed to Nagasaki with all haste, as the *Amagi* was waiting alone for him. The other vessels in the Middle Fleet of Japan had already sailed for Shanghai, where they had been sent to observe the growing tensions between the fleets of France and China. The Japanese were under orders to participate in the observations of a multinational fleet, including ships from Germany, the UK and the USA. This was a great achievement in itself, but secret orders asked for a little more. Tōgō and his fellow captains were urged to pay close attention not only to the posturings of the French and the Chinese, but also to the practises and habits of their fellow 'neutrals'. We may reasonably assume that the Lieutenant Commander received an enthusiastic send-off from Mrs Tōgō, as the couple's eldest son, Hyo, was born nine months later on 28 February 1885.

The Sino-French quarrel was, as ever, concerned with unwelcome incursions by a European power. Humiliated in Europe by defeat in the Franco-Prussian War, the French government had sought possessions further afield, including, among other targets, lucrative potential markets in China. In particular, the French concentrated on 'Indochina', the area now known as Vietnam. Like Korea in the north, the region was nominally a tributary state to the Chinese Emperor, leading to Chinese protests at French incursions. Critical to the French plan was the Red River, which stretched up from its seaport of Haiphong through the old local capital of Hanoi. Mastery of the Red River would allow goods to travel deep into the Asian hinterland, and while not as useful a conduit as the Yellow River and Yangtze in China proper, the river would still help French goods gain access to the Chinese provinces of Yunnan and Sichuan.

The politics of the situation were confusing. The French had signed a treaty with a local king that supposedly acknowledged that the region was still part of the Chinese Empire. However, neither the French, the Vietnamese nor the Chinese had any real influence over a powerful group of bandits, the Black Flag Army, who extracted extortionate tolls from Red River traffic. In fact, the Chinese were secretly encouraging the Black Flag Army, hoping to play the Black Flags and the French off against each other by claiming to each that the other was a local problem that they needed to suppress. Mistakenly believing that the French would have no stomach for war, the Chinese government broke off talks. The French retaliated with a lightning-fast military campaign in Vietnam in late 1883, supposedly against the Black Flags, although much of the military resistance they encountered and crushed was actually Chinese. In the embarrassing aftermath, representatives of China and France concluded a hastily-written treaty in May 1884, the Tianjin Accord, shortly before Tōgō arrived in China.

Tōgō reached Shanghai and paid his respects to his superior officer aboard the flagship. For the young Lieutenant Commander, perhaps it was a reminder of precisely where he stood in the great scheme of things in the Imperial Navy – the Middle Fleet's flagship was that same *Fusō* whose construction Tōgō had witnessed in London, but the vessel was commanded by another, while he was stuck with the ageing *Amagi*. At first, it might have seemed that Tōgō had arrived late, as the Tianjin Accord had already been agreed. There were, however, already questions about the power of the treaty. The Chinese had already mentioned, in a sheepish aside, that the terms of the agreement might be difficult to enforce. While it had been agreed that Chinese soldiery would pull out of the Tonkin region (i.e. northern Vietnam), the inexperienced negotiators had neglected to put an exact date on the withdrawal. Nor was it all that clear who was 'Chinese'. The leader of the Black Flag Army, Liu Yongfu, had been born in China, but was technically a stateless bandit – there was no guarantee that he would heed a single word of the Accord.

Accordingly, the multinational group of neutral observers loitered in Shanghai, waiting for something to go wrong. Tōgō made the best of the situation and struck out on a mission of his own. He turned the little *Amagi* to the west, and steamed upriver on a mission of exploration and observation that took him 600 miles inland, all the way to Hankou (modern Wuhan). The *Amagi* was the first Japanese vessel to penetrate so far into the Chinese hinterland, establishing in the process that the Yangtze remained navigable for gunboats for a surprising distance inland.

Tōgō returned to Shanghai in June 1884, just ahead of the news that something had indeed ruined the treaty. A French force had run into what appeared to be Chinese soldiers in a Vietnamese border area and wrongly assumed they were retreating. Instead, the Chinese tailed the French for several days, ambushing them late in the afternoon of 23 June near the small village of Bac Le. Although the Chinese suffered heavier losses, the French were still forced to retreat with twenty-two dead. Paris demanded reparations, which were not forthcoming from the Chinese. Accordingly, in August 1884, the French struck back.

The French naval commander, Vice Admiral Amédée Courbet, had recommended that his ships should punish the Chinese by seizing strategically important territory close to Beijing. He suggested Weihaiwei or Port Arthur – both valuable seaports that overlooked the Yellow Sea route to Beijing's port at Tianjin. The only consideration that kept the French from doing so was the fear of other powers, since other European nations, particularly Russia, already coveted the area. Instead, Courbet was ordered to keep his reprisals to territory that, while still of use to the French, would not interfere with the actions of other imperialist powers. Courbet decided to sail up the coast from Indochina, bypassing the British colony of Hong Kong and treaty port of Amoy. The next worthy prize was the great naval town of Fuzhou, once the home port of the Africa-bound treasure ships of the Ming dynasty admiral Zheng He, and the power-base of fabled pirates of old. Courbet's flotilla entered the approach to Fuzhou, French flags flying gaily from his masts.

News reached Shanghai of 'trouble' in Fuzhou. Tōgō sailed south immediately, and reached Fuzhou on 1 September. Vice Admiral Courbet and his ships were nowhere to be seen, forcing Tōgō to piece together what had happened from the reports of others and the wreckage strewn around the ruins of Fuzhou's harbour, the waters thick with driftwood and the macabre flotsam of thousands of Chinese corpses, rotting on the shores or floating out to sea.[15]

Fuzhou was technically a river port, set a little way inland on the wide but twisting River Min. The Min delta was guarded by forts with powerful guns whose mountings only allowed them to fire out to sea. As soon as Courbet had steamed past the Chinese forts, their heavy artillery was powerless to stop him. Rather than launch an attack immediately, Courbet had instead lurked in the river for two days, eyeing up the squadron of over twenty Chinese vessels in the harbour – a wooden corvette, and a cluster of gunboats, scouts and torpedo boats. At 2 p.m. on 23 August, Courbet gave the order to open fire.

At close range, the French made short work of much of the Chinese fleet in just twelve minutes. The 'Battle' of Fuzhou dragged on for another two hours and continued in a fashion after nightfall, as the Chinese seized local junks and launched them at the French as fire ships. The following day there were no ships to fight back as Courbet turned his guns on the Fuzhou arsenal. Ground forces, however, maintained a strong defence; and Courbet decided to keep to the water. On 25 August, he turned back downriver and steamed out to sea.

Notoriously, at no point had France declared war.[16] Courbet had received his orders the previous night and had calmly informed the French consul of his plans, as well as the captains of three nearby British ships and an American corvette. In hindsight, it seems suspicious that British and American neutrals should have been in the area, but that the Japanese should only hear about it afterwards – perhaps the Europeans still held the Japanese at arm's length, and did not trust them with advance knowledge of the French plans. But regardless of whether the Japanese absence was intentional or not, Tōgō took special note of Courbet's behaviour. Later, Courbet would assert that he simply could not have announced his belligerent intentions before steaming upriver, as the shore batteries would have destroyed his force before they could reach Fuzhou. It was, in French eyes, a justifiable deception to sneak past the shore batteries under a flag of peace, and to Tōgō's great interest, the European powers largely agreed.

The shore batteries were no longer there when Tōgō arrived. With their guns fixed facing out to sea, they had been defenceless against the departing French, who had pounded them into the ground. Always a few steps behind, Tōgō tailed the French to their new target, the north end of the island of Taiwan. Courbet had only attacked the island under protest, as he still regarded France's interests as best served by taking a peninsula closer to Beijing. However, the harbours of Danshui and Jilong in north Taiwan had both been regarded as ideal spoils by one of Courbet's fellow admirals, who also noted the presence of coal in the Taiwanese hills. But while Courbet was a dab hand at firing guns at forts, he enjoyed less luck with landing forces. Breaking off the assault, the French sailed for Hong Kong, tailed all the while by the *Amagi*.[17] When the French set out in October for a second assault on Taiwan, Tōgō followed them again. As the shore battles continued, Tōgō came aboard Courbet's flagship and asked permission to inspect the fortifications in French hands. Courbet not only granted it, but allowed Tōgō to see his own report of the naval actions against Jilong.

In early October, Lieutenant Commander Tōgō was permitted to go ashore on Taiwan, accompanied by a towering young French engineer officer, Joseph Joffre. Tōgō and his subordinates inspected the ruins with great interest, making careful notes of the kind of damage inflicted by shells against different types of structure. They pored over the coastal fortifications, evaluating what had gone right for the defeated Chinese and wrong for the victorious French. Tōgō also noted the lie of the land, and the place where the Chinese had placed their shore batteries. To the French, this all seemed largely irrelevant, but Tōgō was thinking ahead. The detailed report that he presented back aboard the *Fusō* in Shanghai assumed, rightly, that the French would not stay in Taiwan, that the Chinese would reoccupy but also largely recreate their damaged forts, and that on some unspecified future day, a Japanese force would make use of the knowledge he had amassed.[18]

The public image of Tōgō was based on a single state portrait that showed him with dark hair, recalling his younger days as a captain, not the greying admiral who achieved world fame

5

Princes and Prisoners

Promoted to Commander, Tōgō was ordered off the *Amagi* in June 1885 to a shore posting. With the Japanese now attempting to build state-of-the-art warships at home, Tōgō was ordered to supervise the construction of the *Yamato*, one of three composite sloops under construction in home waters, with twin propeller shafts – a new development for Japanese-built ships. Tōgō was expected to supervise the *Yamato*'s final stages of completion in the light of what he had learned from observing the construction of the *Fusō* in London. Japan still lagged far behind Europe in such matters; the *Yamato* was soon destined to be outclassed by other 'Japanese' ships already under construction in Britain, and her armaments had to be bought in from abroad anyway.[1] Nevertheless, it was a worthy task for Commander Tōgō, who also received the honour of commanding the new ship as she put to sea. In July 1886, Commander Tōgō of the *Yamato* was promoted to Captain in a shake-up of the ranks of the Imperial Navy. The round of promotions was not universal, and seemed designed to quietly halt the careers of officers whose knowledge or attitudes were deemed unsuitable for a modern navy. In achieving the rank of Post Captain at the age of thirty-nine, Tōgō seemed to have been signalled out for further advancement.

Two months later, however, he was struck down by a crippling bout of rheumatism which threatened to end his career. For some time, Captain Tōgō tried to hide the severity of his condition from the Admiralty. He delegated command of the *Yamato* to junior officers while he writhed in pain on a bed in his cabin. When the news got out, he was relieved of his duties in September and sent home to recuperate. On several occasions, he filed reports with the Admiralty claiming to be on the mend, only to shamefacedly retract his applications for reinstatement to active service. Relapses were followed by convalescent periods at hot springs; although for much of the ensuing two years, Tōgō was bedridden, only leaving his house on a handful of occasions. Attended faithfully by Tetsu, he lay in bed throughout the day, attempting to serve the Imperial Navy in a different way by studying textbooks of international law and naval tactics.

Captain Tōgō pleaded that he was on the mend once more in early 1887. In the summer of that year, he served on a commission that investigated a minor disciplinary incident when the corvette *Kongō* had run aground. The doubting Admiralty, still not wishing to put a sick man in charge of a warship on the open sea, then wisely gave him a new position that kept him close to home – a supervisory role at the Yokosuka Arsenal. Technically, Tōgō was also the commander of the *Asama*, an ageing training vessel that remained permanently anchored in Yokosuka harbour, like the *Worcester* of his England days. Even captaining a ship that never moved was too much for the ailing Tōgō, who was soon back in bed. He was, at least officially, captain of the *Hiei* for a period in 1889, before records show him back on land, serving on a court martial investigating an explosion on Navy property.

Navy records have Captain Tōgō returning to active duty in May 1890, although Mrs Tōgō would probably have more accurately dated her husband's recovery to a night in January when the couple conceived their second son, Minoru (born 10 September 1890). The family relocated to Kure Naval Base, whose waters Tōgō had once surveyed in the *Amagi*, where he was now appointed chief of staff to the resident admiral. As the heart of the nation's sea defences, Kure afforded Tōgō many new opportunities to see elements of navy life that would have escaped a mere sea captain. Kure was the centre for navy repairs, for constructing new vessels, and the headquarters of the supply staff. He was seconded to a committee that inspected the marine defences – mainly the sea mines – in the Straits of Shimonoseki and, despite another minor relapse of his condition in the winter, served without incurring any penalties.

Nevertheless, Captain Tōgō had a new opportunity to fight a battle with little more than signals and cunning. With Mrs Tōgō six months pregnant with their next child,[2] Tōgō was called away to the dockside at Yokosuka to entertain some foreign dignitaries. A Chinese squadron had put in at Yokohama. Notably, it was the Chinese squadron with special responsibility for north China's sea environs – in other words, the warships based at the Yellow Sea port of Weihaiwei, charged with protecting the approaches to Tianjin and Beijing, the coasts of Korea and, in the event of war, the ships most likely to fight against the Japanese themselves.

Commodore Ding Ruchang, who Tōgō had last encountered in Korea, was determined to fight a propaganda war of his own. His 'goodwill cruise' was actually an excuse to show off his latest acquisitions: two massive German-built battleships that dwarfed anything the Japanese had to offer. The *Dingyuan* and the *Zhenyuan*[3] (the 'Decider' and the 'Suppressor') had been ordered by Beijing years earlier, but had been interned in Europe at French request during the Sino-French War. Now, Commodore Ding made a point of steaming the two vast warships through Japan's Inland Sea to make it crystal clear that each of his new toys was twice the size of the nearest Japanese equivalent.

Commodore Ding was a frail, cadaverous man in his mid-fifties, a former cavalry officer who had somehow stumbled into commanding China's navy. He was also, like Tōgō, a stickler for correct protocol. He had risked his own life in earlier years by protesting to the Chinese government about inadequate naval budgets – an act bordering on treason at a time when the Empress Dowager had been plundering the naval coffers to fund the ostentatious decorations in her Summer Palace gardens. In 1880, Ding had travelled across the world to the north of England so he could personally sail two other British-built ironclads, the *Chaoyong* and *Yangwei* ('Superhero' and 'Projection of Power') back to China to add to his fleet. Now, he was intent on showing the Japanese that the best course of action in naval conflict with China was *no action at all.*[4]

Commodore Ding's six ships arrived off Yokohama in order to take full advantage of the Japanese media. The classically-educated Ding brought a touch of class to naval events that had recently been dominated by brusque and inscrutable Occidentals; he charmed the Japanese nobility with his off-the-cuff poems and Confucian wit, and successfully gave the impression that much more united China and Japan than divided them. An audience with the Meiji Emperor went without a hitch, although Ding's true purpose was to entice Japanese opinion-formers down to the dockside. Tokyo urbanites were terrified at the sight of the Chinese ships looming over the vessels of the Imperial Navy. The Meiji Emperor's own court chronicle noted the revival in modern idiom of the term 'elder brothers' to refer to the Chinese. In public relations terms, Ding had made sure the Japanese knew who was boss and, for a brief time, revived the old-time awe Japan had once enjoyed for things Chinese.[5]

To make sure that everyone got a good look, Commodore Ding then sailed his military circus down to the waters off Kure, where Tōgō was one of the local dignitaries invited aboard for a tour. Commodore Ding proudly showed off the many refinements aboard his ironclads, their triple torpedo tubes, a desalinisation plant that would make fresh water sufficient for a crew of 300, and even two torpedo boats carried as part of each ship's compliment, so that the 'Decider' and 'Suppressor' might suddenly multiply themselves from two big ships into a ready-made flotilla of six. Not every one of these wonders was news to the Japanese, but oriental courtesy on both sides required that the officers make sufficient noises of appreciation and excitement at each new feature. Alone among the Japanese, Captain Tōgō remained conspicuously unmoved.

His suspicions were justified. At the time of their construction, the two giants were adjudged 'practically invincible', but ships already under construction would soon surpass their speed; and although their guns were monstrously powerful, their mountings made them all but useless in even mildly choppy seas. Furthermore, the ships had already run into difficulties in Europe. While waiting for the Sino-French War to blow over and for the warships' delivery to China to be approved, the *Dingyuan*'s German builders had been unable to resist the opportunity to take her out for a spin. The resultant sea trials had been calculated to annoy the British, but instead led to much smirking from the London *Times*, which gleefully reported:

> ... [I]t was also necessary to test the effect of the concussion of these monster cannon on the corvette itself ... [When the guns were fired] a large quantity of skylight and window glass was smashed, a thick iron rail on the bridge was wrenched off, a funnel was snapped in two, the deck was strewn with coals jerked up from the coal bunker, some wooden furniture was smashed into splinters .... How the Chinese are to face ... any other foe with such disastrous guns is a question well worthy of their considerations.[6]

Unlike his fellow officers, Tōgō remained as suspicious as the British newspapers about the twin giants' actual capabilities. Instead of poking around the ships themselves, he made the acquaintance of two of Ding's captains, and found them to represent opposite poles of the Chinese navy.

One, Lin Taizeng, had none of the excitability of the other Chinese. He sat apart from the proceedings and remained quiet at all times – a man after Tōgō's own heart. Although Tōgō may not have known it, Lin was from a famous family; his grandfather Lin Zexu had been the commissioner whose resistance to the British had sparked the Opium Wars. Lin Taizeng had survived his grandfather's rise and fall, and sought a career with the organisation that he felt best able to protect China from future indignities – the navy. He had even enjoyed similar experiences to the young Tōgō, having travelled to distant Britain with Ding to bring home the two smaller warships on their shakedown cruise.

Lin's fellow warship captain, Liu Buchan, had an even more impressive resumé, but did not seem to live up to it. As a teenager in 1876, he had studied at Greenwich Naval College in England, returning to Europe several years later to pick up a German warship for the Chinese government. He was a prominent captain in the

Chinese fleet, described by his contemporaries as 'suave, polished, clever' and yet already suspected by some of his subordinates of not having what it took to command a ship at war. Captain Tōgō would eventually go into battle against both men, but it was Lin that he would remember as a 'great officer'.[7]

Even when the Japanese had left the ship, and were chattering among themselves about the impressive turret-mounted German guns on the Chinese ships, Tōgō seemed cautious. 'We should need to know a little more about it,' he said.[8]

Captain Tōgō suspected that merely because the Chinese had bought some impressive technology, there was no guarantee that they knew how to use it. As if on cue, it was only a few days before one of Commodore Ding's propaganda fleet, the *Pingyuan* ('Queller') limped into the harbour at Kure for sudden repairs. The *Pingyuan* had been built in Fuzhou to German plans, but seemed to have been operated with customary Chinese neglect. Captain Tōgō elected to go on a new inspection tour, but instead of arriving at the dockside in his uniform, he elected to do so each evening disguised in civilian clothes.

Tōgō was soon horror-struck at the behaviour of the Chinese. Shirts, socks and dirty linen were strung up on washing lines between the *Pingyuan*'s gun turrets. From his harbour vantage point, Tōgō saw the decks of the *Pingyuan* unscrubbed and blocked with clutter. Captain Tōgō's thoughts on the matter were damning in the extreme, and soon reported to his associates:

The Chinese Squadron is not worthy of the respect and fear of Japanese. It is, so to speak, a bright sword on the surface, but it is overdone, burnt up. It looks threatening, but it is brittle. It will be of no use in time of need. Look at the *Pingyuan* – she betrays what the Chinese Squadron really is ... You know, the gun should be regarded as sacred, but the Chinese use it as a pole to hang their laundry on, and that in a foreign country. They do not know that the gun is, as it were, the soul of a battleship. Besides, the deck is dirty and out of order. Their slovenliness bears an eloquent testimony to the loose spirit of the whole navy. A few excellent commanders will be of but little use, if their men are slack and slovenly.[9]

Meanwhile, developments even further to the west would grant Tōgō a new and unexpected mission which had its origins in events a decade earlier. On 4 March 1881, part-way through Tōgō's service on the Imperial yacht, a foreign Head of State had visited Japan for the first time in history. News drifted in from the American minister that King David Kalakaua of Hawaii had embarked upon a round-the-world cruise and would be dropping in on the Meiji Emperor *incognito*.

Protocol, and to a certain extent, the Japanese sense of pomp, demanded that King Kalakaua's visit be anything but unnoticed, leading to a terrific series of 21-gun salutes from both Japanese and foreign warships as Kalakaua arrived in Yokohama as a regular passenger aboard the liner RMS *Oceanic*. All Japan was advised of Kalakaua's visit, a band belted out a perfect rendition of Hawaii's national anthem on the shore, and Kalakaua was driven through streets lined with crossed Japanese and Hawaiian flags.

The next day was a day of firsts for the Meiji Emperor. He received the King of Hawaii in the manner set out by European protocol, meeting him at the threshold of his palace dressed in an ostentatious military dress uniform, shaking the King's hand, and even permitting the giant, brown-skinned monarch to walk by his side – an honour not previously accorded even to the Empress.

Kalakaua's visit, originally planned to last just three days, stretched into two weeks. He was feted at dances, shown the sights, and left in the care of Prince Yamashina Sadamaro, a teenage member of a minor Imperial house, who was studying at the naval academy. Kalakaua charmed the Japanese with his talk of the pressing need for strong Japanese labourers on Hawaiian plantations – a welcome gesture of friendship at a time when the Japanese were deeply unwelcome in California. He also proposed that the two nations strike off the extraterritoriality clauses in their treaties – in another first, it was determined that Hawaiians in Japan and Japanese in Hawaii would honour the laws of their host country.

In a private meeting on 11 March, with even Kalakaua's chamberlain absent, the Hawaiian king proposed an even grander suggestion, that Japan become the leader of an Asian league of nations, to present a united front against the white man. Although Meiji diplomatically demurred, Kalakaua made another proposal – that the charming young Prince Yamashina be betrothed to the Hawaiian king's five-year-old niece and putative heir, Victoria Ka'iulani.[10]

It was a bad idea. After initial attempts to beg off, the matter was left to the Prince himself, who diplomatically wrote to King Kalakaua that he had been betrothed to a Japanese fiancée since his infancy, and hence could not honourably break off one agreement to accept another. The Prince's polite refusal, which left the Hawaiian King, if anything, with even greater admiration for him, was a polite spin on the attitude of the conservative faction within the Imperial Family, which regarded Meiji as a direct descendant of the Sun Goddess, and refused to permit the idea of a Japanese marriage to a foreigner. Politically, both the Meiji Emperor and Kalakaua's own chamberlain disapproved of the idea, as it was sure to have been regarded by the white powers as the beginning of a Japanese take-over of Hawaii.[11]

While the Hawaiian King's efforts at bringing highborn Japanese to Hawaii failed, he enjoyed much greater success with his appeal to the working classes. The reforms in the Japan of Tōgō's youth had not brought wealth and prosperity for all. Some agrarian parts of Japan remained in crushing poverty. Traders in outmoded commodities who were unable to adapt, or peacetime samurai unsuited to the modern military, were forced to search for new means of employment. Many therefore jumped at the chance to ship out to Hawaii to earn an honest day's wage for an honest day's work. At the time of King Kalakaua's royal visit, the Japanese population of Hawaii was but a handful of men. A year later, there were over a hundred Japanese workers in the plantations. Within a decade, there were more than 24,000, mainly single men threatening to crowd out the native Hawaiians, whose numbers were fast declining. Consequently, even though young Victoria Ka'iulani had not married a Japanese prince, the Japanese state was obliged to pay closer attention to developments in the distant islands, to ensure the well-being of Japanese subjects at the very least. It was in this capacity that Captain Tōgō would be sent to Hawaii for an eventful cruise in 1892.

His recuperation finally judged to be complete, Tōgō was given command of a beautiful ship, the British-built steel cruiser *Naniwa*.[12] At first, both captain and ship were put through mild paces, steaming in Japanese waters and facing no adversary more threatening than fellow Japanese vessels in naval drills. Tōgō toured the major harbours, all the better to shill for his own navy in the wake of Commodore Ding's efforts to promote the Chinese. *Naniwa* then returned to Japan before being dispatched on her first cruise of note: a trip to Hawaii.

King Kalakaua's efforts to promote an Asian 'league of nations' had not quite gone according to plan. Despite Kalakaua's gallant offer that the Meiji Emperor lead the coalition, the Japanese ruler had refused, not the least because he knew that such an organisation would be sure to provoke the anger of the Chinese, who were bound to take umbrage at the suggestion that they should treat with any other nation on equal terms. Instead, Kalakaua seems to have reduced his aims somewhat, embarking on the first steps of what might have become a Polynesian confederation if his plans had not been thwarted by unrest at home.

In 1887, Kalakaua was stripped of many of his royal powers by a revolt. His hopes that an Asian union might protect him from the predations of the white man were never realised. Instead, he was forced to accept a form of constitutional monarchy that disenfranchised many of his native subjects and left the government of Hawaii in the hands of Americans, Europeans and their stooges. Kalakaua continued to rule, at least in name, until his death in San Francisco in 1891. His sister, Queen Liliuokalani, took the Hawaiian throne and immediately disappointed the white lobby by proposing to restore the vote to both native Hawaiians and to Asians living in Hawaii. The Queen also suggested that it would be better for her realm if the reigning monarch's power of veto were restored, all the better to resist the intrigues of pro-foreign factions. Meanwhile, in America, the new McKinley tariff forced Hawaiian exports to the United States to compete for the first time with other 'foreign' goods. American plantation owners in Hawaii realised they could restore their profits if they somehow engineered the incorporation of Hawaii into the United States, thereby reclassifying its sugar and pineapple exports as 'local' American products.

On 17 January 1893, a self-styled 'Committee of Safety' acted to overthrow Queen Liliuokalani and seize control of the Hawaiian government. Some 1,500 non-native Hawaiians, supposedly acting out of concern for their own safety on Hawaiian territory, seized government buildings and proclaimed a Provisional Government. The committee then invited the resident US minister, John Stevens, to put ashore troops from the USS *Boston*, supposedly to protect the interests of Americans in Hawaii.

With a similar order to protect his own countrymen, Captain Tōgō was ordered to take the *Naniwa* with all haste to Hawaii. Even at full speed, it was two weeks before the warship reached Hawaiian waters, catching up with the older Imperial navy ship *Kongō*, whose captain had put in at Hawaii on his way home from San Francisco and had decided to wait around. The *Naniwa* was easily the most impressive ship in the harbour, outshining Britain's *Garnet* and a cluster of American vessels. Captain Tōgō fired a 21-gun salute for the Hawaiian flag, followed by 13 for the Americans on the *Boston* – all present and correct.

In meetings with the captain of the *Kongō* and the Japanese consul Fuji Saburō, Tōgō established that the American government had hailed the new government in Hawaii, but that Japan still technically recognised the deposed Queen Liliuokalani. This fact may have escaped the Provisional Government – many foreign consuls and ministers had acknowledged the regime change, but Consul Fuji had fobbed them off with a long-winded note that, when inspected more closely, merely acknowledged that he had informed the Japanese Emperor of the Provisional Government's claims.[13] Back in Washington, a faction tried to push through a treaty that officially annexed Hawaii to the USA, while in Honolulu, Sanford Dole, a man of American ancestry but Hawaiian born, was elected as the ruler of a newly democratic Hawaii.

Already, the rhetoric of the revolution was divided on political lines. To many Americans, the revolution was a re-run of the birth of the United States itself, with free citizens rising up against a deluded tyrant, establishing a democracy in which all men were created equal. Such a claim, however, did not play in the same way with the subjects of the Japanese Emperor, who saw a friendly reigning monarch rudely shoved aside by the same kind of brash commercial interests that had sent warships to Japan to open up the country by force. With this in mind, Tōgō informed his officers that they needed to tread with even greater care than usual.

> I take it for granted that you already know how you are placed here and how you are to behave, but I must remind you of one thing. That our ship has come here means that part of our empire has temporarily been extended here, and you must be prudent in conduct. Every move you make here will affect the dignity of our empire. You must beware of acting rashly lest you should compromise the dignity of our empire, whether there may be disturbance or not hereafter. But should an emergency arise, you must be up and doing in a manner worthy of our empire.[14]

It was precisely the sort of tense political situation for which Tōgō had often cautioned his subordinates to prepare. If the American navy felt able to land troops to 'protect' its own resident citizens, then why not that of Japan? The Imperial Fleet's first duty was to the safety of Japanese subjects in Hawaii – a situation likely to become problematic if the American government announced that it was now the ruler of the islands.

The rumour mill soon intrigued against the Japanese. Somehow, the story got out that Tōgō was less of a captain than a matchmaker, and that he had arrived in Hawaii with a dashing young Japanese prince aboard the *Naniwa*. The plan, supposedly, was to swiftly join the prince in holy matrimony with the deposed Queen's niece and heir, the teenage Victoria Ka'iulani, turning Japan's interest in restoring the old order from neutrality to passionate imperial interference in a family matter.

'There is little doubt,' fulminated the Honolulu *Daily Bulletin*, 'that Japan looks upon these islands with an eye of longing, and that there has been a plan underfoot to bring them under Japanese influence by the marriage of one of the Princes of the Imperial House with Ka'iulani.'[15]

As the Meiji Emperor had already told the late King Kalakaua, there was no chance of that happening. But it is easy to see why the local press had thought otherwise. Clearly, King Kalakaua had been significantly less discreet than the Emperor in discussing his thwarted wedding plans with a home audience. Tōgō's biographers unanimously dismiss the story as poppycock, but despite the brusque denials of the time, Tōgō does appear to have arrived in Hawaii with a dangerously eligible bachelor aboard his ship. After schooling in Britain and a period at a French naval academy, Prince Yamashina had returned to Japan a year beforehand and been given what everyone had hoped would be a safe and trouble-free posting as a marine squad leader on the *Naniwa's* sister-ship, the *Takachiho* in March 1892. Unfortunately for all concerned, he had then been transferred to the *Naniwa* herself as a sublieutenant that same September. Now a dashing young officer in his twenties, Prince Yamashina was indeed aboard the *Naniwa*, and was one of the officers whose responsibility it would be to lead a landing party, should Tōgō decide to wade in on the side of the Hawaiians. Luckily for Tōgō, the putative bride was elsewhere. Victoria Ka'iulani had been sent to England for an education, and by the time Tōgō reached Hawaii, the Princess was already *en route* back across the Atlantic to protest in Washington at her country's treatment.[16]

To ensure that the Hawaiian spring got even more unpleasantly hot for Tōgō, Sanford Dole himself paid a visit to the harbour. The self-styled ruler of Hawaii crossed the water in a small boat, making a beeline for an American warship that was inconveniently close to the *Naniwa*. Seeing a man approaching who had been accepted by the Washington government as a Head of State, the American warship boomed out an entirely proper greeting – a 21-gun salute.

It would now be deemed appropriate for the *Naniwa* to follow suit, an unfortunate position considering Tōgō's past record with naval salutes. Tōgō ruled that the Americans might think Dole was a head of state, but until such time there was a change of policy in Tokyo, Queen Liliuokalani was still the rightful ruler of Hawaii, and Dole was just a pretender. This meant no salute at all: not from the guns, nor even from the sailors aboard the *Naniwa*.

As the minutes passed, it became apparent that the *Naniwa* was making no effort to fire her guns whatsoever. Dole himself peered from his boat at the Japanese warship, and saw Tōgō standing on the after-bridge, staring back at him impassively through a pair of binoculars. Then, in a gesture sure to be misinterpreted, Tōgō turned his back on Dole and stared out to sea. By Japanese principles, it was a polite means of pretending that nothing was amiss; to the slighted Dole, it added personal insult to diplomatic injury.[17]

While Tōgō busily courted diplomatic disasters on the *Naniwa*, the *Kongō* was having an altogether easier time of it on an island cruise. The lesser warship took a week-long tour of the Hawaiian archipelago, largely to make sure that the majority of the Japanese nationals in the region, on the Big Island rather than on Oahu, were safe. The *Kongō* returned to Tōgō, reported all was well and then steamed off towards Japan.

Tōgō was soon to have just cause to wish that he were onboard the *Kongō* himself, or at the very least, that he had kept her in the harbour for just one more day. Instead, even as the *Kongō* steamed out to sea, Tōgō received a unwanted guest aboard the *Naniwa*.

Imada Yasaka was neither prince nor president, but a convicted murderer. A Japanese migrant worker on the island of Maui, he had killed a fellow Japanese labourer with a hatchet, for which he had been sentenced to twenty-one years hard labour. Only three months into his sentence on 16 March 1893, Imada was one of a work-gang shipped over from Oahu Prison to undertake work on the Quarantine Station in the harbour. At a moment when his wardens were fatefully looking elsewhere, Imada broke free of his captors, sprinted down the wharf and dove into the water. A strong swimmer, he powered across the waters, snatching hold of the *Naniwa*'s gangplank sufficiently far ahead of a pursuing outrigger canoe to be able to introduce himself to Tōgō's deck officers and claim asylum. By the time word reached Tōgō of the new arrival, all those involved had come to appreciate the delicacy of the situation. Even if Imada had not been wholly forthcoming about his resumé, there was soon a flotilla of police launches and canoes in the water around the *Naniwa*, demanding that Tōgō hand the escaped prisoner back. Tōgō, however, reacted in a fashion that would not have surprised anyone who had witnessed his previous attitude towards the letter of the law. 'I am here to protect my countrymen generally,' he said. 'Therefore I cannot deliver up to you this subject of Japan.'[18]

When Imada's jailers failed to elicit the desired compliance from Tōgō, the matter fell to the police. When Tōgō politely told the police the same thing, the matter was passed up to the same Provisional Government that Tōgō had already refused to recognise. Realising that Tōgō was not listening, officials instead leaned on the Japanese consul, Fuji Saburō, who was at least within reach on land. Fuji pleaded with Tōgō to relent, and when this failed, passed the buck by asking him to write an explanation of his legal and diplomatic situation.

Contentious as ever, Tōgō wrote a long assessment of the legal precedent and protocols, and did so in the beautifully-formed Japanese characters that one might expect from a classically-educated samurai boy from Kagoshima. A flustered Fuji protested that none of the plaintiffs could read Japanese, to which Tōgō bluntly replied that he was the captain of a warship, and had better things to do than translate legal documents into English for a crowd of self-styled revolutionaries.

Now as exasperated as the whites, Fuji sent a cable to Tokyo asking for orders. His problem, as far as he could see, was that Tōgō was not necessarily in the wrong. As one local newspaper had already pointed out:

As there is no extradition treaty between this country and Japan, doubtless the Japanese authorities are in no way bound to comply with the request of this Government for the return of the prisoner. If the *Naniwa* were a merchantman, she would be under Hawaiian jurisdiction, but the case is difficult with vessels of war, which carry their national sovereignty with them. The *Naniwa* is as it were a piece of Japanese territory, subject to Japanese laws, and merely temporarily set down in Honolulu harbour.[19]

What was at issue, and what the Admiralty ultimately decided for itself, was that the stubborn Captain Tōgō was hardly protecting a political refugee or saving an innocent civilian. Instead, he was offering sanctuary to a man who had buried an axe in the skull of a fellow Japanese. Was Tōgō expecting to bring Imada home for a new trial? Imada had already been convicted of second-degree manslaughter, and it seemed churlish to risk an international incident to protect the questionable rights of an escaped convict. Moreover, when the late King Kalakaua had made his historic visit to Japan, he had publicly agreed with the Meiji Emperor to drop extraterritoriality from the agreements between the two countries. In other words, while Tōgō might be adhering to the letter of international law in refusing to hand Imada over to an unrecognised government, the *spirit* of that same law was that Imada had been found guilty by a Hawaiian court in the closing days of the reign of King Kalakaua, with whose laws the Japanese Emperor had agreed his subjects would abide. What was good enough for the Meiji Emperor was surely good enough for Captain Tōgō.[20]

Even when Tōgō was faced, not for the first time in his life, with a stern countermand from Tokyo, he refused to give up. Rather than hand Imada over to the Hawaiian authorities – whom neither Tōgō nor Tokyo recognised – he dumped him on Consul Fuji with these words:

> I must obey orders, but, as you know, this prisoner is our countryman and, when he needs our protection, I cannot refrain from extending it to him. I am not delivering him to the officials of the *de facto* government, but to you, another representative of Japan. If you find it necessary to surrender him, do it where I cannot be a witness.[21]

In later years, Tōgō was occasionally heard to wonder what difference his stand would have made. Would Imada Yasaka have enjoyed a more fortunate fate if he had been permitted to return to Japan? Consul Fuji was not troubled by any such musings and promptly handed Imada over to the Hawaiians again.

The loopholes that Consul Fuji had made for himself were now closed – if Tokyo was ordering Captain Tōgō to hand over Imada, then it would seem that the Provisional Government was recognised after all. As the weeks passed, the news came back from America that Hawaii had been recognised as a Republic, and hence no longer required the 'protection' of the American marines. The Stars and Stripes was taken down, the Hawaiian flag raised once more in the government offices and, it was hoped, normality restored.

Captain Tōgō left on 11 May, taking the *Naniwa* back to Tokyo for two months' recuperation, followed by an uneventful cruise that took her up to Vladivostok and around the island that had once been called Ezo – now renamed Hokkaido. He was back in Hawaii on 11 November, fast behind the rumours of new troubles brewing. As the guns of American ships in the harbour sounded to mark Tōgō's return, the British sailors of HMS *Champion* discovered to their great embarrassment that they did not have a Japanese flag on board. Protocol demanded that they raise the flag of the new arrival and then salute it.

In what must have been a tense wait, while the etiquette-minded Captain Tōgō looked on in bafflement, sailors from *Champion* launched one of their boats and rowed frantically over to the *Philadelphia* to borrow the Americans' flag. Purloining a Rising Sun, the sailors then rowed back, dashed aboard, hoisted the colours and let off their thirteen guns. Although Captain Tōgō surely noted the delay in the British salute, it is not clear that he ever understood the reason behind it; had he known, it would surely have amused him.[22]

Tōgō arrived back in Honolulu during a brief and unsuccessful attempt by the USA to persuade the Provisional Government to step down in favour of the deposed Queen Liliuokalani. Such machinations would continue for several more years, ending with the election of a new American president who would officially annex Hawaii to the United States. Consequently, while diplomats blew hot and cold over the correct procedure to follow with regard to the the government of Sanford Dole, Tōgō remained stuck amid thorny protocol issues little different from those that he had hoped to have left behind.

A year after the original change in regime, Dole's officials announced a day of national celebration, scheduled for 17 January 1894. Dole's Foreign Minister notified the ships in the harbour that he expected to see them decked out in full dress as for a naval gala, and that they should fire a noon salute in recognition of the anniversary of the revolution. Captain Tōgō went aboard the British and American vessels in the harbour and informed them that he would be taking no such action. The foreign captains agreed that it would be inappropriate, leading to the bizarre situation whereby the government of Hawaii celebrated on land, while in the harbour the ships of the rest of the world behaved as if there was nothing special about the day. On that occasion, the British and the Americans joined in with Captain Tōgō's very Japanese policy, and simply acted as if Dole and his cronies were not there.

The sinking of the *Kowshing* by Japanese men-of-war in 1894. An
illustration by a Chinese artist for a contemporary English newspaper

6

Sink the Kowshing

Upon Tōgō's return to Japan in 1894, he spent six weeks at Kure before being reassigned to the *Naniwa*. It did not take a brilliant military brain to calculate where he would next see action. Tensions already ran high between Japan and Korea, following the assassination of a prominent pro-Japanese Korean revolutionary in Shanghai in March 1894. The crisis point arrived shortly afterwards, with countrywide unrest by conservative rebels calling themselves the Donghak – 'Eastern Learning'. Like the conservative samurai who had been crushed in Japan, the Donghak were locals who refused to accept foreign incursions. Anti-Japanese and anti-Western agitators joined forces with disaffected peasantry in the countryside, determined to overthrow the old order. As in Japan a generation earlier, this revolt was couched in terms of 'loyalty' – in this case to Korea as an old-world, secluded Hermit Kingdom, with no dealings with foreigners. Unlike Japan, the revolt was tinged with elements of class struggle, as if many of the peasants were determined not merely to oust foreigners, but to overturn Korea's ruling class in favour of a new elite.

Despite early defeats by government troops, by May 1894 the Donghak rebels presented a serious threat to Seoul, causing the government to call for Chinese aid in suppressing them. The decision by the Chinese to send troops brought a critical difference of opinion to light over the wording of the Tianjin Accord. As far as the Chinese were concerned, they were merely obliged to *notify* the Japanese if they dispatched troops to Korea, which they duly did. Japan strongly protested that the Tianjin Accord meant nothing if both parties could do as they wished, and that notification required *consultation* and *approval*.

It was too late: 3,000 Chinese troops were already on their way to Korea. Japanese troops were mobilised in the next of a tense series of moves that threatened to end in an exchange of fire and outright war between China and Japan on Korean soil. Although the Donghak rebels were suppressed, both Chinese and Japanese soldiers remained in Seoul, with their leaders trying to steer the Korean government towards new policies favourable to their own. Chinese and Japanese troops continued to arrive, in a build-up that was sure to end in conflict. The Japanese struck on 23 July, with the sudden arrival of two small detachments of troops in Seoul, who took over the palace, informed the Korean king that he had been 'rescued' from the intrigues of the family of Queen Min, and sent for the disgraced former regent, the Daiwongun, with the news that he had been re-appointed to a government position. Two men were killed in the ensuing scuffles, but the day ended with announcements that a new era was dawning in a Korea free from Chinese influence.

Captain Tōgō sailed aboard the *Naniwa* in July 1894, escorting a Japanese expeditionary force in five troop transports. He reached Chemulpo and successfully navigated its tides and treacherous waters with the aid of the charts he had helped to draw during his previous visit. Tōgō steamed out of Chemulpo harbour on 25 July, heading down the coast towards the site of the Chinese troop landings.

The order of events that followed was a matter of delicate international politics, and excruciatingly tense brinkmanship. As far as the Japanese were concerned, the regime change in Seoul had been a policing action, a minor skirmish involving Japanese military men and Korean rebels. The Korean king was still technically the ruler of his country; there had, on paper, been no coup. Moreover, none of this was considered to be any business of the Chinese.

The Chinese, of course, saw things very differently. Shots had been fired in the Korean capital. The Japanese had seized control of Seoul, and it was incumbent upon the Chinese to come to the rescue of their Korean allies. Considering the relative speeds of the available ships, the Chinese and the Japanese were sure to run into each other first somewhere in the Yellow Sea. And yet, war had not yet been declared. A Sino-Japanese war, although clearly looming, still awaited official sanction from either government.

As Tōgō steamed down the Korean coast in the *Naniwa*, he spied the smokestacks of two vessels approaching from the south. The new arrivals were sure to be Chinese warships and were getting closer by the minute. Protocol demanded that Tōgō should fire a salute, but the awful prospect remained that the sound of a blank charge might be mistaken for live fire.

The two smoke columns drew steadily nearer, while Tōgō weighed the situation. He was sure that the approaching commanders would be having similar thoughts. They could fire a salute, and risk being mistaken for belligerents. Or they could take advantage of Tōgō's *politesse*, wait until they were at point-blank range, and then let loose with live ammunition. Whoever attacked first would be forever remembered as the instigator of the Sino-Japanese War. The defender, however, would be unlikely to have a chance to retaliate – he would already be dead. The other ships were still mere dots on the horizon, but Tōgō could not afford to take any risks. He ordered his men to load the saluting gun. Then he issued the order for Battle Stations. The *Naniwa* was prepared for any eventuality.

As the ships drew nearer, Tōgō's worst fears were realised. They were the *Zhenyuan*, one of the twin behemoths that had scared the Japanese a few years earlier, and the *Pingyuan*, the same vessel which Tōgō had once spied on in the Kure dockyards. Through his binoculars, he saw that the sailors on both vessels had also manned their guns, unsure of whether battle was about to commence.

Neither the *Zhenyuan* nor the *Naniwa* would deviate from their course. They were all but head-on, sure to pass within a stone's throw of one another. Tōgō's men waited silently by their guns, their hands sweating on the triggers, ready in a split-second order to unleash hell. The noise of the *Zhenyuan*'s engines thrummed on the water as the ship drew close enough, so close in fact that Tōgō could see the face of his opposite number. There, on the *Zhenyuan*'s bridge, was the unmistakeable form of Captain Lin Taizeng, the same quiet officer he had met on the earlier goodwill cruise. The two men stared at each other in melancholy recognition, before Tōgō stood sharply to attention and saluted. Captain Lin returned the gesture, and the moment passed along with the ships. The *Zhenyuan* continued north, the *Naniwa* continued south, with a salute of sorts given but not a shot fired. [1]

The tense encounter between the *Naniwa* and the *Zhenyuan* is a crucial event in late July 1894, in particular for the impression it gives us of Tōgō's razor-sharp grasp of protocols and precedents. He was not, as his detractors would soon imply, a trigger-happy captain looking for trouble. Far from it: in his encounter with the *Zhenyuan* he had done everything possible to avoid bloodshed or political damage. Such considerations are important in the light of events of 25 July, in which Tōgō would twice be accused of firing the first shot of the Sino-Japanese War.

Tōgō was soon back in the area, ordered there in search of Chinese troop transports. One body of Chinese troops would have to march down from Chinese territory, crossing the Yalu River in the north and making the long journey on foot. The Japanese knew that other units would attempt to make a more direct crossing by sea, and sent a handful of warships, the *Naniwa* included, to sweep the area.

Just after dawn on 25 July, two Chinese vessels came out of the channel leading to Asan – the aging cruiser *Qiyuan* ('The Aider') and a smaller torpedo boat, the *Guangyi*. This time, there was no waiting for a salute. It is unclear who fired first. The Japanese certainly believed it was the *Qiyuan*, recording her first shot at eight minutes to eight – a muzzle flash from one of her guns, followed by a plume of water from a stray shell. Other accounts suggested that nervous Japanese sailors saw a torpedo in the water that only existed in their imaginations. Tōgō responded to this attack, real or phantom, with the order to open fire. The other two Japanese vessels followed suit, and answering guns from the Chinese were mere seconds behind.

As the ships closed on each other, the *Qiyuan* took the worst of it, including a direct hit on her conning tower that threw the ship into chaos. At some point in the proceedings, possibly before battle had even commenced, her steering gear jammed, causing her to execute a series of bizarre manouevres that the Japanese at first mistook for bold tactics. Suddenly, the engineers on the *Qiyuan* managed to get her steering gear working again, but even then the *Qiyuan* was sending contradictory signals. A white flag of surrender ran up her mast, followed by a Japanese ensign, but the *Qiyuan* was plainly turning and running south-west, back towards Weihaiwei. Soon after, the heavily damaged *Guangyi* ran aground while attempting to avoid the *Akitsushima*.

Aboard the *Naniwa*, Tōgō prepared to join another Japanese ship in a cautious pursuit of the *Qiyuan* – the captains remained unsure whether the white flag was genuine, or a trap designed to lure the Japanese towards other Chinese vessels lurking nearby. However, Tōgō then sighted two other ships out to sea. The first was a Chinese warship, which appeared to be changing course and fleeing after receiving a signal from the *Qiyuan*. The departing warship had been escorting a tramp steamer, which she was now abandoning to her fate.

While another Japanese vessel pursued the fleeing escort, the *Naniwa* drew close to the transport ship. She was the *Kowshing* ('High Promoted'), a British-registered steamer with a Chinese crew and an English captain, Thomas Galsworthy.[2] Although he was not aware of the irony at the time, Captain Galsworthy was a fellow alumnus of the naval training college aboard the *Worcester*, graduating two years behind Tōgō himself. He had been hired by the Chinese to transport troops the short distance from Tianjin's sea-port to Asan. He had 1,100 troops aboard his ship, as well as Constantine von Hanneken, a German army major who was travelling as a 'civilian' but was actually in Chinese military service. Now, the *Kowshing* was alone, deserted by her escort, and with no protection available but a few rifles and the British Red Ensign fluttering at the mast.

Captain Galsworthy was already confused. He had understandably mistaken the fleeing *Qiyuan* for a Japanese ship, as she had been flying a Japanese flag. Unsure why the *Qiyuan* had steamed right past him without acknowledging any of his own signals,

Galsworthy assumed that all Japanese ships in the area were on a mission of their own and would not trouble him.

Aboard the *Naniwa*, Tōgō ordered a signal raised commanding the *Kowshing* to shut down her engines. The *Kowshing* complied, but her captain noticed that the Japanese warships were not changing course. Instead, they were steaming past in pursuit of the *Qiyuan*. As the *Naniwa* neared, Captain Galsworthy raised a polite signal flag of enquiry: 'May I proceed?' His eagerness to press on may have been the crucial factor that gave him away. Instead of continuing his pursuit of the fleeing warship, Tōgō ordered the *Naniwa* close to the merchant ship and sent over a lieutenant, Hitomi Zengorō, to ascertain what was going on.

Captain Galsworthy protested to Lieutenant Hitomi that he was the British captain of a British ship and that the Japanese had no right to interfere in his lawful passage. Hitomi begged to differ – regardless of the flag at the masthead, Galsworthy was knowingly transporting over a thousand soldiers to Korea, along with four-teen field guns and their ammunition. Galsworthy confirmed this himself, showing Hitomi his ship's manifest with the weapons and ammunition aboard; the *Kowshing* was the third of three transports chartered to help the Chinese war effort. Had he reached Asan the day before, he might have got away with it, but the morning's exchange of fire between Tōgō and the Chinese amounted to an outbreak of war.[3]

Galsworthy had not been witness to the morning's skirmish, but he had seen the *Qiyuan* running for cover, so must have suspected something. Nevertheless, there had not been an official declaration of war and he still hoped to tough it out. Hitomi, however, was insistent. 'Your vessel shall follow our warship the *Naniwa*,' said Hitomi. 'She shall,' replied Galsworthy curtly, disappointed to have been thwarted in his mission, but understanding that the situation had changed and that his cargo was likely to be forfeit.[4]

Back on the *Naniwa*, Hitomi reported to Tōgō, noting that Galsworthy understood the situation, but that 1,100 belligerent Chinese might not have such a good command of the laws of the sea. Tōgō signalled for the *Kowshing* to follow, and prepared to head back towards home, but there was no sign of any movement from the British ship. Instead, after a pregnant pause, the *Kowshing* signalled: 'Urgent matter to discuss. Please send boats.'

Tōgō immediately guessed the problem. 'See if the Chinese troops are unwilling to obey any orders,' he said to Hitomi, 'and ask the Europeans what the urgent matter is about. Then, if you find the captain and all the non-combatants anxious to board our ship, take them over in our boat.'

Aboard the *Kowshing*, the Chinese passengers had become increasingly agitated at the arrival of the *Naniwa*, her threatening two-shot signal to stop, and the baffling series of coloured flags being used by both vessels in a coded conversation that the Chinese could not follow. Eventually, a British engineer was able to read the signals for the German officer von Hanneken, who passed on the news to the commanders of the Chinese troops. The stiff but amicable conversation between Galsworthy and Lieutenant Hitomi had an unforseen side-effect. To the Japanese, keen to follow a law of the sea that was largely written by the British, it was a textbook exercise in restraint and civility. Galsworthy, while understandably annoyed, still recognised that the Japanese were behaving impeccably. Many Chinese, however, witnessed the ongoing conversation and concluded that if the two men were acting in such a calm manner amid such a threatening situation, that something was amiss. Several among the Chinese assumed the worst – that Galsworthy was not negotiating over the safety of his ship, but of the size of a bribe from the Japanese. Deciding that, as far as they were concerned, their captain was selling them out to the enemy, the Chinese protested to Galsworthy, boasting that they outnumbered the Japanese and were determined to fight to the death.

'The Chinese generals,' wrote Galsworthy later, 'learning the meaning of the signals ... objected most emphatically.'

They were told how useless it would be to resist, as one shot would sink them in a short time. The generals then said they would rather die than follow Japanese orders, and as they had 1,100 men against 400 on the *Naniwa*, they would fight sooner than surrender. They were told that if they decided to fight, the foreign officers would leave the ship. The generals then gave orders to the troops on deck to kill us if we obeyed the orders of the Japanese or attempted to leave the ship. With gestures, they threatened to cut off our heads, to stab, or shoot us; and a lot of men were selected to carry out the order. [5]

When Lieutenant Hitomi rowed over a second time, Galsworthy attempted to meet him at the gangplank. Even as Galsworthy tried to explain his situation to Hitomi, he was surrounded by a gaggle of irate Chinese, yelling at him that he was under orders from their government, and that if he obeyed the Japanese, they would kill him. Hitomi heard someone else (the list of suspects is short and favours von Hanneken) pointing out: 'This vessel is possessed by a British company. However wild Japan may be, she will certainly not inflict any injury upon a ship of a neutral country.'

Galsworthy offered Hitomi a compromise. He could turn his ship back around for its port of origin, the Dagu forts near Tianjin. The Japanese would thereby prevent the arrival of 1,100 Chinese troops at Asan, and Galsworthy would not be beheaded by his passengers. Hitomi sternly warned Galsworthy that the occupants of the *Kowshing* were obliged to come quietly or to swim home, but that there was no other compromise on offer. If the Chinese had mutinied and were impossible to control, then Hitomi offered Galsworthy a last resort – he and his fellow Europeans could be ferried to safety aboard the *Naniwa*.

Captain Galsworthy was in an impossible position. The Chinese would kill him if he tried to leave, and the Japanese had already promised to blow his ship out of the water if he stayed. Meanwhile, Tōgō was similarly troubled – it was his duty to sink or capture the *Kowshing*, despite her official registration as a British ship. He was also well aware that time was passing and that it would only take the arrival of a Chinese warship to tip the delicate situation once more in the *Kowshing*'s favour. Tōgō weighed the many precedents in his head and reached a difficult conclusion. The *Kowshing* had lost its claim to be a British ship when her captain had been forcibly overruled by his passengers. It was effectively in a state of mutiny, and one that had essentially transferred its ownership into Chinese

hands. 'Four hours had been consumed in these fruitless negotiations,' Tōgō wrote, 'and there was no longer room for hesitation, so
I signalled ML [quit the ship immediately].'[6]

Galsworthy's return signal was hopeless: 'We are not allowed
to leave.' Tōgō stared at the distant flags with his arms folded.
On his orders, the *Naniwa* was already raising a single red signal
flag, a symbol that she was about to open fire. Captain Tōgō's face
remained impassive. His cheeks filled with air – known by his subordinates to be a sign of their captain weighing a difficult situation
in his mind. Suddenly, he blew out the air in an explosive sigh. He
had made up his mind. 'Sink her,' he said.

The *Naniwa*'s propellers whirred into life, and the warship
began to approach the helpless merchant vessel. A single torpedo
whooshed into the water, and then all the *Naniwa*'s guns opened
up. Despite the target being a sitting duck that had not moved
for four hours, the *Naniwa*'s torpedo somehow managed to miss
the *Kowshing*. The ship's guns, however, had an easier time of it,
and landed five devastating shells on the defenceless vessel in two
thunderous salvos. Something hit the *Kowshing*'s bunkers amidships, and the middle of the ship exploded in a black cloud of coal
dust and smoke, so thick that 'day became night.'[7]

The Europeans on the *Kowshing* dove overboard. The Chinese
ran to the rails with their rifles and began taking futile potshots at
the distant Japanese warship. Deserted by his panicking captors,
Captain Galsworthy took his chance, grabbed a life-jacket and
jumped into the water on the far side of his ship, the *Kowshing* herself shielding him from any stray shots from the *Naniwa*.
The *Kowshing* was already listing in the water, beginning to sink
at quarter past one on a hot July afternoon. But as Galsworthy
bobbed in the water, noting the sporty von Hanneken swimming
steadily for shore, he was astounded to hear not only the continued discharge of rifles from the sinking ship, but the unmistakeable whoosh of bullets around him in the water. Up on the deck
of the *Kowshing*, some of the Chinese had decided to take aim at
Galsworthy himself. [8] Gifted with a vast supply of ammunition,
the Chinese soldiers kept up their barrage of rifle-fire for the
next half-hour. Unwilling to put his ship's boats in the line of fire,

Tōgō was forced to wait until the *Kowshing* finally slipped below the waves.

A handful of men from the *Kowshing* managed to swim ashore. Others appear to have put to sea in two of the ship's boats and rowed in a suicidal attack against the *Naniwa*, cut to pieces by the *Naniwa*'s deck-mounted machine guns. Still more stayed aboard the sinking ship, firing into the floating bodies of their own countrymen. Galsworthy's chief officer, Lewes Tamplin, initially began swimming towards the shore, but decided that he stood better chance of surviving in Japanese captivity than marooned on an island with hostile Chinese.

Tamplin, however, also claimed that the Japanese had joined in the shooting in the water:

> I was not swimming long when I saw [the *Naniwa*] lowering two of her boats, and one coming towards me, I was picked up. I explained to the officer the direction in which I had last seen the captain and the major swimming, and he directed the other boat to pull that way. No attempt was made to rescue the drowning Chinamen. Two volleys were fired from our boat with the object of sinking two of the lifeboats, which, having got clear of the ship, were filled with Chinese. Our boat was then recalled and I was taken on board, and dry clothes given to me.[9]

By firing upon a vessel flying the British flag, Captain Tōgō gained worldwide notoriety. His decision to sink the *Kowshing* led to outraged protests in Britain comparing him to a pirate, while the commander of Britain's naval squadron in the Far East sent a passionately worded admonition to the Japanese Admiralty. Itō Hirobumi, the Japanese Prime Minister, commented: 'I wonder what the Japanese navy will do to cope with the grave international complications created by this.'[10]

Journalists and inquisitive passers-by soon attempted to elicit commentary from Tōgō's own family, who remained at his Tokyo home. They were shooed away by his venerable mother Masuko, who refused to make any comment except a pious statement of loyalty to the Emperor and a heartfelt wish that her prayers would be answered and that the Imperial forces would return home in triumph. Although it might sound like an attempt to avoid being drawn out on the incident itself, this seems to have been a fair summary of Masuko's general state of mind regarding military matters – her old-time samurai attitude never quite left her.[11]

Clearer heads eventually prevailed, even in London, where the letters page of the *Times* became a battleground between legal minds. The sinking of the *Kowshing* was a hot topic for several years to come, but much of the opposition to it, particularly in Britain, was based on early reports that muddled the facts. Eventually, the consensus went in Tōgō's favour – although war had not been officially declared, there was clearly a state of belligerence between China and Japan, and nobody aboard the *Kowshing* could seriously pretend that they were not going to Asan to shoot Japanese soldiers. With that in mind, it was the right of the *Naniwa* to sink the *Kowshing* if the *Kowshing* refused to surrender. Far from being pilloried by the international community, Tōgō was instead widely praised for his incredible patience in the many hours of prolonged negotiations, during which he had diligently tried to save the lives of all aboard the *Kowshing*.[12]

Tōgō fared less well over his treatment of the Chinese survivors. It was, as many noted at the time, deeply suspicious that the *Naniwa* had only rescued European survivors. Von Hanneken openly asserted that the the Japanese had shot at the men in the water, and he was not alone in this accusation. Galsworthy, however, could not have been clearer in his testimony: 'I can positively say I did not see the Japanese fire upon the Chinese in the water.' Testimonies universally agree that many Chinese 'in the water', and even in the lifeboats, were not awaiting rescue at all, but continuing their futile attack against the *Naniwa*, rendering it impossible for Tōgō to save them. Galsworthy's own testimony made it clear that it was the foreign officers who were in danger from the Chinese, and it was these men that Tōgō fished out of the water.[13]

Some time later, when the *Naniwa* put into her home port, Tōgō's launch was met at the jetty by a fellow captain, Yamamoto Gonnohyōe, and his roommate, a Mr Matsunami. Matsunami reported that Yamamoto enthusiastically grabbed Tōgō by the hand and congratulated him, while Tōgō replied with nothing but a mumbled monosyllable. Yamamoto introduced Matsunami as a scholar of maritime law, which was Matsunami's cue to tell Tōgō that he had examined the evidence and that his behaviour had been exemplary. 'I did it,' said Tōgō, 'because I thought it right, but I feel easier when I am assured by a scholar.'[14]

Politicians and soldiers were already scurrying to make good on Tōgō's act. On 29 July, four days after the sinking of the *Kowshing*, Japanese forces overwhelmed Chinese forces at Asan that were at least 1,100 men short thanks to Tōgō's actions. Two days later, with southern Korea already in Japanese hands, the Meiji Emperor tardily declared war on China. Even then, the Emperor hedged his bets by leaving such business in the hands of politicians. He did not officially go on the record by ceremonially reporting hostilities to his ancestors until 11 August.[15] By 16 September, Japanese troops had occupied Pyongyang, and all Korea was effectively under Japanese control. The Chinese forces retreated north across the Yalu River into Chinese territory. The Japanese would soon follow.

The Battle of Yalu River during the First Sino-Japanese War of 1894–1895. Fought between Qing Dynasty China and Meiji Japan for the control of Korea

7

The Angry Dragons

The Yalu River was not merely a border between the territory of China and Japan. Its mouth also marked the boundary of Chinese waters. This was not the decision of Ding Ruchang, now Admiral of the Chinese fleet, who would have much preferred to take the battle to the Japanese, perhaps even landing a body of Chinese troops somewhere behind Japanese lines in Korea to mount a counter-attack. Instead, Admiral Ding was fettered by the decisions made by bureaucrats in distant Beijing, determined to draw a line that they were sure the Japanese would not dare cross.

The Japanese, of course, wasted no time in crossing it. On 10 August, with the battle still raging in north Korea, Admiral Itō Suk-eyuki steamed the short distance across the gulf and fired some desultory shells at the fortifications of Weihaiwei, Admiral Ding's headquarters. However, Itō did not hang around for long, instead turning tail and running back towards open water. If he had been hoping to lure the two Chinese behemoths, the *Dingyuan* and *Zhenyuan*, out of hiding, he was to be disappointed. Nor did Admiral Ding rashly send his two giants chasing after the Japanese tormenter – Ding was no fool, and would not readily run into a Japanese trap.

In Weihaiwei, the stronghold of Ding's navy, the Chinese rushed to prepare their ships for a new encounter. There was, as Captain Tōgō might have wryly observed, no longer any talk of laundry strung between the gun barrels. Many of the ships' guns were stripped of their 'protective' shields, since they had been found to be an additional hazard for glancing blows and no help at all in the case of a direct hit. Sails, too, were dismantled and disembarked. It had been decided that they were next to useless in the close-quarters manouevering of the Yellow Sea and were likely to be a fire hazard.

The 'Chinese' fleet was not wholly Chinese. In a scheme that had already caused ructions within the fleet, many Chinese commanders both with and without the necessary skills and experience shared their commands with foreign advisers. The question of precisely who was in control had already cost the Chinese fleet its foreign admiral, a British officer who had quit in disgust when Liu Buchan had scrambled ahead of him on the promotion ladder.

Whereas most foreign officers had been purged from the Japanese fleet, Admiral Ding still had a number of white faces among his men – perhaps, it was unkindly alleged, to ensure that foreigners could take the blame in the event of defeat and thereby allow their Chinese colleagues to keep their heads, execution being the Chinese punishment for military failure. Ding's own flagship, the *Dingyuan*, was technically captained by Liu Buchan, who supposedly shared his authority with the English Captain Nicholls, and her chief engineer was Albrecht, a German. Also aboard was von Hanneken, survivor of the *Kowshing*, and William Tyler, another Englishman. There was a similar division of labour on her massive sister-ship, the *Zhenyuan*, with a nominal Chinese captain, but a ship's master from Britain and an engineer from Germany; also a maverick American officer, Philo McGiffin, described by Tyler, even before the Battle of the Yalu supposedly drove him mad, as 'not quite all there'.[1]

Admiral Ding led his fleet in a dogleg course across the gulf to the Liaodong Peninsula, where the Chinese ships were able to take on new supplies of coal at Dalian. He then hugged the coast of Liaodong all the way down to the mouth of the Yalu River, where he unloaded several troop ships for the Chinese war effort. Then, Admiral Ding turned back and sailed back on a course that would take him back towards Shandong. He did not steam directly towards Weihaiwei, as that would have been tempting fate. Instead, he steered a few degrees further towards the west, in order to take his fleet behind the small island of Haiyang.

The Japanese, meanwhile, had sent much of their fleet on a wide sweep of the area, approaching Haiyang Island from the other direction. Admiral Itō had suspected that the Chinese might have been using Haiyang harbour as a way station, but, finding no evidence of the Chinese fleet there, gave up on the search and headed for home. His ships consequently rounded Haiyang and headed back towards the mouth of the Yalu, putting them on a collision course with the Chinese coming in the opposite direction. Each unaware of the other, the two fleets were converging on the same point, sure to run into each other within a few hours.

The Japanese were the first to realise. At 11:30 a.m. lookouts spotted a shroud of what initially appeared to be mist on the sea in the distance. It was a cloudless day, and the experienced sea captains realised that only a rival fleet could put so much smoke into the air that it would be visible on the horizon. The Chinese, whose clocks seem to have been set an hour earlier, on Beijing time, sighted the Japanese shortly afterwards, at what for them was lunchtime.[2]

The Chinese, realising that there was still a little time before the fleets would be close enough for action, went back below and hastily bolted down their meal. Meanwhile, on the *Naniwa*, Tōgō called his officers around for a pep talk.

'The pick of the enemy's fleet is over there,' said Tōgō to his subordinates. 'Not very far away now. A glorious battle is imminent. I would not waste my words on you brave and loyal subjects of the Emperor. Only I would like to say at the last moment that the brave action of an individual and that of a squadron is based on that of an individual ship. I trust that you will bear this well in mind and do your duty and destroy the enemy, thus answering to the gracious blessings of the Emperor.'[3]

The Japanese vessels were strung out in a long line, with Tōgō's *Naniwa* fourth from the front. Behind the *Naniwa*, there was a gap of several thousand metres, and then the slower Japanese ships, mainly the older, less efficient vessels like the aging *Fusō*. As for the Chinese, it had been Admiral Ding's plan to meet his enemy in a similar fashion, with his ships strung out in an oblique line. However, aboard Ding's own flagship, the *Dingyuan*, Liu Buchan gave a signal that ordered the Chinese vessels to form a crescent, with the two giant battleships in the centre and the smaller vessels strung far out in front on the tips of the horns.

Aboard the *Dingyuan*, William Tyler was aghast. By the time anyone noticed the error, the fleet had already formed up, and it was deemed too late to change formation, lest that lead to further confusion. Tyler later wrote of his suspicion that Liu's 'mistake' had been nothing of the sort, but a calculated decision to push the smaller Chinese vessels on the southernmost flank of the fleet into the sight of the Japanese first, thereby drawing fire from the Japanese and reducing the chances of any shells landing on the *Dingyuan*. When Tyler tried to get Liu to turn four points to starboard, all the better to bring his big guns into firing range, Liu at first pretended not to hear him, then gave the order and immediately countermanded it. Incensed, Tyler rushed down to complain to Admiral Ding, who was standing on a temporary platform built above the *Dingyuan*'s huge 12-inch guns. Even as Tyler told Ding of Liu's bizarre behaviour, Liu gave the order to open fire, in the full knowledge that the first discharge of the guns would blow the wooden viewing platform to pieces. The first casualties of the Battle of the Yalu were hence Admiral Ding himself, who was badly burned, and Tyler, who was blown thirty feet away by the force of the explosion and gradually regained consciousness, his ears ringing, with a stabbing pain in his left eyeball.[4]

Aboard the *Naniwa*, Captain Tōgō saw the puff of smoke from the distant Chinese ships, followed shortly by the distant rumble of the *Dingyuan*'s gun. At the time, the *Dingyuan* was some 6,000 metres away from the *Naniwa*, and the shell splashed harmlessly into the sea some distance from the Japanese. While Tōgō and his fellow captains looked on in bafflement, the other Chinese ships similarly commenced firing. On the foremost ship of the Japanese, the *Yoshino*, the fastest warship in the world, the signal flag still flew for the Japanese to hold their fire.[5] This they did for fifteen minutes, while the Chinese guns threw hundreds of shells in their direction. Vast plumes of water erupted from the sea, but the Chinese fleet was hitting nothing.

It was not until the range between the fleets had closed to 3,000 metres that the order came for the Japanese to open fire.

The *Naniwa*'s guns targeted three Chinese vessels in swift succession, seeing several bright explosions light up on each as shells found their target. The Chinese returned fire, with one shell landing in the water so close to the *Naniwa* that Captain Tōgō was drenched by the splash. James Allan, a British observer on the shore, commented:

> Terrific indeed it was – a wide dense pall of smoke, which there was little wind to carry off; through the haze the huge, reeling shapes of the fighting vessels, looming indistinctly, vomiting flame like so many angry dragons, and several of them burning in addition, having been set on fire by shells; and above all the appalling concussion of the great guns, like the bursting of incessant thunder-bolts.[6]

Quite by coincidence, Tōgō's gunners were firing on the two ships that a younger Admiral Ding had once steered home from England, the *Chaoyong* and *Yangwei* ('Superhero' and 'Projection of Power'). As Tōgō led the *Naniwa* out for another turn, the ships were subject to a second attack from an unlikely source. The Japanese vessel *Saikyō* was not even a proper warship. Instead, she was a hastily converted liner, a glorified transport that happened to be carrying Admiral Kabayama, the Japanese navy's chief of staff, in an observational capacity. Kabayama, a former army officer whose meddling in naval matters was not always welcome, does not seem to have been able to resist involving himself in the battle as well and emptied his ship's defensive guns into the heavily damaged Chinese vessels. James Allan saw it all:

> Meanwhile, the Chinese ships had been forced still nearer the land, and the *Chaoyong*, an absolute ruin, drifted helplessly ashore, half a league from where we stood. By the aid of our glasses we could perceive her condition clearly – her upper works knocked to pieces; her decks, strewn with mutilated bodies, an indiscriminate mass of wreck and carnage. Her crews were abandoning her, struggling to land as best they could.[7]

The *Chaoyong* was the first to go, suddenly listing far to starboard and sinking with great speed. Shortly afterward, the *Yangwei* erupted in flames and fled for the coast, where she ran aground.

However, the *Saikyō*'s charge was not without ill effects. Her unprecedented race into action left her open to retaliatory fire from several Chinese ships. She was hit by 12-inch shells, one of which wrecked her steering, while two passed clean through her without exploding. Wheeling out of control, the helpless *Saikyō* careened past one Japanese warship and straight for the *Naniwa*, missing the prow of Captain Tōgō's ship by a hair's breadth. [8]

From a distance, any problems among the Japanese were disregarded. To James Allan, watching the action from a nearby cliff, the Japanese remained promptly obedient to their signals and did not let up their barrages, while the Chinese were clearly getting the worst of it: 'The Japanese vessels, working in concert and keeping together, as we began to perceive, seemed to sail around and around the enemy, pouring on them an incessant cannonade, and excelling them in rapidity of fire and manoeuvering. Some of the Chinese vessels appeared to me to present an appearance of helplessness, and there was no indication of combination as amongst their opponents.'[9]

Aboard the *Dingyuan*, the wounded, half-blind William Tyler stumbled through the carnage. His ears were still ringing from the blast, and would continue to do so for the rest of his life. Up ahead he saw a friend of his, Lieutenant Wu. Even as they exchanged greetings, a man standing nearby was torn apart by an enemy shell, smearing gore and entrails across the deck. 'So this is civilisation,' said Wu. 'This is what you foreigners are so keen to teach us.'[10]

The survivors on the *Dingyuan* tried to give as good as they had got. Even with Admiral Ding suffering from terrible burns, with one leg left crushed by the stupid opening salvo of Captain Liu, his ship made a beeline for the *Matsushima*, the flagship of the Japanese commander Admiral Itō. The two ships pounded each other for an hour, with one shell from the Chinese vessel scoring a direct hit on one of the *Matsushima*'s guns. Scandalously, the shell broke open to reveal that it was filled not with explosives, but with cement. Another shell from the *Dingyuan* proved to be of higher-quality manufacture, setting off a pile of ammunition on the

Matsushima. The Japanese flagship was left listing and in flames, many of her guns out of action as Admiral Itō steered her out of harm's way.[11]

Itō hoisted a new signal: 'Disregard movements of the Commander-in-Chief', in order to make it clear that he was merely dealing with his own damage, and that his removal of the *Matsushima* from the line of battle was not a sign of a general retreat. No such options were open to the *Dingyuan* – even if Admiral Ding had wanted to retreat, Nicholls was dying below decks. Tyler manned one of the short-handed guns and the selectively obedient Liu was still steering the ship, but the *Dingyuan* had lost most of her masts. There was, in fact, no longer any mast on which Admiral Ding could hoist any signal, even if he had wished to.

The Japanese ships continued to tear at the Chinese. 'Throughout the fight', commented Tyler with sour admiration, 'the enemy was as orderly as in manoeuvres; in general, [the Japanese] … circled around us, we steaming on an inner circle. Gradually, the vessels on that inner circle became, from one cause or the other, fewer and fewer.'

The Chinese had begun the day with ten ships. Now, only four remained in the fray, with the others either sinking or fleeing for safety. The captain of the *Zhiyuan* ('The Deliverer') had gone down with his ship after trying to ram the lead Japanese vessel, the *Yoshino*. From the shore, James Allan saw the *Zhiyuan*'s final moments:

> [The *Zhiyuan*] had evidently been for long in difficulties, labouring heavily, with the steam pumps constantly in requisition, as we could tell from the streams of water [that] poured from her sides. Bravely she fought on, unsupported, and her upper deck and top guns were served until she sank. At length her bows were completely engulfed; the stern rose high out of the water, disclosing the whirling propellers, and bit by bit she disappeared. We could hear distinctly the yelling sounds of triumph that rose from the Japanese ships as she went down.[12]

Other Chinese participants had found less heroic ways to leave the battle. The *Qiyuan*, that same ship that had deserted the *Kowshing*, did not even enter the battle, but steamed immediately for Port Arthur, her captain signalling that she was suffering from technical difficulties. Later, it was discovered that her crewmen had sabotaged their own guns with a sledgehammer.[13]

Amid such chaos, the *Naniwa* steered almost entirely unscathed, with only one man wounded. Only a single Chinese shell struck the *Naniwa* during the whole battle, smashing through the ship's hull just below the waterline but failing to explode. Instead, it all but plugged its own entry hole, and spent the rest of the battle where it had ended up, nestled snugly but dangerously inside one of the ship's coal bunkers.

Not every Japanese vessel had the same luck. The *Hiei* ran so close to the enemy that the exchange of fire was virtually point blank, devastating the Japanese vessel. The small *Akagi* came to the *Hiei*'s rescue, dragging herself into a fight with the *Laiyuan* ('Advent'), an armoured Chinese cruiser four times her size. A lucky shot from the *Akagi* took out the *Laiyuan*'s bridge, but the gunners on the cruiser tore the *Akagi* apart in retaliation. Engineers on the *Laiyuan* remained diligently at their posts, as fires raged through the ship, the temperature in the engine room rising close to 200 degrees Fahrenheit, leaving them blinded, maimed or dying. All the while, the crew of the *Naniwa* maintained their calm routine of aiming, firing and reloading, pouring rounds into Chinese vessels distracted by other Japanese ships nearby.[14]

The fire aboard the *Dingyuan* seemed out of control; the massive warship was now a tower of flames on the sea, as the Japanese ships circled nearer like sharks. Suddenly, a second iron giant swept through the smoke. It was her sister-ship, the *Zhenyuan*, bravely placing herself in the line of fire while the crew of the flagship struggled to get the fires under control. The Japanese shells now concentrated largely on the two behemoths, while aboard the *Zhenyuan* the quiet Captain Lin calmly returned fire.[15]

By now, the light was fading. As the fires aboard the *Dingyuan* were replaced by smoke, it came to Admiral Itō's attention that the sun was setting and it was becoming harder to see. His chief concern, considering the number of Chinese vessels that had fled from the scene unharmed, was that they might even now be planning to send out a flotilla of unlit torpedo boats under cover of darkness, to sink the victorious Japanese even as they claimed to have won the day. After a signal from Itō, the Japanese broke off. The next time their vessels circled out of range, they simply did not return.

The Chinese, who had not actually thought far enough ahead to plan any stealthy night attacks, were left baffled by the Japanese departure. Aboard the smoking *Dingyuan*, von Hanneken and the concussed Tyler celebrated at the base of the bridge ladder with champagne and biscuits, and pointedly did not offer any to Captain Liu. On her sister-ship, the *Zhenyuan*, Philo McGiffin was similarly mystified. 'Had they stayed with us a quarter of an hour more,' he wrote, 'our guns would have been silent and our ships defenceless.'[16]

According to popular myth, a falcon trailed the Japanese fleet for much of the day. As Itō turned from the battle, it swooped out the sky and put to flight a flock of terrified crows. The falcon settled on the mast of the *Takachiho* and was supposedly captured by the sailors and later presented to the Emperor as a divine omen of Japanese victory. It became the first of many supposed portents of divine approval.[17]

Itō's fleet steered a course that looped back towards the open sea, from where the most badly damaged ships were detached for repairs, or, in the case of the *Matsushima*, the long limp back to Japan. Itō transferred his command to the relatively undamaged *Hashidate* and took the ships on a long circle out of harm's way that brought them back in the vicinity of Haiyang at dawn the next day. The Chinese, however, were nowhere to be seen.[18]

Two ships were sent out to ascertain what had happened to them: the *Akitsushima* and Captain Tōgō in the *Naniwa*. It was, however, not much of a mystery. Weihaiwei had no dry dock facilities, so any heavily damaged Chinese vessels were sure to have run for Port Arthur at the end of the Liaodong Peninsula – the only place where they could repair themselves to any great degree. Not all of them had made it. On the beach at Dalian Bay, just a few tantalising miles short of Port Arthur, Tōgō found a beached gunboat that had clearly foundered only partway home. His men used the ship for target practice and blew her up, although subsequent Chinese reports suggested that the Chinese had done so themselves on seeing the approaching Japanese in order to stop her falling into enemy hands.[19] At Port Arthur itself, Tōgō saw signs of several Chinese ships undergoing repairs. He noted the visible masts and flags, and then turned back towards Korea to make his report.

The Chinese fleet had been badly beaten, but it was still in possession of its two giants, the *Dingyuan* and the *Zhenyuan*, as well as several smaller vessels. Amazingly, in one of the unexplained decisions of the war, it also had a month's respite, as the attentions of the Japanese military turned to the land war. Even if the Japanese were wary of Port Arthur's coast defences, it would have surely been wise to keep a naval presence off shore, ready to attack the Chinese if they left Port Arthur, as they were sure to do as the Japanese army drew ever closer along the Liaodong Peninsula.

Instead, Tōgō and his fellow captains were back on duty escorting the army. Even as the Japanese prepared to cross the Yalu into Chinese territory, a massive 'Second Army' was assembled in Hiroshima. The fleet returned to Kure to pick them up, transporting them across the strait and along the coast of Korea, dropping them off at Huayuan ('Flower Garden'), a harbour on the Liaodong Peninsula itself, eighty miles from Port Arthur. The Chinese offered no resistance, and the Second Army was landed without a shot fired. It was a plan typical of the Japanese military's bias. As in his younger days in the war against the Shōgun, Captain Tōgō was a glorified bus-driver for the army. The landing at Huayuan was a military masterstroke from the army's perspective, leapfrogging the defenders of the Yalu and leaving them to the First Army, while the Second Army charged along the Liaodong Pensinsula with naval support.

Meanwhile, in Port Arthur, the Chinese war machine was not as efficient as the Japanese might have suspected. William Tyler's first action on reaching safety was to organise a media clampdown, less for military ends than to prevent the vainglorious Philo McGiffin from sending telegrams back to America boasting of his naval prowess. For the first week that the Chinese fleet was in Port Arthur, the officers bickered among themselves about who was responsible, while the hulks of their warships sat in disrepair. Two weeks after the Battle of the Yalu, an officer aboard the *Dingyuan* stumbled across the rotting corpse of one of her sailors, left to decompose where he had fallen. Von Hanneken had had enough of the sea and voted himself a commission on land. Admiral Ding's new 'vice-admiral' was John McClure, an alcoholic tugboat captain deemed by many of the surviving foreigners to be a disaster waiting to happen.[20]

Eventually, on 3 November, the fleet was ordered to leave Port Arthur and chase the Japanese from local waters. Admiral Ding's superior, the Viceroy Li Hongzhang, protested that the Chinese fleet was reduced to six ships and two torpedo boats, against fourteen Japanese vessels with seven torpedo boats. A requested reinforcement of five ships from China's southern fleet had been refused, which left the Chinese fleet, even with the two giants, hopelessly outclassed in a pitched battle against the Japanese.

This explanation, at least, seemed to convince the authorities in Beijing, who instead ordered that Admiral Ding's ships be used to transport army reinforcements from Tianjin to Port Arthur, ready to fight the coming Japanese onslaught on land. Admiral Ding, however, had already given up Port Arthur as lost, regarding it as a site that was doomed to fall as soon as the land route to it had fallen into enemy hands. Instead, he led his fleet out of Port Arthur, abandoning it to its fate, and fleeing across the gulf to Weihaiwei.

On the morning of 7 November, Tōgō's *Naniwa* was part of a main force covering the army's advance on Dalian Bay. Five smaller boats swept ahead in search of mines, but found nothing. With the sun above the horizon, Tōgō fired some exploratory rounds at Dalian's fortifications, but elicited no response. The entire harbour was eerily quiet. It was three hours before Admiral Itō began to suspect that what he had thought to be a trap was actually another Chinese failure. He nudged his ships closer to land, at a range that would have put them within deadly danger from the guns of the forts. Through his binoculars, Captain Tōgō saw movement in an area around Dalian. But the uniforms were clearly Japanese. As he watched with mounting surprise, there was a flurry of activity on land, and a flag was run up a pole on one of the forts. It reached the height and snapped into view in the wind – it was the Rising Sun. Other forts began flying Rising Sun flags of their own. The Chinese torpedo boats in Dalian harbour, that might have offered some (admittedly suicidal) resistance to the Japanese, were later found to have surrendered practically without a fight. The capture of Dalian gave the Japanese a fully-serviced, operational harbour, deep in Chinese territory, close to Port Arthur and readily resupplyable from both land and sea. Intelligence gathered at Dalian, quite possibly from the surrendered gunboat commanders, told the Japanese of Ding's dash for Weihaiwei. Admiral Itō sent the *Naniwa* and a dozen other ships to see for themselves on 11 November. Sure enough, Tōgō could see the remainder of the enemy fleet nestled behind the Weihaiwei forts. But the Japanese did not advance any closer, nor did the Chinese come out to fight.

The Chinese could not even retreat without inviting disaster. Admiral Ding himself protested at the suicidal behaviour of some Chinese commanders. He understood, he said, that suicide was a traditional exit strategy for the Chinese, but complained that the cost of training captains was so high that suicide should be discouraged.[21] Unknown to Captain Tōgō, the brave, quiet Lin Taizeng, whom both he and Admiral Ding so admired, had become a casualty of what should have been a simple sailing from one port to another. As the massive *Zhenyuan* approached Weihaiwei, she had struck an underwater hazard and suffered some damage. Captain Lin was inconsolable – he knew that there were no adequate facilities to repair her. Divers did what they could to fix the hole, pouring cement into an 18-foot gash in the double hull, but the *Zhenyuan* was no longer suitable for putting out to open sea, and was now rendered little better than a floating fort in the habour.[22] The news of her condition was hushed up, but Captain Lin could not bear the shame, and committed suicide. At his funeral, people spat in his coffin.

Abandoned by her maritime defenders, Port Arthur fell within a fortnight to a Japanese land assault. The Chinese defenders could have held out for considerably longer had they not decided to abandon their outer ring of forts, affording the Japanese with ready-made positions from which to bombard the remaining strongpoints. They also tempted fate by posting grisly trophies on the approaches to Port Arthur. With each new area of ground gained, the Japanese soldiers would encounter fellow countrymen, killed, mutilated and strung up as warnings. When Port Arthur eventually fell, there was a massacre of the inhabitants by the infuriated Japanese. Supporters of the Japanese, of whom there were many, glossed over the slaughter as the reaction of the Japanese to Chinese taunts and atrocities. Opponents of the Japanese instead fretted about the behaviour of the Japanese army towards its defeated foes, raising concerns that had ominous foreshadowings of the war crime trials that would follow the Second World War.

Tōgō's part in the capture of Port Arthur was minimal. He was with the Imperial Fleet as it shelled some of the town's outlying forts and was a likely participant in the apprehension or sinking of several fleeing despatch boats in the seasonal mists. On 21 November, an approaching storm threatened to dash the fleet into the rocks of the coasts, and the ships were ordered out into deeper water where they would be safer. When Tōgō returned to Port Arthur a couple of days later, the town was already in Japanese hands, and with it the entire Liaodong Peninsula.

Within days, the 25 July fight near Phung-do Island en route to Asan became a subject for Japanese artists. This woodblock print by Kobayashi Kiyochika is dated August 1894, and shows a fire aboard the *Guangyi*.

8

Though Your Swords Be Broken

Across the gulf at Weihaiwei, Admiral Ding did not rate his chances of a successful sea battle against the Japanese. Instead, he dug in at the sea port, hoping perhaps for a diplomatic end to the onslaught before he was obliged to defend the area. Rather than send out his remaining ships against the better-prepared Japanese, Admiral Ding planned to wait out the Japanese for as long as possible in Weihaiwei itself, his great battleships little more than floating forts.

The Japanese, for their part, saw little reason to change the strategy that had worked so well at Port Arthur. Tōgō on the *Naniwa*, along with the *Akitsushima* and the *Yoshino*, was sent across the gulf ahead of Japan's Third Army, a body of troops embarking at Dalian and obviously intended for a landing somewhere on the Shandong Peninsula.

On 18 January 1895, Tōgō steamed out of a snowstorm into range of Dengzhou, eighty-five miles west of Weihaiwei. Just to make sure that everyone was awake, he let off several blank charges before commencing a bombardment with live ammunition, unleashing salvo after salvo against whatever defenders Dengzhou might have assembled in its fort. The fort returned fire; and as each hurled shells at the other, a small boat put out to sea on the choppy waves, flying the Stars and Stripes and a white flag. To Tōgō's great surprise, the boat contained an American missionary, who hoped to talk him out of any further hostilities. Unfortunately for the missionary, he need not have bothered – Tōgō's mission was a bluff, intended to lure as many Chinese as possible away from Weihaiwei and west along the peninsula, in order to ensure better odds for the *real* landings, thirty-five miles *east* of Weihaiwei at the sheltered harbour of Yongzhong.[1]

The deception worked, up to a point. The Third Army, comprising fresh troops from north Japan and the Kumamoto Division of the Second Army, staggered ashore in the middle of a thick snowstorm on 20 January 1895 to find themselves under fire from Chinese positions. Some 300 Chinese riflemen were in the area, but fled soon after the Japanese began returning fire in force.

It was not long before the news reached the Chinese in Weihaiwei. Tōgō's superior, Admiral Itō, did everything in his power to win over Admiral Ding by peaceful means, leaning on HMS *Severn*, a neutral British observer, to carry a message up the coast to the besieged Chinese. Itō had the deepest respect for Admiral Ding, and his offer of terms shows that, for the Japanese Navy at least, gallantry was not dead. Part of it read:

I have the honour to address you, Admiral Ding. Unfortunate circumstances have made us enemies, but wars in this world are wars between nations, and not hostilities between individuals, so my friendship for you remains unchanged and is as warm as it was in the old days. I beg that you will not consider this letter an attempt to persuade you to surrender ...

The present condition of your country is not due to the fault of a few persons in power, but is really a result of the system of government. You select a man for a post solely on account of his literary attainments, which is a custom dating from thousands of years ago. Those who wield political power are all men of high literary accomplishments, and though I do not say that this system is absolutely bad ... it is now obsolete ...

You are well aware in what a painful position the Japanese Empire was placed thirty years ago, and how we managed to escape from the difficulties which beset us by throwing away the old system and adopting the new. Your country also must asdopt this new way of living. If your country does this, all will be well, but if it rejects it, it cannot but disappear sooner or later.[2]

Itō knew that Admiral Ding faced execution or suicide if he was defeated, but also knew that Ding was not to blame for the situation in which he found himself. Ding's colleagues, the Viceroy who had supplied him with dud shells, the officers who had countermanded his orders, the sailors who had sabotaged their own vessels with hammers: all these had some part in his defeat, as did the administration in Beijing that sent him into battle against Japanese ironclads after the naval budget had been squandered on decorations for the palace garden. Itō still regarded Ding as a worthy opponent and as a friend with misguided priorities, and offered him sanctuary in Japan until, he implied, the political situation changed in China and Ding could return to his command under a better regime.

Admiral Ding's fleet stayed huddled in the harbour, functioning, as Ding had ordered, as artillery positions to make life difficult for the soldiers, but still refusing to engage the Japanese warships at sea. Nor were Tōgō or any other commanders willing to make a suicidal run through Weihaiwei's obstacles and minefields for the chance to fire at the Chinese fleet where it hid. Instead, the Japanese favoured night attacks by torpedo boats, while ships such as the *Naniwa* remained at a safe distance.

However, the Japanese siege was not without its miscalculations. The lack of communication between the Japanese army and navy began to cost lives. On 31 January, Japanese soldiers in a newly-occupied fort turned their captured artillery pieces on a shadowy flotilla of torpedo boats that turned out to be vessels from their own navy making a sneak attack on the Chinese.

February began with a hellish, icy storm. Much of the Japanese fleet was pulled back into sheltered harbour, with only a handful of ships left to ride the rough waves on guard duty. Tōgō was one of the unlucky commanders given that difficult responsibility – effectively running the *Naniwa* on the spot to maintain her position against treacherous tides and winter waves. Tōgō had to keep the *Naniwa* within sight of the entrance to Weihaiwei harbour, which was dangerous enough with reduced visibility, but all the more risky when every surge threatened to pitch his ship against the cliffs, onto a beach or into the Chinese minefield.

On 3 February, the storm finally died down. Tōgō resumed the attack as one of a constant shift of ships, maintaining a steady shelling of Weihaiwei that lasted for nine days and nights. Tōgō and his fellow captain kept up a relentless bombardment from offshore. Although the Japanese vessels were able to peel away from the fleet for rest and recuperation, there was always at least one close to Weihaiwei, blasting through the night, ensuring that the Chinese never had a moment's respite. One by one, the outlying forts fell to the Japanese land forces, each becoming a new bridgehead for the assault on the next.

Among the foreign officers in Chinese service, William Tyler noted that Admiral Ding was actively courting his own demise:

> That fine old man had already been degraded by Imperial Decree – stripped of his rank and honours. He had wished so much to be killed in action; when we bombarded forts he stood exposed, praying for relief …[3]

When confronted, Admiral Ding revealed to his men the awful burden of command within the Chinese military machine. Pending an unlikely miracle, Ding was a dead man walking, sure to be executed for his inevitable defeat. With little remaining authority over his fractious troops, he pleaded with them to stay at their posts, not for victory, but in order to assure their good treatment in defeat.

> If you wish me to live, fight on. Fight on even though your swords be broken and your ammunition exhausted. If you surrender after fighting in this way, your enemies, who place *bushidō* above all things, will treat you with the respect due to you. You will then not only save your lives, but your honour.[4]

Torpedo boats from the Japanese came in fast whenever the storm let up. On 4 February, some vessels from the Chinese fleet mounted what would have been a last-ditch effort to prolong the siege, planning to engage the Japanese and break out of Weihaiwei – not for a true naval battle, but to destroy some nearby forts in order to make it harder for the Japanese to bombard Weihaiwei itself. At the last moment, the expedition was cancelled due to technical trouble in some of the ships. The Japanese, however, did not sleep. At 2 o'clock that night, the Chinese sailors were woken by warning flares from outlying patrol boats. The Japanese torpedo boats were dangerously close. One scored a hit on the *Dingyuan* itself, from suicidally close quarters. The Japanese crew were wiped out by the great jet of steam that erupted from the side of the holed *Dingyuan*. Aboard *Dingyuan*, Tyler heard the whoosh of the escaping steam and then 'a dull thud and a quivering shock'. Something had exploded deep within the *Dingyuan* and the ship's bugler was already sounding the signal to close all watertight doors.[5] But the damage was too great. Tyler sadly advised his Admiral that the best they could do was deliberately run the *Dingyuan* aground while she was still level in the water, thereby ensuring her guns might still be turned on any new attackers. Accordingly, the Chinese fleet's pride and joy was rammed unceremoniously into a beach.

The next day, her crew fussed miserably over the wreckage, with Tyler waist deep in freezing water on the lower decks. Admiral Ding transferred his flag to the *Zhenyuan*, which was almost as impotent as her sister-ship. The following night, at 4 a.m., another Japanese torpedo attack cost the Chinese four more vessels.

The demoralising effect on the Chinese was palpable. Tyler noted that the sailors were now openly disobedient. Even those who understood the plan to use the hulk of the *Dingyuan* as a gun platform could see how little use it was likely to be. A single night, huddled together for warmth, frostbitten by the cold wind whistling through the half-flooded wreck, was enough to convince many of the men that it was all over. For some, a kind of claustrophobia set in when they realised that they were little more than captives aboard the beached *Dingyuan*. At knife- and gun-point, Tyler was obliged to promise the men that they would be taken off the wreck and brought ashore, but this was not enough.

On 8 February, the Chinese soldiers in Weihaiwei were in open mutiny, demanding that Admiral Ding's surviving ships be used to evacuate them ahead of the Japanese occupation. With rumours drifting in of a massacre at Port Arthur, the Chinese feared that a Japanese occupation would lead to a bloody massacre unless the Chinese surrendered. The foreign officers, also justifiably, fretted that news of their problems would be sure to reach the Japanese imminently and lead to a massed assault on Weihaiwei within 24 hours. 'Ding declared at first,' wrote Tyler, 'that capitulation was impossible; but later he said he could arrange it by committing suicide, and hence save the lives of many.'[6]

Pure negligence was costing Chinese lives. Tyler prevented two stretcher-bearers taking a man straight to the morgue, even though he was demonstrably still alive and eventually recovered from his wounds. On 9 February, the Japanese vessel *Itsukushima* steamed perilously close to Weihaiwei, and the damaged *Zhenyuan* responded with a barrage of shellfire. The *Zhenyuan* scored a direct hit on the *Ikutsushima*, but the shell failed to explode, saving dozens of Japanese lives and plunging the Chinese deeper into despondency.[7]

On the evening of 11 February, Admiral Ding made a fateful decision, the nature of which has been heavily romanticised in Japanese sources. The first Tōgō knew of the change in circumstances came when a ceasefire signal went up from the *Matsushima*. Through his binoculars, Tōgō saw a small Chinese gunboat pulling out of Weihaiwei harbour, flying a white flag. An exhausted pair of Chinese captains were taken aboard and delivered a message from their Admiral to Admiral Itō:

> It was my intention to fight it out to the last vessel and to the last man, but on second thought I can hardly bear the idea of killing so many of my men for nothing. I now put my vessels, ammunition and Liugong Island at your disposal and entreat you to stop fighting, and let my men and civilians go to their native places to enjoy the rest of their lives. If you will comply with my request, I will carry out my terms to the letter asking the Commander-in-Chief of the British Squadron to act as witness. I trust that you will kindly give consideration to the above.[8]

The Japanese were ecstatic, but Admiral Itō kept his reply graceful and honourable. He sent Admiral Ding a hamper of champagne and restated his offer for Admiral Ding to seek asylum with the Japanese.

The guns now silent on both sides, the ships and forts waited for a reply. After several hours, the gunboat returned. The Chinese captains brought back the hamper with them, unopened, and a short note from Admiral Ding:

> I have just received your letter and thank you on behalf of my officers and men. I cannot, however, accept your present, owing to the state of war which still exists between our two countries. I nevertheless appreciate your motives in sending me the hamper, and I thank you.[9]

The Chinese captain who had delivered the message had one final thing to say to the Japanese. 'Our Admiral wept at the thought of your kindness,' he said. 'After which, he bowed in the direction of Beijing and, swallowing poison, died immediately.'

Over on the *Naniwa*, Tōgō received a new signal from the flagship. All vessels of the Japanese fleet were to lower their flags to half-mast.

The suicide of Admiral Ding, facing impossible odds, caught the Japanese imagination, although even at the time the stories of it were muddled. One woodblock print, published at the time for a Japanese audience hungry for news, presented the sad Admiral sitting at his desk in a study bright with garish oriental colour, reading a brutal command from the Chinese Emperor instructing him to take his own life. A fat, cowering messenger hunches obsequiously nearby, while on a nearby table is a bottle of poison, and outside the window, flurries of the symbolic February snows lurk in a barren garden.

The reality was nowhere near so poetic. Admiral Ding had commanded his captains to scuttle their ships, but his subordinates were already thinking of their own futures and did not want to anger the inevitable victors by willfully destroying ships that the Japanese were sure to want as the spoils of war. Meanwhile, Ding was surrounded by demands from his own side, both open and implied, for a surrender. That night, the insubordination of his own men had reached the stage when a number of them approached him with knives drawn. Politely, Admiral Ding begged their pardon, locked himself in his cabin and took a lethal late-night overdose of opium.[10]

Whatever the precise sequence of events surrounding the death of Admiral Ding, the Chinese fleet was gone. Most of it was at the bottom of the sea; some ships, like the *Zhenyuan* and the *Qiyuan*, were later repaired and incorporated into the Japanese fleet. In a final gesture of defiance, Yang Yongling, the newly appointed captain of the former, waited until the Japanese boarding party was clambering aboard and then shot himself in protest.[11] The terms of the treaty between the two admirals allowed for Ding's defeated men to return home 'in civilian clothes' – i.e., that their lives were to be spared so long as they left their equipment behind. However, despite the gallantry of Admiral Itō, the Chinese did not fare so well within their own service – many of those officers who did not take their own lives in defeat later had their lives taken from them by Imperial decree in Beijing.

Captain Tōgō was no more. As of 16 February 1895, he was Rear Admiral Tōgō, and soon dispatched south to make good on Japan's northern victory.[12] What passed for China's modern army was defeated in the north, and Japanese troops were facing increasingly less experienced and less modern opponents as they advanced. It was almost as if the Japanese army was advancing backwards in time, first fighting uniformed riflemen supported by artillery, then scruffier local militia with irregular equipment, then musketeers and swordsmen. China had put the best of its fighting force first on the Yalu border, and the Japanese were finding each victory easier than the last.

It was only a matter of time before China would be forced to sue for peace. The Japanese hoped to retain the Liaodong Peninsula in the aftermath, and Japan's suzerainty in Korea seemed guaranteed, but Rear Admiral Tōgō was sent on a new mission southwards with orders to take Taiwan. Strategically, Taiwan had little value in the Sino-Japanese War. The decision to invade it in the dying days of the conflict seemed to be a move by the Japanese to secure an all-new naval zone of influence. Taiwan offered an extension of Japanese waters, an addendum to the Ryūkyū Islands chain that stretched southwards from Tōgō's home domain of Satsuma.[13] Taiwan was also the famous last redoubt of Chinese sea power. The island had only become part of China in the 17th century, during a Qing dynasty expedition to quell offshore rebels. To the land-based minds of the Beijing authorities, Taiwan was beyond the horizon, out of sight and mind, but to the Japanese Admiralty there was a tantalising possibility of adding it to Japanese possessions. Mastery of Taiwan would present a naval power with a powerful base from which to launch further expansion, be it south to the Phillipines or west to China's Fujian province.

On 15 March 1895, Li Hongzhang, Viceroy of the Chinese northern maritime region, left Tianjin for Shimonoseki, ready to begin negotiations over a possible armistice. By luck or by design, the same day marked a massed departure of a Japanese fleet from Sasebo, heading south in a final dash for acquisitions before the navy might be ordered to cease hostilities.

Tōgō was tasked with capturing a seemingly insignificant dot on the map – the tiny archipelago known to the Chinese as the Penghu Islands and to the world at large as the Pescadores, which sat at the halfway point between China's Fujian province and the island of Taiwan. The islands were named for the occasional groups of fisherman who used the islands as a staging post, temporary harbour or as a place to dry their catch. Storm-swept, largely barren and lacking in fresh water, the Pescadores had only one true asset – a massive natural harbour sufficient to act as a staging post for any fleet that hoped to invade either Taiwan or Fujian. Whoever controlled the Pescadores could, in times of war, be regarded as the master of the strait and hence prevent the large part of any Chinese reinforcements from coming to the aid of the garrison on Taiwan itself.

The fleet included the *Naniwa*, but Rear Admiral Tōgō had transfered his flag to the faster *Yoshino*. The other ships were largely veterans of the war in the north – the *Ikutsushima* that had had such a lucky escape, the *Hashidate* and *Chiyoda*, along with the 4th

Torpedo Boat squadron and five other ships – transports for troops, artillery and munitions, and a surprising amount of 'peaceful' equipment. The Pescadores expedition was not merely a military venture; it had set out with the expectation of turning Taiwan into a fully operational Japanese colony, and was sailing with a ready-made administration aboard, including the putative Japanese 'Governor of the Pescadores', the retired Admiral Tanaka Tsunatsune.[14]

Tōgō also had a time limit. The capture of the Pescadores needed to be accomplished in less than a fortnight, as by early April most of the troop transports would be required back in the north for a renewed advance on China. That, at least, was the official explanation. The more complex one was that the Chinese, too, would be hoping to reach an agreement with their enemies before the spring thaw and would be crazy not to sue for peace before the Japanese advanced any further. The expedition to the Pescadores was hence a realistic and somewhat cunning scheme – the best chance the Japanese had of seizing a delineated and defensible pocket of new territory before the expected armistice.

Tōgō did not take the direct route from Japan, but instead steamed along the east coast of Taiwan, a region largely regarded as lawless and 'unoccupied' except for aboriginal tribesmen. This tactic ensured that the approach of his fleet avoided any chance contacts with China's southern navy. Tōgō rounded the southern tip of Taiwan and headed back north, approaching the Pescadores from the opposite direction that anyone would have expected. If any Chinese vessels had been lurking in Taiwanese waters on the lookout for a Japanese attack, they would have had nothing to report. Tōgō had effectively sneaked up on the Pescadores from behind.[15]

The *Yoshino* and the *Naniwa* approached the islands in rolling seas, with a grey, overcast sky that made it difficult for them to see the sun. Twenty miles off his planned course, Tōgō ruled that the seas were too rough for smaller boats to put ashore and instead reconnoitred the islands from a distance. Tōgō was surprised to see a French flag fluttering above the Pescadores' main town of Magong. Worried by the presence of the French, the rough seas and the notorious shoals and reefs of local waters, Tōgō decided to attack the island from the open sea, rather than sailing into the sheltered harbour. The greater part of his ships were to bombard the outer fort while the *Akitsushima*, with her shallower draft, was to steam into the harbour itself, drop anchor at the closest possible approach to land, and then fire her guns into the town to cover the arrival of the troop ships behind her.

However, as the Japanese fleet manoeuvred into position, there was a sudden, grinding shudder aboard the *Yoshino*. The helmsman had not seen one of the treacherous reefs and had inadvertently run the *Yoshino* right onto it. Notably, Tōgō said nothing. As the overall commander of the expedition, he was not responsible for any incidental issues aboard the *Yoshino*, and so stood quietly to one side while the ship's captain attempted to get her off the rocks. Eventually, it became apparent that the *Yoshino* was unlikely to get herself free before high tide, whereupon Tōgō transferred his flag to another ship.

It was therefore aboard his old command, the *Naniwa*, that Rear Admiral Tōgō led the assault on the Pescadores Islands. The fleet made four runs at the shore batteries, looping in from 6,000 to 4,000 metres' range, before circling out for another pass. On each occasion, the Japanese vessels hit targets on the shore, while the Chinese fort failed to score any damaging hits against their attacker. On the fourth run, the fort seemed to have fallen silent, and the *Akitsushima* began her dash for the shoreline. When her captain judged that it was unsafe to advance any closer, she dropped her anchor, which was the signal the troops had been waiting for.

As the landing boats sped from behind the *Akitsushima* towards the shore, the guns in the fort suddenly opened up again, this time aiming at the soldiers and marines as they splashed through the shallow waters onto the beach. 'The enemy replied,' wrote Tōgō with characteristic understatement, 'but though their aim was often good, their range-finding was faulty and we did not suffer any damage.'[16]

Tōgō lent support from the sea while the troops struggled to set up their own field guns. Once the land forces had their own artillery pieces up and running, the capture of the Pescadores was a foregone conclusion, and the resistance faded away. On 24 March, the Japanese flag was raised at Magong. The British warship HMS

Leander arrived in Magong harbour that same day and fired a 21-gun salute in honour of the Rising Sun – Japan's acquisition had been acknowledged by a foreign power.

Not every British Empire presence in the area was as welcome. Tōgō remained suspicious that the Chinese might be using foreign vessels to run guns across the strait. Over the next two weeks, he made two patrols of the surrounding area, and boarded a British merchantman, although the ship was found to be transporting no suspicious items. The worst attack, however, came in an invisible form. One of the 'Japanese' troop transports had been a British vessel, acquired for Japanese use shortly before the outbreak of hostilities. A veteran of the East Indies trade, the ship had supposedly been disinfected before entering Japanese service, but was the likely vector for an outbreak of cholera on the Pescadores which claimed many more lives than the invasion itself. Safe from such afflictions at sea, Tōgō busied his own crew with more mapping. As the *Yoshino*'s brief distress had shown, the Japanese were still lacking charts of local waters, and Tōgō took the chance to survey some of the coastal areas along the Fujianese coast.

While Tōgō and the rest of the Pescadores expedition poked around south Chinese harbours, the negotiations in Japan proceeded. Notification reached the Japanese fleet on 24 April that an agreement had been signed and that the fleet was to be recalled. Tōgō consequently reached port in Sasebo on 5 May.

The initial terms of the peace treaty showed the scale of the Japanese victory. The Japanese would stay in Weihaiwei until such time as the Chinese government had paid a massive war indemnity. Port Arthur and the Liaodong Peninsula would remain in Japanese hands. China unilaterally recognised the independence of Korea – this carefully worded statement ensured that Korea was out of the Chinese sphere of influence, but by no means safe from future Japanese interference. The terms of this agreement, however, did not please other powers.

In particular, the Japanese occupation of the Liaodong Peninsula was seen by Tsarist Russia as a threat to its own interests in the region. The Russians, joining forces with the French (who owed them a favour under the terms of another treaty), and the Germans (who would do anything to keep the Tsar focused on Asia instead of Europe), lodged a formal protest in what is now known as the Triple Intervention.

While Japan might have been confident in the victory against China, she was in no condition to fight a war against one or more European powers. In a humiliating climbdown, Japan pulled out of Liaodong in return for a slightly higher indemnity payment. Russia then rushed in to occupy much of Liaodong itself, while other European powers swiftly seized nearby ports in order to counter-balance Russian interests. To the Japanese, who had hoped to be one of the imperialist powers themselves, it was as if their own interests were rudely shoved aside by the longer-serving members of a club that still refused to admit them. The sole exception was Taiwan, which neither the Chinese nor Europeans cared enough about to fight over. Much of what the Japanese had fought for in the north of China was lost to them by the terms of the Triple Intervention. Ironically for Tōgō, he and his men had laboured hardest and longest over the Yellow Sea area, but won their most enduring victory over Taiwan, which would remain Japanese territory until 1945.

As the man who led the Japanese acquisition of Taiwan, Tōgō remained a hero, while many generals, admirals and politicians of the Sino-Japanese War were tainted by their association with the Triple Intervention. The Triple Intervention was to signify the beginning of a new era in Japan. It led to riots in the streets and protests from the right wing, and was the first visible sign in Japan that the country would not simply be made welcome among the other powers if it imitated their behaviour. By expanding its sphere of influence into mainland Asia, Japan had also inadvertently found itself a new potential enemy – Tsarist Russia, which had ambitions in northern Chinese territory.

None of this, however, was the Navy's problem. Tōgō's more immediate concern was a return to Taiwan as an escort for the occupation force. Caught up in the arguments over the coasts of the Yellow Sea, China had given relatively little thought to the fate of Taiwan. Only a few years before, the Chinese government had even dared to claim that tracts of Taiwan remained lawless and free from the Emperor's jurisdiction. The island was long regarded as a haven for pirates, ne'er-do-wells and tropical diseases; and in some quarters of Beijing, its handover to Japan was regarded as a subtle revenge. The Chinese had only conquered Taiwan in the first place to prevent piratic rebels from using it as a base, and the mood in Beijing was generally one of good riddance.

That, at least, was the official story. However, as in Vietnam and Korea, the Chinese gave the appearance of disinterest while secretly favouring 'local' groups with pro-Chinese sentiments. The Japanese fleet that sailed for Taiwan to occupy this spoil of war did so with the expectation of trouble, which arose soon after Tōgō sighted land.

Allied forces advance on the Imperial Palace in Beijing during the Boxer
Rebellion of 1900. Lithograph by Kasai Torajiro

9

Republicans and Rebels

Even as the Japanese fleet had been underway, the abandoned residents of Taiwan sought a new protector, to the extent of asking if the island might be admitted to the British Empire. This strange request being refused, the Chinese on Taiwan pursued a cunning diplomatic option. Even if abandoned by the Chinese Empire, the people of Taiwan could refuse to be co-opted into that of the Japanese. Accordingly, even as Tōgō was lowering boats at the mouth of the Danshui River that led to the city of Taipei, officials on land proclaimed the Republic of Formosa.

Tang Jing-song, formerly the Governor of Taiwan, was now its President. Liu Yong-fu, like Tang a veteran of the Sino-French War, was dragged out of retirement as the commander of the new Republic's army. The Republic's troops were, of course, largely comprised of those same men who had until the previous day thought of themselves as Chinese subjects. Consequently, although the Sino-Japanese war had been declared over, Rear Admiral Tōgō was sailing into an unexpected coda – a war of conquest against an all-new enemy that proclaimed itself to be an independent Taiwan.

Off the Danshui fort, Tōgō saw a new and unfamiliar flag flying in the rain – a writhing yellow tiger, set on a sea-blue background with thunderbolts and crashing breakers. Tōgō did not recognise the new flag, but soon understood its implications when land forces began firing on the *Naniwa*'s boats.

The newly-proclaimed Republic's hold on the local people was unclear, but the resistance at Danshui was enough to persuade Tōgō to seek another place to put his marines ashore. Leaving two ships at Danshui to guard the river entrance, Tōgō headed to the north-eastern tip of Taiwan. He bypassed Jilong, where he had once scouted on shore in the company of the French, and found a place suitable for a landing. The soldiers were put ashore without trouble and faced a march over rocky terrain to Jilong. The date for the attack on Jilong itself was fixed for 3 June, with temperatures in Taiwan already soaring and many of the soldiers still misguidedly equipped for a Manchurian winter.

Tōgō made no secret of his intentions. On 2 June 1895, the *Naniwa* led three other ships in a leisurely, uneventful pass of Jilong and the fortress above it. Tōgō wished to reacquaint himself with the fortifications he had last seen some ten years previously. The following day, he took up position some 3,000 metres off the coast and began a bombardment of Jilong. However, driving rain made it difficult for Tōgō's spotters to ascertain where the shells were landing, and the final assault on Jilong was largely an army matter.

With Jilong in Japanese hands, Tōgō returned to Danshui and bombarded the fort there, awaiting the arrival of reinforcements overland. With both routes to Taipei now in the possession of the Japanese, the inland city fell soon afterwards. Safe aboard a navy vessel anchored off Jilong, Admiral Kabayama solemnly took his oath of office as the Governor of Taiwan, but Tōgō was not present. Like many of the other navy vessels, the *Naniwa* was patrolling Taiwanese coastal harbours, still wary of anti-Japanese insurgents. Other vessels shipped Chinese prisoners home by the hundreds, dumping them in Fujian where only some of them truly belonged.

Tōgō suffered a relapse of his rheumatism in the hot, muggy Taiwanese summer, but refused to admit it. Instead, he allowed himself the indulgence of a chair on the bridge of the *Naniwa*, and continued to direct operations. Taiwan had three major population centres, Taipei, Taizhong and Tainan – literally Tai-north, -central and -south. The south and central regions of the island remained the epicentre of resistance, particularly around Tainan, which had been the island's capital during the period of Chinese rule.

In a reflection of the progress of conquest, and its proximity to a new authority, Taipei became the new capital. Tōgō was present at a marine assault on Xiangshan near Taizhong in July. In October, he was put in charge of picking up the soldiers he had left on the Pescadores and bringing them over to Taiwan itself for more active service. This began sooner than expected, as insurgents were waiting on the beach at Putai. Instead of peacefully disembarking his soldiers, Tōgō found himself running into a two-hour battle.

By 21 October, the Japanese net was closing around the local resistance. Tōgō's report of his campaign against the Republicans is over in only a few lines – a repetitive series of encounters in which the ships engaged the coastal forts, providing cover for a landing party which then took the forts by storm. This simple scheme worked on at least three separate occasions, until Tōgō and his marines took the final prize: Tainan.

Five thousand defenders made their last stand at Anping, a coastal fortress on the outskirts of Tainan. Originally built by Dutch merchantmen as Fort Zeelandia, it had been captured in the 17th century by the 'pirate king' Coxinga, and had been used as the centre of government during his descendants' brief hold on the island. Tōgō was present as commander of naval forces when Admiral Kabayama made a pious procession to the temple in Tainan dedicated to Coxinga. The 'pirate king', as the Japanese never tired of reminding the locals, had been born in Nagasaki to a Japanese mother and hence could even be regarded as the first *Japanese* ruler of the islands. In that regard, so claimed Kabayama, he could be seen to be liberating the island from unwelcome Chinese usurpers and restoring it to Japan, where it belonged. Just to make matters clear, Coxinga was deified soon afterwards and added to Japan's Shintō pantheon.[1]

Rear Admiral Tōgō was himself recalled home on 16 November 1895, after five months at sea. He was decorated for his achievements in Taiwan, and appointed a member of the committee of the Admiralty. He received a hero's welcome everywhere but in his own home, where his mother received him back under her roof with stoic impassivity. She ushered him into the place of honour in the family's living room, knelt before him, and bowed low. 'It is,' she said gravely, 'the power of His Majesty the Emperor.' Tōgō did not ask if she meant the victory, or his safety, or something else. He merely bowed in return, and, true to form, said nothing at all.[2]

As Tōgō approached his fiftieth birthday, he was ordered back on land, as director of the Higher Naval Academy, a Tokyo institution for advanced training of naval officers. He was determined to push the trainees under his command into thinking more like European officers, and tried several experiments. One was to encourage them in games of strategy, which he recommended in a memo:

> As I perceived that for increasing the power of rapid judgement in questions of tactics, it would be useful to make the head alert by means of such a game as chess, I commenced recently to study the Englishman Jane's book on chess and although I have not yet been able to attain the results expected, still, if I can get new ideas and make some improvements, it cannot be said to have been a waste of time. If we exploit the idea of this game, we shall surely reach points which will be of use to the study of the art of war.[3]

Tōgō also encouraged the young officers to ask themselves how their counterparts in other navies were thinking or were being encouraged to think. Secretly, he commissioned a translation of a book on naval strategy by Vice Admiral Stepan Makarov, a prominent Russian naval officer. The translation was eventually printed and kept on the shelf of the academy library, but Tōgō purloined an advance copy for himself and pored over it line-by-line, making detailed annotations and notes in the margin. He kept the manuscript with him on his flagship for several years, and appears to have hidden it from his subordinates.[4]

The academy appointment gave him considerably more time at home with his family than he had previously enjoyed, and also led to several opportunities to serve on courts martial. Compared to the action he had seen in Chinese waters, it was uneventful. A trip to a hot springs in 1897 suggests that the aging sailor continued to be troubled by rheumatism; however, promotion to Vice Admiral in May 1898 implies that this was not serious enough to worry his superiors. In 1897, he represented the navy at the funeral of the Meiji Emperor's stepmother, the Empress Dowager.[5]

Tōgō was a respected figure in the Japanese military, but still lowly in comparison with some of the senior admirals. More exciting foreign junkets went to his superiors, including the coronation of the new Russian Tsar, Nicholas II, where a group of Japanese diplomats attempted to broker a deal with the young ruler over the situation in the Far East.

Ever since the Triple Intervention, Russia and Japan had continued to clash over Korea and Manchuria. While Tōgō had been in Taiwan, a group of Japanese agents had murdered the influential Queen Min of Korea in a botched attempt at a coup, leading her husband King Gojong to seek sanctuary in the Russian legation.[6] In February 1896, Russian troops in nominal support of King Gojong landed at Chemulpo and marched on Seoul, in much the same fashion as the Japanese had once done themselves. The coup undid much of the advances that the Japanese had made since 1882, leading some Japanese diplomats to wonder aloud if Japan and Russia should not agree to divide Korea between them at the 38th Parallel.

But while the Japanese attempted to agree on Korea and Manchuria with the Tsar, it was their old enemy, Li Hongzhang, who came home with a deal. Unlike his right-hand man, Admiral Ding, the old Viceroy of maritime China had survived the purges following the defeat of the Sino-Japanese War. Discredited but still in power, he made a number of secret deals with the Russians, designed, in old-style Chinese fashion, to pit one enemy against another and so to keep China from having to fight either of them. Fatefully, the Tsar's ministers wanted to interest the Chinese in the Trans-Siberian Railway – a wondrous monument to Western civilisation intended to stretch from the Pacific coast all the way to Moscow. It would, they said, work wonders for trade and make it easy for China's new-found Russian friends to come to their aid in case the Japanese launched a new attack. Li's treaty with the Russians was also concluded in the utmost secrecy – the deal appears to have been done without the knowledge even of the Chinese Empress Dowager, and its existence did not properly come out until 1922.[7]

Instead, the Japanese were left to puzzle over the effects of the secret treaty without even knowing for sure that it existed. In July 1897, Russian military advisers arrived in Korea to train local troops. In November that same year, German forces occupied the port of Jiaozhou in Shandong, only a few miles from where Japanese occupiers still held Weihaiwei in lieu of payment of the Sino-Japanese War indemnities.[8] Worried about the German presence, Li Hongzhang invited Russia to occupy a port of its own in the region to maintain a watch over the Germans. The Japanese were thus faced with the great insult of hearing that Port Arthur, which had been so hard fought for in the Sino-Japanese war, was now being handed over free to the Russians, who already hoped to build a railway from their new, beautifully-appointed warm-water port on the Yellow Sea, up to Harbin in Manchuria, where it would link to the Trans-Siberian Railway. The Japanese were less unhappy about another concession: Great Britain demanded, and received, occupant's rights in Weihaiwei in order to 'counterbalance' the Russian occupation of Port Arthur, possibly to Japan's own benefit.

In 1899, Vice Admiral Tōgō was moved to a new post, as commanding officer of the naval base at Sasebo. Although it still appeared to be a shore appointment, it put the 52-year-old officer in an enviable new position, overseeing not only the daily operation of the station, but also the construction of new ships in its dockyard. With the new threats on the Asian mainland, Japan was preparing a new fleet, and the locally built vessels would be chaperoned by full-sized, foreign-built battleships like the *Mikasa*, currently taking shape in England. His next assignment would be to put Japan's might to use as part of an international effort, designed to save expatriates from America, Europe and Japan from death at the hands of a Chinese religious cult.

The Chinese interest in pitting foes against one another did not only apply on the borders. In 1900, the Beijing government made a fateful decision to look the other way while a new religious cult, dedicated to the removal of foreigners from Chinese soil, took direct action. The Society of the Harmonious Fist, otherwise known as the Boxers, was a grass-roots movement that first arose in Shandong province, where some of its adherents had murdered European missionaries. Not unlike Saigō Takamori's Satsuma Rebellion in Japan, or the Donghaks in Korea, the Boxers were a blunt assertion of 'traditional values' – in this case a China free of white influence, with a quasi-religious element that held that true-hearted Boxers were impervious to foreign bullets. Although this claim was demonstrably untrue, the Boxers successfully massacred several enclaves of Europeans in China, and the Beijing faction managed to surround the Legation Quarter in Beijing. When the Empress Dowager claimed to have no control over Boxer activities, the foreign governments resolved to sent an international relief force.

The Yellow Sea was the route to Beijing. The international effort needed to sail past Russian-owned Port Arthur and British-occupied Weihaiwei, straight for Tianjin, the nearest sea-port to Beijing. The Boxers and their sympathisers held not only Beijing, but also the Dagu Forts, a maze of gun positions set around the S-bends of the Hai River where it met the Yellow Sea. Control of the Dagu forts controlled access to the port city of Tianjin, at one end of a railway that led to Beijing itself.

On 12 June, a member of the Japanese legation in Beijing was murdered and his body mutilated. As a mark of the seriousness of the situation, Tōgō himself was ordered out to China. While Tōgō was *en route*, the Chinese in one of the Dagu forts opened fire on the railway station, where many of the foreign troops had assembled. This attack came in concert with rioting by pro-Boxer parties within Tianjin itself and a series of attacks on Christian churches. The Japanese in town, 300 marines newly arrived from Sasebo, fought alongside Russian Cossacks led by Major-General Anatoly Stoessel. With the Japanese concession under attack, the marines still spared squads of men to back up their similarly beleagured allies at the French and German concessions.

Amid this chaos, Tōgō's subordinate Captain Nagamino was obliged to make a political decision. Representatives of the foreign powers were unsure how to deal with the Dagu forts – the British and Germans favoured an all-out attack on the forts before they could do any more damage; the Americans refused to get involved in any attack until war was officially declared. Nagamino threw in his lot with the British and Germans, signing a joint ultimatum to the fort commanders to give up their forts before dawn or face the consequences.

A rag-tag fleet of three Russian craft formed a flotilla alongside a single boat each from France, Germany, Britain and Japan. All seemed to doubt their chances, volunteering their oldest and most expendable vessels – in Captain Nagamino's case, the 13-year-old composite wood-and-iron gunboat *Atago*.[9]

The *Atago*, however, developed engine trouble and was instead left to guard the river bank near the flotilla's point of embarkation. This appears to have been a genuine technical problem, as several hundred Japanese marines were still committed to the overland assault, as a similarly multinational force landed upriver with orders to storm the North-West and North Forts.

The other ships steamed gingerly downriver, with little choice but to form a single file, as the banks were barely 60 metres apart. It was hoped that the sight of them would be enough to persuade the occupants of the forts to leave; but in the event that the bluster failed, the flotilla would be a series of sitting ducks. Uncharacteristically for the Chinese, the watching artillerymen did not immediately open fire. Instead, they watched the ships as they rounded the S-bend on the approach to the first fort. The forts opened fire at one in the morning, with an instant reply from the waiting gunners on the ships. The flotilla continued its slow progress downstream, taking heavy damage from the onshore batteries, but giving as good as it got.

The land forces were right behind the bombardment, a united force of Germans, British and Japanese, blowing their own hole in the walls. The eager Japanese Lieutenant Shiraishi mounted a foolhardy single-handed charge over the wall, dropping down inside and fighting off Chinese defenders with little more than a broken staff, before unbolting the gates to let his fellow soldiers inside. As the hand-to-hand fighting continued within the fort, Shiraishi dashed for the roof, where in unseemly enthusiasm and unnecessarily violent competition with a rival coalition member, Shiraishi reached the flagpole on top of the fort, only to discover that he had somehow lost the flag he had saved for the purpose. Infamously, Shiraishi grabbed a large white cloth and daubed it with a ragged dot of fresh Chinese blood to make a rough approximation of the Rising Sun. It was this gory trophy that ran up the flagpole of the North West Fort, and signalled it had fallen to the alliance sometime around dawn.[10] The North Fort fell soon afterwards, and then the South Fort. A second assault unfolded south of the river, as marines scrambled from two other boats to board several Chinese destroyers in the naval yard.

It was a superb victory for the international alliance, although the misgivings of the Americans and even some of the participants were soon realised. In firing upon Chinese government soldiers, the international alliance was blatantly lumping all Chinese in together as enemies, counting the loyal servants of the Empress Dowager as little different from the Boxer fanatics. It was the ideal excuse for the Empress Dowager, who convened an emergency council and decreed that all foreigners were henceforth banned from China. The foreigners in Beijing were expected to leave immediately, along the impossibly dangerous road to Tianjin, where they were sure to be massacred. Instead, the inhabitants of the Beijing Legation Quarter decided to make their stand where they were, barricading themselves within the small cluster of city blocks where all the foreign legations could be found. A mere stone's-throw from the Forbidden City, the legation staff and their families blocked their entranceways, pooled their resources, and prayed for a swift rescue.

Tōgō arrived at the captured Dagu forts on 22 June 1900, too late to contribute to the assault. His presence seems to have been ordered more for political reasons than anything else, as there was considerable one-upmanship among the coalition forces as to who should be in charge. As a Vice Admiral, Tōgō outranked many of the lesser commanders, many of whom were already in open disagreement about how to proceed.

With the sea-route to Dagu already in friendly hands, Tōgō could expect little naval action. Some of his smaller vessels might make brief forays upriver, but it was understood that much of the relief action of the Tianjin and Beijing foreigners was going to be a matter for the land armies. Consequently, Tōgō saw to it that the Japanese army was best served. Eight well-equipped Japanese troop transports arrived soon after him, and began unloading their men and supplies onto the beach. Tōgō immediately ordered that the Japanese warships send their ships' boats to aid in the landing operation, effectively doubling the speed with which the Japanese could get ashore. However, Tōgō seemed to display a largely academic interest in the situation. He went upriver to Tanggu on an inspection trip, but otherwise preferred to lurk off shore within view of the coast, in the presence of the other coalition admirals.

On 29 June, the Russian battleship *Petropavlovsk* arrived, commanded by Vice Admiral Yevgeny Alexeiev. Ever inistent on the correct protocols, Tōgō made ready to pay a courtesy call on the new arrival, as Alexeiev outranked him. However, before Tōgō could set out, the over-enthusiastic Alexeiev rowed over to say hello. A tense meeting followed, with Alexeiev effusing loudly and at great length about the new-found alliance between Russia and Japan, while Tōgō offered little more than polite nods.

Tōgō remained aloof from much of the further squabbles among the coalition commanders. He attended one meeting of the assembled commanders, but pronounced it a waste of time, and sent a subordinate to further conclaves. Tōgō only broke his new rule when the British Admiral Sir Edward Seymour returned from the hinterland, in order to congratulate his colleague on his rescue. In all his dealings with the coalition commanders, Tōgō remained cagey with the Russians and cordial with the British – a sign, perhaps of future enmities and alliances, but also of the underlying tone of the coalition. The Russians were rushing to the area in order to balance what they regarded as a potentially unwelcome number of Japanese troops. With Japan so close to the Yellow Sea, it was a relatively simple matter for it to pour troops into the conflict, much to the concerns of the other powers, except for the British, who seemed glad of the asssistance. Notably, the Germans swiftly rushed over a Field Marshal, in order to prevent the Japanese land commander from being the highest ranking officer present.

While the admirals bickered and dealt over such matters as who landed first, who commanded which divisions, and which supplies were most crucial, Tōgō busied himself with one of his old hobbies – spying on everyone else. His report to Japan concentrated less on the minutiae of landing troops, for which Tōgō was once again little more than a riverbus driver, but on aspects of his coalition allies, particularly the over-friendly Russians.

> I mainly directed my observation to the Russian warships, and my conclusion is that the Russian navy is not so formidable as is supposed by the world. It leaves very much to be desired. For one thing, it lacks discipline. What surprised me most, however, was the fact that Russia used warships as substitutes for transports, carrying soldiers and ammunition on board. This is evidently ignoring the true mission of a war vessel.[11]

In this assessment, Tōgō was being a little unfair. The Russians were, after all, arriving in the Yellow Sea in the full expectation that there would be no sea battles to fight. Tōgō himself had tasked boats from his warships to aid in the landing of Japanese troops, and none of the coalition forces were expecting to fight *each other*. However, for Tōgō this was no excuse, and, moreover, was a sign of a larger malaise.

> A warship will thus have its energies wasted for what it is not intended, and will be of little use in case of emergency. This is what a naval man must be aware of most of all. Russia has at the same time betrayed by this that she is devoid of the proper means of transportation and that she is not likely to be able to despatch troops in a proper way at a moment's notice.[12]

Meanwhile, the land forces steadily advanced upriver to Tianjin, and onwards towards Beijing. In Tianjin in late July, Tōgō's curiosity got the better of him when he decided to try his hand at horse-riding. All of the other coalition officers were proceeding on horseback, and Tōgō's legendary reticence, tinged perhaps with a touch of pride, did not allow him to admit that he had relatively little experience with horses. He borrowed a mount from a Japanese lieutenant-general, and having been warned that the animal was jumpy, kept his reins tight and moved the horse along at a slow pace.

Lieutenant Commander Takarabe Takeshi, riding alongside Tōgō, mistakenly assumed that it was the horse that was over-cautious and cracked his riding crop across the animal's rump. The horse immediately bolted, while the stoic Tōgō clung on for dear life. Eventually, he regained control and walked the horse back towards the other Japanese.

'He ran pretty well, didn't he?' enthused a breathless Takarabe, only to be greeted with one Admiral Tōgō's monosyllabic grunts. It was several years before Tōgō confessed his true feelings about the incident:

> I was never so greatly troubled as I was then. I clung to the back of the horse so as not to fall, feeling pretty much in the same way as a man at the helm would suffer in stormy weather. The staff officer acted out of his good will and kindness and I could not complain. But I was very much troubled.[13]

If Tōgō was messing around on horseback in Tianjin, then he was plainly not performing much of an admiral's duties any more. His presence had been wise, if not vital during the early flurry of activ-ity off the Dagu forts, when the multinational expedition force was still unsure if it was a rescue party or an invading army. With the fall of Dagu and Tianjin, the further advance of the troops towards Beijing was now an army matter, and Tōgō could offer little assist-ance. Consequently, he was called home to Japan, arriving back at Nire at the same time as the news that the besieged foreigners of the Legation Quarter had been rescued from the Boxers after fifty-five days of fighting and waiting.

The sinking of the Russian flagship *Petropavlovsk* off Port Arthur, 13 April 1904. Admiral Stepan Makarov and 630 crew members were lost

10

Port Arthur

Tōgō's journey home was not without incident. He took a zig-zag route across the Bohai Gulf to Zhifu and back towards Korea, seemingly patrolling the old demarcation line that had once hemmed in his old foe Ding Ruchang. Leaving his ship at Chemulpo, he made the familiar journey inland to Seoul, where he was received in audience by the Korean ruler and made several courtesy calls on diplomats from some of the other nations involved in the Boxer strife. He then entertained two Korean ministers back aboard his ship, and steamed off down the coast of Korea. *En route* for Japan, he found a Russian ship stuck on a shoal and delayed his trip to come to her rescue, successfully towing her out of trouble.

Uneventful months followed at the naval academy; although in February 1901, Tōgō requested and was granted a brief compassionate leave. His mother Masuko, now eighty-seven years old, was in failing health, and Tōgō rushed to her bedside to nurse her in her final days. She remained a Satsuma samurai to her last breath, dying with the words: 'Be loyal in your service.'[1]

Tōgō's observations in Tianjin were not misspent. In the years that followed, the Japanese Admiralty re-assessed the greatest threat to Japan as issuing from Russia, and continued preparations to avenge the indignity of the Triple Intervention. Tōgō was called to Tokyo for secret talks on 15 October 1903. The summons found him once more bedridden with rheumatism, but he dragged himself to his feet, sure that if he did not, he would lose his chance to command the fleet. He was not to be disappointed. In a meeting with his old Satsuma friend, Admiral Yamamoto Gonnohyōe, Tōgō was informed that war was imminent and that he was to command the fleet. Tōgō was ecstatic at the news, but, true to form, merely acknowledged it with a curt nod and a salute. Even when being given the chance of a lifetime, he never went beyond bare monosyllables. He took his leave of his wife and family, and treated this sight of them as his last. To Mrs Tōgō, he left with a parting entreaty that she should look after his dogs if he never came back.[2]

Although the result of his summons was a blunt statement in the official gazette that he had been appointed to a new post as Commander-in-Chief of the Standing Squadron, the discussion of his new position took several hours. Saying nothing to his subordinates, Tōgō threw his new squadron into a continuous round of drills, much of it in deliberate preparation for dealing with the naval tactics that he might expect from a pupil of Stepan Makarov – the admiral whose manual he had ordered to be translated some years earlier.

Tōgō would have several months to prepare, until 4 February 1904, when an Imperial Order was sent to both the army and navy:

> We are now compelled to conclude that the Russian Government has no sincere desire to maintain the peace of the East. The integrity of the territories of China and Korea has a close connection with the independence and self-protection of our Japan. We have, therefore, ordered Our Government to break off the negotiations with Russia and have decided to take free action for the maintenance of our independence and self-protection.[3]

The precise meaning of this was clear to Tōgō and his superiors, who had in fact been discussing the best course of action for months; the Emperor himself had accepted the inevitability of war since January 1904. Behind the scenes, the Japanese military had been squabbling over the best moment to initiate hostilities, and the navy had been causing the delays. Technology had been one issue – the Japanese Admiralty wanted wireless telegraphy installed aboard its ships, which was only completed at the end of 1903.[4] Meanwhile, two impressive new Japanese warships, the *Nisshin* and *Kasuga* (the latter named after the famous vessel on which the teenage Tōgō had served), were *en route* from Italy, and the navy did not wish to find itself in the same embarrassing position of the Chinese a decade earlier, entering a war with their two best weapons impounded in a foreign port. It was thus only when the new acquisitions reached Singapore that the navy approved the escalation of hostilities, knowing that their new prizes were only a fortnight away.

After midnight, Vice Admiral Tōgō called a meeting aboard his flagship, the *Mikasa*. The huge ship was crowded by a swarm of smaller vessels, cutters, picket boats and torpedo boats, and Tōgō's cabin was packed to the gunwhales with expectant officers. Tōgō's officers assembled around his table, which was bare of the usual maps and charts. Instead, a ceremonial tray sat in the centre of the table containing nothing but a unsheathed dagger – the last resort of the trapped samurai, a symbol of final, noble suicide. None commented the ominous blade, and Tōgō made no mention of it himself; but it was to become a regularly repeated scene in the Tōgō legendarium for years to come.[5]

> Perfect silence reigned for a few minutes. The Admiral was simply looking at the sword. From this eye hint, commanders, captains and other officers comprehended the meaning of the Admiral. The hint was: 'If defeated, don't return, but use the sword.'[6]

Tōgō informed his officers that their orders were to 'destroy the Russian Pacific Squadron and command the sea'. The Japanese fleet was to split into two squadrons, with Vice Admiral Uryū taking one group for a surprise attack on Chemulpo. Uryū's mission, already underway, was to wipe out the Russian naval presence at Chemulpo and to watch over the ensuing landing of Japanese troops. As Tōgō knew from his own personal experience, seizing Chemulpo would leave Seoul itself open to the Japanese and hasten the Japanese seizure of Korea. However, the bulk of the fleet, including three entire divisions and the entire destroyer complement, were to be placed under Tōgō's command and given the more difficult job

– destroying the Russian Pacific Sqaudron, currently rumoured to be anchored at Port Arthur.

'Upon this war,' noted Tōgō dourly, 'depends the safety of our country, and I intend with you officers, by doing our utmost, to crush the enemy without fail and ease His Majesty's mind.'[7]

> I hope that we shall all meet again when your mission has been accomplished; but if any one of you has to die, his is the greater glory, that of having sacrificed his life for the greatness of Japan, and history will place him forever among its heroes.[8]

Records of Tōgō's address to his men do not include any mention of a more pressing strategic concern – that under any reasonable analysis, a Japanese attack on the Russian navy was an act of suicidal daring. The Russian navy had more than twice the tonnage of the Japanese at the time, and the Admiralty in Tokyo had resigned itself to losing perhaps half its ships in a desperate scramble for mastery of the Yellow Sea. Even if Tōgō were successful, he would only buy the land forces a few weeks to seize Korea before the inevitable Russian counter-attack, which was expected to come by land along the Trans-Siberian Railway and by sea from one of Russia's European squadrons.

The vast harbour at Sasebo was packed with ships at dawn, as the sun streaked the clouds in the sky overhead with warm colours. Tōgō signalled his fleet to leave in a pre-arranged order – a further sign that the 'surprise' departure of the Japanese had been in the planning stages for some time.

On the other side of the world in St Petersburg, the Japanese minister Kurino Shinichirō received a telegram on 6 February ordering him to break off diplomatic relations. He informed the ministers of Tsar Nicholas of his order, and noted that the Japanese would now 'take such independent action as they deemed appropriate'. Meanwhile in Tokyo, the Russian ambassador Roman Rosen was called in to hear the same news. Rosen returned to his legation, only to hear that the Japanese fleet had already put to sea in two battle-ready squadrons. He was thus, perhaps, the first Russian to realise that the 'independent action' was no idle threat or brinkmanship, but a *de facto* declaration of war. He rushed to warn St Petersburg, only to discover that all foreign telegraph traffic had been suspended. Tōgō was already underway, and there was no hope of warning the Russians in Port Arthur.[9]

The crews of the Japanese ships were not informed of their objective until the fleet was already at sea. That night, as the ships steamed towards the Yellow Sea, Tōgō ordered all vessels to watch for torpedo boats. Although the Russians were oblivious as to the approaching danger, Tōgō saw no reason not to regard the countries to already be in a state of war.

Instead of preparing for trouble, the Russians in Port Arthur were preparing for a party. The city was decked out in celebration of a forthcoming feast day, and many officers had been given extended leave to attend a round of banquets and balls. 'Many houses,' noted one Russian officer, 'gave banquets to celebrate the day and a gay atmosphere pervaded the streets. One could see people staggering tipsy along the streets.'[10] Among all the festivities there were two must-have tickets. The wife of Vice Admiral Oscar Stark, leader of the Russian Pacific Squadron, would be holding the party to end all parties to which many high-ranking naval officers had been invited. Across town, Lady Sonnenbrin, the wife of the chief surgeon attached to the 10th Regiment, planned a rival shindig favouring the army. Both parties were to be held on the night of 7 February, but many officers appeared to have been getting in the mood with a round of pre-parties that left them hungover or bedridden the next morning.

Consequently, there was nobody of sufficient intelligence or rank on duty that morning when a steamer put into Port Arthur from across the gulf. Onboard was the Japanese consul from Zhifu, who paid his respects to what few staff were on duty at the naval base. He made no secret of his mission; he had come to pick up the Japanese residents of Port Arthur and to take them to safety. This, it seems, was misinterpreted as a reiteration of Japan's decision to break off diplomatic relations and not as the rather obvious statement of intent to commence hostilities that hindsight affords. Nor, it seems, did the Russians notice the behaviour of the consul's fellow passengers, as the Zhifu steamer was crammed with naval officers disguised as common sailors and labourers. While the consul dropped in on several woozy and delicate officials, still recovering from the night before, his spies fanned out across the harbour and diligently noted down the disposition and condition of every vessel in sight.

While the Russians in Port Arthur carried on regardless, Tōgō was already at the tip of Korea. At Mokpo, in the south-west of the Korean peninsula, Tōgō left behind his 'Third Squadron' – a creaking collection of condemned ships and outdated tubs, many of them once-proud combatants in the Sino-Japanese War, including the legendary *Zhenyuan*. Under the control of the aging Vice Admiral Kataoka, the Third Squadron was charged with keeping the Yellow Sea safe from any unexpected Russian attack from the rear. However, there was little chance of that. The Japanese spy network was remarkably thorough, and it was known that only a handful of ships from the Russian Pacific Squadron were outside the Yellow Sea area and presumably far out of harm's way in Vladivostok.

The crossing to Korea was not uneventful. Tōgō's fleet ran into and captured a merchant vessel, whose name, the *Russia*, was taken by all the Japanese to be a great omen. Less happily, the *Takachiho* literally ran into something else, ramming an unfortunate whale on the open sea. However, the damage was not fatal, at least not to the *Takachiho*.

Uryū's squadron peeled off for Chemulpo, while Tōgō and the main fleet continued on their course for Port Arthur. Tōgō's own observations during the Boxer Rebellion had taught him that the Russian ships were not at peak performance, slowed by barnacles and diminished by poor discipline and corner-cutting. Intelligence reports told him more – that the Russians had not yet bothered to dredge the approaches to Port Arthur. This meant that the largest and most powerful Russian ships could only enter or leave the harbour at high tide. At all other times, they would either be unable to flee into the harbour or unable to steam out of it to aid in the port's defence. Twice a day, the Russian commanders had to decide whether their ships were in the right position and to stick to that arrangement for the next twelve hours.

Assuming (wrongly, as it turned out), that the Russians would have the guns of Port Arthur fully manned and garrisoned and ready to return fire, Tōgō hatched a scheme that would keep the most valuable of Japanese warships out of harm's way. On the starlit but moonless night of 8 February, he intended to send in his destroyers with torpedo boats to deal with any of the Russian ships that rode at anchor outside the harbour. A second, smaller group would mount an assault on the harbour at nearby Dalian, just in case Tōgō's intelligence was wrong and there were any Russian ships in that port.

At the final briefing, Tōgō cautioned his captains to make every effort to run dark. There should be no lights on the boats, and all should run at low speed until the very last moment so as to avoid any telltale sparks flying from the smokestacks. Pouring champagne for the captains, Tōgō did what he could to impress upon them the momentous importance of their mission:

> Let me especially remind you that the attack must be delivered with the greatest energy possible, because, gentlemen, we are at war, and only he who acts fearlessly can hope for success. Your duty, gentlemen, is very simple, and I make only one request, a request which … has produced excellent results in cases much more complicated than this: Show yourselves worthy of the confidence which I place in you, and for which I am responsible to His Majesty the Mikado.[11]

After the champagne toast, Tōgō shook each man's hand – a strangely European gesture that shows the continued foreign influence on naval etiquette in Japan.

The attack began at 10:30 p.m., before the imminent moonrise brought unwelcome additional light to the dark waters. The Dalian group found nothing and turned back, heading directly for Chemulpo as agreed beforehand. The others knew they would have better luck in Port Arthur, but, running dark themselves, were entirely unprepared for the sight of most of the Russian fleet, lit up like Christmas trees, riding obliviously at anchor in the waters outside Port Arthur. The Russian viceroy, that same Yevgeny Alexeiev who had once tried to charm military secrets out of Tōgō during the Boxer Uprising, had remained convinced there would still be a diplomatic solution to the quarrels between Japan and Russia, and had made no effort to prepare for hostilities.

They ran into two Russian destroyers on patrol and took hasty evasive action, although the Russians did not open fire. With no lights or means of signalling, the Japanese squadron was now functioning entirely independently, with no ship truly able to coordinate with any other. It was 12:20 a.m. when one of the groups decided to take the initiative. The torpedo boats worked in as close as they thought possible, releasing their torpedoes at a distance of half a mile. Although the Russians seemed oblivious to the risk of Japanese attack, the vessels off Port Arthur were fitted with torpedo nets – extensive skirts of wire mesh designed to prevent a torpedo striking the sides of the ship. The Japanese torpedoes were fitted with net-cutting blades but these often dragged them off course. Those that did reach the nets did so without enough force to tear through the mesh, but three torpedoes still managed to hit their targets. As the moon rose, the Japanese torpedoes slammed into the battleships *Tsetsarevich* and *Retvizan* and the light cruiser *Pallada*. The *Tsetsarevich* opened fire on the torpedo boats while sailors on the other vessels scrambled to action stations. The torpedo boats retired, while the Russian ships limped back for Port Arthur, grounding themselves close to the harbour and further blocking the channel for their fellow ships.

The noise of the initial explosions, and of the Russians opening fire, was heard clear across town at Lady Sonnenbrin's party. A curious guest phoned the naval station, only to be told that the *Retvizan* had been ordered to conduct midnight firing practice and there was nothing that need concern the partygoers.

'The firing ceased for some time,' wrote a reveller, 'but half an hour later guns were again heard, this time more violently and in quick succession. An expression of uneasiness spread again over the countenance of every one, but, conscious of the invincible power of our fleet, [everyone] kept his seat complacently at the banquet table.'[12]

By the time someone on shore sounded a proper alarm, Tōgō's torpedo boats were already on their way home. Fearing a Japanese landing, the Russians scrambled to their posts, in such a panic that many got lost or arrived at the wrong fort. In a triumph of bad preparation, the 10th Regiment reported for duty but neglected to bring any ammunition.

Tōgō had, if anything, been overly cautious. Unwilling to believe that the Russians would be so entirely unprepared, his own flagship was still an hour away at dawn with the bulk of his fleet; nor had he dared send troop transports in ready for a landing. As the sun rose on Port Arthur, the only Japanese ships in the area were the light cruisers of Rear Admiral Dewa Shigeto. Dewa urgently radioed Tōgō with the news that the three holed ships had blocked the harbour entrance and that the Russian Pacific Squadron was trapped offshore in whatever state it had been in the night before. From what he could see, several of the Russian ships had not even raised steam. There would be little chance of coaling or resupply before the Japanese could arrive. If there was a time for the Japanese to engage the Russians in open battle, it was right now.

By 11 a.m., when Tōgō arrived aboard the *Mikasa*, the element of surprise had been lost. The Russians had had all morning to man the guns in the coastal forts to offer some modicum of cover to the ships. Tōgō raised a signal inspired by his youthful instruction in Nelson's career: 'Victory or defeat depends on this first battle. Let every man do his duty.'[13]

The *Mikasa* led the charge herself, taking a heavy pounding from the forts and ships. One shell actually hit the ship's main bridge and would have killed Tōgō had he not chosen to command from the smaller forebridge, as was his habit. The Japanese and Russians fired at each other for an hour, until it became plain to Tōgō that he would not achieve anything unless he could either lure the Russians away from the covering fire of their coastal forts, or land troops to deal with the forts directly. At half past noon, Tōgō gave the order to retreat, leaving the Russians in disarray and despondency. As one Russian captain recalled:

As our fleet had been ordered by the viceroy not to go beyond the range of the forts, we were unable to pursue the retreating enemy. While the enemy sang triumphal songs and were thus able to stimulate the morale of the whole fleet, our petty officers and men, on the other hand, became obsessed with the idea that the Japanese were unconquerable.[14]

Tōgō steamed for Chemulpo, confident that Uryū's mission would have been successful. Sure enough, Uryū had been able to land thousands of troops in full view of the Russian battleship *Variag*, without any attempt at stopping him. Uryū warned the foreign ships in the area to stay out of the way, despite protests from the future British admiral Lewis Bayly that his acts were in violation of Korean neutrality. The Russian presence was limited to a single battleship, the *Variag*, and an insignificant vessel called the *Korietz*. The Russians tried to make a break for the open sea, but were heavily outnumbered by the Japanese, and retreated, battered, to the port, where the ships were scuttled. When Tōgō arrived, Uryū was able to inform him that the new American-built *Variag* had been sent to the bottom of the harbour without so much as a scratch on any Japanese man or ship.[15]

While Japanese troops poured into Korea, ready to advance into Manchuria and Liaodong, Tōgō kept watch over Port Arthur. His strategy baffled the Russians, who continued to expect an all-out assault; but Tōgō much preferred to wear them down. In an ideal world, he hoped to block the Port Arthur harbour entrance with wrecks so that Russian ships could get neither in nor out, trapping the best ships in harbour, and ensuring that none of those outside had the chance to make repairs. Tōgō ordered a second torpedo boat attack on 13 February, striking in the midst of a driving snow-storm. Visibility was so poor and the seas so rough that only two of Tōgō's boats even located Port Arthur. They returned without scoring any hits.

Although the fame of the devastating attack soon spread, at the time there was grumbling among the lower ranks about Tōgō's *lack* of preparation. Some officers dared to suggest that Tōgō should have been more pro-active in his assault. A significant proportion of the Japanese were aghast that Tōgō had not been more ready to exploit his immediate advantage. 'It is to be hoped,' wrote one captain, 'that the inactivity of the Admiral that night will not be repeated.'

All naval history goes to prove, and the English in some measure also teach us, that only an attack delivered with energy and determination can be successful. I do not think that Nelson with his squadron would have remained inactive before Port Arthur, as Tōgō did.[16]

Over the weeks that followed, Tōgō tried several more attacks on the Russians. In March, he decided to use condemned Japanese vessels, intended to be sunk as blockships at the harbour entrance if the Russians would not oblige by allowing themselves to be hit. Tōgō asked for a handful of volunteers to pilot the doomed ships. He received 2,000 applications, some of them earnestly written in blood. Tōgō invited the successful applicants to dinner aboard the *Mikasa*. 'You have a great task before you,' he said, with his usual sparse words, 'and I hope you will succeed.'[17]

Five blockships, disguised as coal ships, chugged away from Tōgō's fleet on the night of 23 February. Their approach was timed to coincide with the setting of the crescent moon at half past midnight. Safely in place, the ships waited in silence until the early hours of 24 February, going into action at 4:30 a.m. One struck a reef and was unable to go on. The second and third raced for the harbour mouth under enemy fire and scuttled themselves in approximately the right positions. The fourth and fifth had less luck, misreading signals from other vessels and misjudging their position, opening their valves and sinking in less advantageous positions. The crews managed to escape with only one dead and a few wounded. Three crews made it to the torpedo boat that was waiting to pick them up; two others were blown out to sea, but were later picked up by Japanese ships.

Tōgō continued to keep the Russians bottled up in Port Arthur, while the Japanese marched on Seoul from Chemulpo, then north to Pyongyang. The Russian response remained sluggish. The ships in Vladivostok were kept busy by a small squadron of Japanese cruisers. Meanwhile, the much-lauded Trans-Siberian Railway was found to be ill-equipped for mass mobilisation. Despite the Tsar's boasts of his strong communication links with the East, the Trans-Siberian Railway still lacked a vital 40-mile section of track spanning Lake Baikal in Siberia. In summertime, train carriages were ferried directly across the water; in winter, the Russians relied on running tracks across the ice, which was forever shifting and heaving, thus delaying any attempts at crossing. While the Russians struggled with this bottleneck, the Japanese continued to head north largely unopposed. The winter, however, took its toll on them, as did the lack of transport available while much of the navy remained occupied guarding against the Russians. The Japanese dug in around Pyongyang and did their best to make friends with the Koreans, dutifully paying for anything they requisitioned and awaiting the spring thaw.

For the Russians at Port Arthur, the prospects looked bleak. As winter turned to spring, the Japanese were sure to advance out of Korea and into Liaodong, where they might be expected to cut off Port Arthur from any hope of being relieved by land. With Port Arthur under siege, there would be little hope of relief from the railway line that stretched north across Manchuria to Harbin, the junction with the Trans-Siberian Railway. By the time Russian reinforcements arrived in Harbin, they would face an uphill struggle to come to Port Arthur's aid.

But before the Japanese could cut off the railway, the Russians got the closest thing to a saviour – the respected Vice Admiral Stepan Makarov arrived on 8 March to take charge. Makarov was the best that the Russian navy had to offer, a great captain who had been shunted aside into a pointless onshore post by the politics of the Russian military aristocracy. Now, he raised his personal flag aboard the *Petropavlovsk*, regarded as the battleship in the best state of repair in Port Arthur.

'Makarov is coming! Makarov is coming!' the excited cry went up among the men, and when his flag fluttered in the spring breeze from his flagship's mast, there were reports of sailors doffing their caps and crossing themselves in devout gratitude. Makarov's fame was based in part on his military service record, but also on his grasp of naval theory. He had produced many standard sea charts and was credited as the inventor of a new class of steam-powered ice-breaker. Best of all, his fame had spread far and wide through the publication of a textbook on naval tactics. Unknown to the

Russians, Tōgō had kept a copy, heavily annotated, by his side for the previous decade.[18]

With Makarov's arrival, the Russians suddenly began behaving like they were at war. The *Retvizan*, which had been little more than a hulk-fort at the harbour entrance for several weeks, was now refloated and repaired. The Russian ships were scraped clean and made ready for battle; and the next time Japanese ships appeared in the vicinity, a party of Russian ships sallied out to engage them.

Tōgō now faced reports of occasional skirmishes between Russian and Japanese vessels, with mounting casualties. One unnamed Russian destroyer took several damaging hits that left her dead in the water. The Japanese boarded, only to find the Russians waiting for them with swords and pistols in hand, ready for a savage battle from deck to deck. Before the Japanese could seize the ship, the crew opened her valves and sank her.[19] Makarov was instrumental in this new-found Russian valour. His flag leapt from ship to ship, flying from whichever vessel was in the best position to lead an attack, even if it was not the best armed or armoured. But with the waters receding and the harbour approach still not dredged, Makarov was forced to run back to port and wait for the next high tide.

Tōgō took full advantage of the lull, sending a group of ships over to shell the harbour indirectly from the other side of the mountains, while other vessels closer at hand spotted the fall of shot and telegraphed their observations in real time back to the gunners. Russian plans for Port Arthur had included the building of additional forts to prevent such a bombardment; but as with the dredging, they had never quite got around to it. Instead, the Russians were left fuming as the Japanese shells crashed into the supposedly safe anchorage. The damage was minimal, but it wounded Russian pride. On the bridge of the *Petropavlovsk*, Makarov lamented his enemy's ability to exploit Russian weaknesses:

> Tōgō is a shrewd fellow to have taken advantage of low tide, when we cannot go out, to make indirect firing upon the harbour and then withdraw before high tide. It is quite provoking to be handled

in this way. But I must admit that he knows his business all right. Well, he shall soon catch it for this![20]

Late in March, the land forces were drawing near. Advance units of the Russian army had made it across Lake Baikal and reached the critical junction of Harbin in north Manchuria. Now they had streamed down the southern Manchurian railway from Harbin towards Mukden, the capital of Manchuria. Meanwhile, the Japanese were still on the Korean side of the Yalu river. Neither land army had yet reached the Liaodong Peninsula, leaving Port Arthur's fate still unsure. Unknown to Tōgō, his actions had already made him an international celebrity – 19 May 1904 saw Tōgō's portrait gracing the cover of the *Illustrated London News*, along with several conjectural reports of his naval actions against Makarov.

On 22 March, Tōgō was back for a rematch, and noted with interest that the Russians had improved their preparations. Battleships returned fire when the Japanese attempted to fire over the mountain tops again; and every fort was ready to open fire on any ship that strayed within range. One Japanese ship, the *Fuji*, sustained heavy damage and was only saved by her watertight compartments – in the course of the conflict, the *Fuji* often bore the brunt of the bad luck, such that Japanese sailors began to give her a superstitiously wide berth.

By this time, Makarov had ordered the approaches to Port Arthur to be heavily mined against any further Japanese assaults. Remembering similar hazards at Chemulpo many years earlier, Tōgō had his officers keep meticulous records of the courses taken by Russian ships out of the harbour. Any strange alterations in course were sure to reflect the location of mines below the surface, and Tōgō wanted that information to hand. Tōgō put the observations to use in April, in a meeting with the commander of the Combined Squadron's mine-laying force, Oda Kiyozo.

'As you perhaps know,' mused Tōgō, 'Makarov comes out of port with his fleet every time we make an attack on Port Arthur. He always takes the same movement, wheeling round in the direction of Xiansheng-cui. Admiral Shimamura and Captain Akiyama will tell you just what route the enemy's fleet is in the habit of taking.

I wish you to lay your mines on that route on the night before our next attack.'[21]

Tōgō's plan had to wait until the spring storms had died down. On the night of 12 April, Oda put to sea with his minelayer, a vessel whose arrival had been long awaited. There was still a fierce drizzle in the air, creating a haze that reduced visibility to winter snow-storm levels and severely affected the performance of the Russian searchlights. Oda's ship was the *Koryo*, a light civilian vessel that had been requisitioned as a minelayer soon after it was built.[22] From the deck, guarded by a small flotilla of silent torpedo boats, he looked on as the *Koryo* carefully laid mines in what all believed to be the likely path of Makarov's fleet. Then, satisfied that Tōgō's orders had been carried out to the letter, the small group of ships slipped away to safety.

At dawn on 13 April, the night-long rain began to dry out into spring mist. A group of Japanese destroyers, originally placed in the area to watch over the *Koryo*, were still in the vicinity when they ran into a hapless Russian vessel, the *Strashini*. Outnumbering the *Strashini* four-to-one, the Japanese made short work of her – she was dead in the water within ten minutes, and sinking fast. A Japanese rescue operation to fish the Russian survivors out of the water was called off by the arrival of a new Russian ship, the *Bayan*, ready for a new fight. The *Bayan*, too, faced overwhelming odds, but wisely ran back towards Port Arthur before she could take any fatal damage. As Tōgō might have hoped, the *Bayan* was only seeking a temporary respite. She was soon back with rein-forcements – a veritable parade of the cream of the Russian fleet, including Makarov aboard the *Petropavlovsk*. In the meantime, Tōgō arrived with his own forces to reinforce the destroyers, leading many to assume that the months of waiting were finally over, and that the long awaited, decisive 'Battle of Port Arthur' was finally about to take place.

Makarov, however, had come to slap down four foolhardy destroyers, not to engage the entire Japanese fleet. As first Tōgō's *Mikasa*, and then ship after ship of the Japanese navy materialised out of the mist, Makarov sensed that he was being lured into a trap and signalled an immediate withdrawal. With none of their earlier haphazardness, the Russian fleet acted as one, all turning at the same instant, rushing back within the relative safety of the range of the coastal forts. Sure that the Japanese would not venture any further, Makarov began his characteristic parade to starboard, right into the path Tōgō had outlined for his minelayers. Crucially, in his haste to chastise the destroyers, Makarov had not ordered his customary mine-sweeping of the outer harbour before charging out.

On the bridge of the *Petropavlovsk*, Makarov thought he saw a shadow in the water – a long, dark shape sliding in the shallows. He raised a new signal, warning his men to watch out for enemy submarines, unaware that the Japanese had none. Tensely, expectantly, Tōgō watched through his binoculars. As the Russian ships receded, they faded back into the mist, until he was no longer able to tell one from the other. The seconds ticked past and Tōgō let his binoculars fall, scowling into the featureless haze. The officers around him on the forebridge, who were all aware of the plan, did not dare breathe a word of doubt about the *Koryo*'s mission.

Suddenly, a vast plume of black smoke erupted through the grey air. Milliseconds behind it came the thunderous rumble of an explosion. The black cloud rolled with terrifying speed over the outline of a Russian ship, as the officers around Tōgō cheered. Even Tōgō permitted himself an uncharacteristic smile, as the smoke cleared and the vessel's outline was nowhere to be seen. Anxiously, Tōgō's deck officers asked him how they should phrase their report, as it was not clear which ship had been hit and to what extent she had been damaged. Expressionlessly, Tōgō announced that it was sure to have been the *Petropavlovsk*, and it was sure to have sunk.

He was right. Amid the elation on the *Mikasa*, the Japanese had perhaps failed to note the sound of not one but several explosions. Survivors on the *Petropavlovsk* reported that the entire ship had been violently shaken by the first explosion. They had barely struggled to their feet when a second blast covered the deck with a pall of yellow-blue smoke, sure to have been the detonation of the *Petropavlovsk*'s eighteen torpedoes. Third and fourth explosions from within the hull were her bursting boilers and exploding magazine, practically ripping the *Petropavlovsk* in two. The ship listed dangerously to the side, her rear propellers already out of the water. She sank in less than two minutes, taking 630 sailors with her. Makarov, badly wounded by the explosion, went down with his ship.

The Russians launched boats to rescue the survivors, fishing barely eighty men from the water. Other boats poured round after round of ammunition into the sea, falsely believing that the Japanese had a submarine somewhere in the vicinity. In fact, the dark shadow Makarov had reported was a very unlucky shark; but by the time the Russians had worked this out, a second vessel had wandered into the *Koryo*'s minefield.[23] A new explosion tore through the hull of the *Pobieda*, although she was spared the fate of the *Petropavlovsk*. Leaning perilously close to the water, the damaged *Pobieda* limped back into Port Arthur, where distraught land forces were already at prayer and in mourning for the loss of Admiral Makarov.

Tōgō refused to give the Russians time to grieve. On successive nights, he sent warships around to the far side of the hills, to continue his characteristic indirect bombardment of the harbour. Meanwhile, he instructed other vessels to launch Holmes Lights towards the harbour mouth. Originally designed as distress flares, these buoys contained calcium carbide, which would transform into acetelyne gas on contact with the water. A second chemical, calcium phosphide, would combust in the water and ignite the gas, turning each buoy into a floating torch, liable to burn unchecked until its fuel ran out. Seeing lights on the water, the Russians diligently took aim and blazed away, wasting their ammunition by shooting at ghosts.

In distant St Petersburg, the Tsar's chief of staff made a fateful decision. The war in the Far East had been regarded for months as a minor irritation – an unpleasant itch that would all too easily be dealt with by a fraction of the Russian military machine, just as soon as they arrived in the theatre of war to chastise the Japanese. Response had been sluggish, but the death of Admiral Makarov seemed to galvanise the Russians. On 30 April 1904, it was announced that the Russian Baltic Fleet was to be renamed the Second Pacific Squadron. The implication was clear: a heavy, overwhelming flotilla of reinforcements would shortly be on its way. The slight Russian advantage in tonnage would be increased by a huge number of new arrivals – sufficient tonnage to outclass the Japanese two-to-one. It would take many months, to be sure, but a Russian relief force was coming. The Russians had started a countdown for the rescue of Port Arthur by sea, and were sure to keep the Japanese in the dark as to when the fleet would arrive.[24]

Tōgō ordered another mission to close the harbour with block-ships. After screening thousands of volunteers, a handful of men was sent in on the cloudy night of 2 May, in command of eleven vessels. A strong wind blew up into a gale by the appointed hour, leading Commander Hayashi, in charge of the mission, to call it off – it was more important to Tōgō that the ships be sunk in the right position than it was to merely harass the Russians. However, only three vessels received, or admitted to receiving, the commander's orders. The other eight, fired up with suicidal fervour, continued their mission despite the countermand.

The ships were commanded by eager lieutenants of the Japanese fleet, determined to make a name for themselves. Five of the ships successfully ran the gauntlet of enemy fire, scuttling themselves around the harbour mouth with varying degrees of success and varying losses of life. In some cases, the crew successfully made it off with minimal casualties. In others, the ship's crew took heavy losses before reaching their target destination – sinking in flames or off course due to a dead helmsman. In still another, the crew successfully disembarked, only for their lifeboat to be overturned on the rough sea – some were picked up by the Russians, others drowned. On hearing the news that most of his vessels had 'diso-beyed' his order, Commander Hayashi ordered his own boat to turn back and join them, only to be left inconsolable by a jammed steering mechanism that prevented him seeking a similar death.

The Russians watched from the relative safety of the shoreline as many Japanese sailors trudged out of the waves onto the shore. The Russians waited expectantly for the Japanese to surrender, only to look on aghast as the hopelessly outnumbered handful of men charged Russian positions with pistols and rifles. Others reported similar small-arms attacks from the Japanese that made it ashore, or in one case, a stricken lifeboat whose passengers fired upon would-be Russian rescuers. Still another beached Japanese ship was the site of a gruesome end – Russian soldiers arrived to take the men into custody, only to discover a sword-wielding officer calmly beheading his fellow survivors. Of the 158 Japanese that had manned the eight ships, only 63 were picked up offshore. Another seventeen were later found in Russian custody, having been apprehended unconscious. The rest either died in the assault, drowned in the aftermath, or were killed in a series of suicidal charges against the Russian forts.

Regardless of Tōgō's orders or Commander Hayashi's wishes, the attitude of the blockship crews was a curious development. In March, during a similar assault, reporting of Japanese actions centred on the heroism of one Lieutenant Hirose, who died when he entered a sinking ship in search of one of his fellow officers. The emphasis, in March, was on Hirose's devotion to his men and his duty. Less than a month later, the attitude of the officers seems markedly different. One Lieutenant Shiraishi, who died in the May assault, openly announced before setting out that he intended to scuttle his ship as ordered, before taking his escape boat and heading straight for one of the Russian forts, apparently with the intention of capturing it, despite the certain likelihood of dying in the attempt.[25]

Hence, while Tōgō maintained his inscrutable smile and habitual calm in May, we might suppose that others in his service were becoming more eager for victory. Despite an outward appearance of cooperation, there may have still been a certain rivalry between the land and sea forces, and it was only a matter of time before the army literally walked up to Port Arthur and subjected it to a different form of siege. But Tōgō was quite satisfied with the continued blockade. Russian naval strength was still significantly greater than that of Japan, but was almost entirely impotent as long as it was trapped at Port Arthur. Tōgō did not need to sink the Russian fleet; he merely needed to keep it from sinking his own, and from sinking the troop transports and supply ships that plied the narrow straits between Japan and Korea.

With Makarov gone, the notorious Viceroy Alexeiev assumed control of the Russian fleet. Alexeiev reinstituted a passive, waiting strategy; although since Tōgō was unaware of this, he maintained a constant, 24-hour series of patrols, happy to keep the Russians bottled up in Port Arthur for as long as the Japanese land forces were advancing. Alexeiev, sensing what was to come, cleared out of Port Arthur in early May before his escape route could be cut off, leaving the fleet under the charge of Rear Admiral Wilhelm Vitgeft. Although he had enjoyed a marine career of sorts in his younger days, Vitgeft was in the Far East as Alexeiev's chief of staff, not as a naval commander. But with Port Arthur about to be cut off, Vitgeft was in the wrong place at the right time, the only available officer with enough experience. Vitgeft, too, favoured Alexeiev's policy of sitting tight. In a perfect world, the Russian fleet ought to be able to make a run for it, smashing through Tōgō's blockade, cutting a chaotic swathe through the Straits of Tsushima, and seeking sanctuary in Vladivostok. But for now, Vitgeft preferred to hide in Port Arthur and pray for relief via the Trans-Siberian Railway. Tōgō's luck could not hold out forever.

Admiral Togo's flagship *Mikasa* engages the Russian fleet during the Battle of Tsushima 27 May 1905

11

The Battle of the Yellow Sea

Since the outbreak of hostilities, Tōgō had led a charmed life. The only Japanese vessels sunk thus far during the fighting over Port Arthur had been old hulks scuttled at his orders, loaded with stones and cement, as blockships. This all changed in mid-May, when Alexeiev appeared to embark on a new strategy designed to test the rules of war.

International law had been a pet subject of Tōgō's ever since his days as a bedridden invalid with a stack of legal books. His knowledge had been put to the test over the sinking of the *Kowshing* and in subsequent courts martial on which he served. He had advised his men to maintain a keen knowledge of maritime law to avoid bad decisions in situations where the fates of nations depended upon it. He had observed the behaviour of other powers in the execution of war, most particularly those of the French in their dastardly attack on the Chinese at Fuzhou. He had, in a sense, fired the first shots of both the Sino-Japanese and Russo-Japanese wars, both of which were the subject of some debate over their declaration and pursuit. It was, then, perhaps with an element of poetic justice that Alexeiev played Tōgō at his own game.

At first, the news was chalked up to misfortune. One of the Japanese torpedo boats struck a mine and sank on 12 May. The next day, the gunboat *Miyako* also struck a mine. Soon afterwards, the *Kasuga* rammed the *Yoshino* in the fog, causing Tōgō's old flagship from the Taiwan campaign to capsize and sink in mere minutes with the loss of 319 lives. Once the fastest ship afloat, the *Yoshino* came to an embarrassing end, rammed by one of her own comrades.

After so many weeks without a single ship lost, Tōgō began to suspect that the Russians were making their own luck. According to the rules of engagement set during the Hague Convention of 1899, floating mines could only be laid within the boundaries of territorial waters. This boundary, at the time, was defined as being within the range of coastal batteries – a directive to which the Russians had so far been adhering. However, as Tōgō had already demonstrated with his intermittent naval bombardment of the harbour, the modern range of heavy guns was substantially greater than that assumed in 1899. Tōgō had, perhaps a little too trustingly, assumed that the Russians would continue to adhere to the Hague Conventions, perhaps because the 1899 Hague Conference had been convened by Tsar Nicholas II himself.

Instead, Vitgeft had sent minelayers beyond the officially recognised boundaries of his own territorial waters, using the cover of more mists to lay mines right in the courses patrolled by Tōgō's own ships. On 14 May, Vitgeft's deliberate bending of the rules paid off, when a mine floated into the stern of the majestic battleship *Hatsuse* at 10:50 a.m., the explosion flooding her engine compartment and disabling her port propellers. Moments later, a second mine blew a hole in the *Yashima*.

The crews of the damaged ships waited meekly for their colleagues to tow them out of harm's way. The *Hatsuse* had come off the worse; her stern was already underwater when she struck a second mine, which touched off her magazine and blew her apart. Another ship was able to get a line to the *Yashima*, but the attempt to tow her to safety was soon revised. She was filling up with water far too quickly to reach a safe harbour; and as time passed, it became obvious that there was not even enough time to beach her in shallow waters. As more water rushed in, she became all the harder to tow, leading her captain to sound the order to abandon ship that afternoon. The last survivors made it to the lifeboats mere moments before the *Yashima* sank beneath the waves. As if this were not bad enough, the depleted flotilla suffered another casualty on its way home, as the *Tatsuta* ran aground and damaged her hull.

'This is a most unlucky day for the Navy,' Tōgō wrote curtly in his report. He listed the catalogue of calamities in his report to the Admiralty, and added: 'I am very sorry to report this to you, but I assure you we are doing our best to ward off future disasters.'[1]

Two days later, there was another collision in the fog, costing Tōgō a support vessel. The day after that, the destroyer *Akatsuki* struck a mine close to Port Arthur and sank with the loss of twenty-three lives. It all amounted to the worst possible week.

Not all the news was relayed back home. The loss of the *Yashima* was hushed up until the end of the war. Nevertheless, the loss of eight ships in less than a week was a resounding blow to Japanese confidence at home. Letters of support and condolence poured in to the Admiralty in Tokyo, including one in the spidery handwriting of a young schoolgirl. It read simply: 'Mister Tōgō, please take great care of yourself.'[2]

For the previous month, Tōgō had been aware of the next stage in the Japanese offensive. He had been instructed to cooperate closely with the Japanese land forces, and was to make ships available to ferry them across the Yalu and to survey suitable beachheads on the Liaodong Peninsula itself. In the meantime, a feint would be made against Vladivostok by a small naval squadron, in order to make the Russians think that the Japanese intended to approach the Trans-Siberian Railway from its eastern end, not from its southern terminus at Port Arthur. In fact, the plan was now and had always been to seize the southern Manchurian railway at Port Arthur and head north. Despite Tōgō's heavy losses in mid-May, he was still successfully keeping the Russian fleet out of play while maintaining Japanese naval strength. The Japanese war machine would capitalise on that by advancing down the Liaodong Peninsula and placing Port Arthur under siege.

General Nogi, commander of the forces intended for Port Arthur, landed at Dalian on the Liaodong Peninsula on 26 May. He had been there before during the Sino-Japanese war ten years earlier, and knew what to expect. Japanese troops advanced slowly southwards, closing in on Port Arthur, but not with the speed that one might have hoped. The Russians had strung the area with a fiendish new invention – barbed wire – which hampered Japanese charges and gave the first intimation of how war would be conducted in the early 20th century. Barbed wire had been employed against cattle for several decades, but it was at Port Arthur that it was first recorded in a military application.[3] Moreover, several howitzers intended for the Japanese land attack had failed to arrive, sunk along with three transport ships in the Strait of Tsushima in June by the all-but-forgotten group of Russian ships that had been hiding in Vladivostok. This timely reminder forced Tōgō to send a few more ships to patrol the Strait, and further diminished his own naval presence.

Viceroy Alexeiev was now at Ying Kou, a coastal town at the north-east end of Liaodong. Ying Kou was much removed from the fretful conditions of Port Arthur, blessed with an easy escape route north along the railway to Mukden and Harbin, it was still connected to the Russian homeland. Some thirty miles inland along the Liao river, it had been a treaty port since 1858, when it was seized by the British, who soon tired of its unnavigable waters and moved their interests downriver to the sea port of Niuzhuang. Regardless, Ying Kou was a place for Viceroy Alexeiev to live the high life – it is perhaps no coincidence that Ying Kou was the epicentre of the Far East's brothel industry, where young Russian ladies offered paid companionship and a home away from home for lonely officers.[4]

But with news of the Japanese advancing ever closer to Port Arthur, Alexeiev graciously took a break from his champagne and caviar to send a stern message to Vitgeft. It was, he thought, time that the Russians took the fight to the Japanese. Despite such orders from the armchair admiral, Vitgeft was reaching that conclusion himself – it was only on 20 June that he received confirmation of the losses suffered by Tōgō in mid-May. On 23 June, Vitgeft left Port Arthur. His minesweepers came first, dropping buoys to mark a clear path for the full complement of the Russian fleet. Watching nearby, Rear Admiral Dewa immediately sent a wireless signal to Tōgō at 8:30 a.m., giving Tōgō sufficient time to bring up his entire fleet ready for action by 11 a.m.

It was a false alarm. It was already late in the day by the time the two fleets drew near to each other. Vitgeft was spooked by Tōgō's speedy maneouvres and realised that he was about to be surrounded by Japanese ships. As the sun began to set, Vitgeft turned and ran back towards Port Arthur. Instead of the ultimate showdown between Russia and Japan, the day turned into a scattered series of skirmishes. Tōgō's large ships held back, while torpedo boats chased the Russians back to their shelter.

At 9:30 p.m., Vitgeft reached Port Arthur to face a frantic series of twists and turns as he attempted to re-negotiate his own minefield. Tired and harassed, he gave up and decided to drop anchor outside the harbour an hour later. Japanese torpedo boats tried to take advantage of the easy targets, but were themselves thwarted by the bright moonlight. The day ended with only one casualty – the battleship *Sevastopol*, which struck a mine, quite possibly one of the Russian fleet's own. However, the damage was not fatal, and the *Sevastopol* was able to make it back.

The Japanese fleet remained watchful, fully expecting the Russians to try another breakout. On land, the army's advance put it within range of the Port Arthur fortifications, intensifying the pressure on the harbour, which was now truly under siege from both land and sea. Among the Japanese, the younger officers began competing in ways to harass the Russians, with the winning entry surely that of a Sub-Lieutenant Yokō, who requisitioned one of the torpedoes from the *Fuji* and three volunteers. The men then swam with their torpedo, unaided, for three kilometres towards Port Arthur through the summer seas, hoping to blow up a Russian patrol boat at anchor, quite literally by hand. Yokō's mission was a failure, but a great boon to Japanese morale.

So too was the arrival of the *Manshū*, a liner bearing many of the journalists (foreign and Japanese) who had been obliged to kick their heels among the Tokyo Press Corps. For many weeks, they had been frustrated in their attempts to gain hard facts about the campaign and had soon tired of attempts by the Japanese to keep them occupied – including, in one patronising task, an attempt to get them all to contribute to a book of their best war stories. Now, at last, they were shepherded in sight of the Japanese fleet, whose off-shore location had been kept a carefully guarded secret.[5]

It was only as the *Manshū* drew near the Elliott Islands off the Shandong coast that the captain informed the passengers that they were approaching Admiral Tōgō's secret redoubt.

> There was considerable excitement on board, especially among the correspondents. We were now nearing 'A Certain Place' – the mysterious naval base whence all those sharp and incisive attacks on Port Arthur by the Japanese came from. Soon, the greyness passed away, and bright patches of blue sky gradually lit up the islands; but there was no sign as yet of any naval life in these waters, not even a scouting torpedo boat … . [A] wide bay suddenly opened out, a dense cloud of smoke hanging over it, and in the centre, near a lofty grey rock, with a crown of emerald grass on its summit, the victorious fleet lay at anchor. The sun was setting behind this rock, whose shape was as sheer as that of Gibraltar, turning everything into tones of russet and molten gold; the black pall of smoke above looked like a curtain about to descend and shut out the picture.[6]

Some forty Japanese ships were clustered in the natural harbour, all ready for immediate action – their banked fires the cause of the smoke overhead. The foreign correspondents squinted eagerly at the ships' name as the *Manshū* steered between them, reading the names on the drab, slate-grey hulls of ships made famous by Tōgō's earlier actions. The Elliott Island group had been secretly converted into an impregnable fortress of the sea, 'small islands threaded together by ten miles of booms, composed of steel hawsers and lumber, to avoid a torpedo rush by the enemy. Perfectly snug and comfortable, the Tōgō fleet had been there since the first attack on Port Arthur, and the Russians had not been able to locate them or dared attempt a raid.'[7]

At last the foreign correspondents understood the nature of Tōgō's prolonged siege of Port Arthur. Each time the Russian fleet prepared for an exit, the sight of their banking fires was relayed to a wireless post outside the harbour. The message then leapt in a matter of minutes from staging post to staging post along the coast of Shandong, allowing the fleet in the Elliott Islands to immediately deploy. From the first sign of a Russian move to the arrival of the Japanese fleet to curtail it, this speedy system allowed a time frame of barely four hours. By this method, Tōgō could almost magically appear to shoo the Russians back into Port Arthur at every breakout attempt.

Ushered aboard the *Mikasa* itself, the journalists patronisingly pronounced its condition as rivalling that of a British ship, and that they had 'never seen a deck more trim'. Tōgō himself was carefully ignoring them as he watched his men go about their duties, his hands on his hips. Nearby, several of his officers imitated their commander's characteristic gesture, as if by copying his stance they might inherit his talents.[8]

The journalists had arrived from a Japan that was crazily enthusiastic for victory against Russia; and their enthusiasm was a reflection of the feverish excitement in the Japanese press and among the Japanese public. The foreign journalists were no less awestruck – delighted at last to be permitted somewhere near the action, and only mildly resentful that they had been kept away from it until, it seems, the Japanese believed that they were assured of victory. Japan's fight against Russia was the ultimate underdog story, but Tōgō in the flesh would prove to be a disappointment. If the foreign journalists were expecting a towering, flamboyant naval figure, perhaps with a piratical eyepatch or a stirring line in rhetoric, they were to be disappointed in the sight of Tōgō with his regulation haircut and his crumpled uniform.

The myth of Tōgō, British-trained, fluent in English, unsurpassed in naval skill, known to his men as 'The Devil', was arguably far stronger and more malleable when he was out of sight. The truth of Tōgō, preoccupied, tired, reticent, resolutely Japanese-speaking, must have been a disappointment. He was not, in 1904 or at any other point in his career, the kind of man who enjoyed a PR event or a press call. In particular, in June 1904, he was a man responsible for the safety of thousands of subordinates, at a secret anchorage in hostile territory, facing a powerful foe in a state of war. Tōgō had other things on his mind, and refused to trot out his English as a party-piece to entertain journalists. He was, as his teacher had noted so many years before aboard the *Worcester*, a plodder: resolute, unstinting, anonymous, but nothing like the glittering celebrity that the foreign journalists had dreamed about in their space-filling speculations from the Tokyo press club.

And so began another cycle of the Tōgō myth, as the journalists began to clutch at straws. His every move and every utterance was spun into new columns on samurai spirituality, or speculations on the oriental mind. Tōgō only had to sit in his cabin and smoke a pipe, or stare out to sea in a state of quiet contemplation, for his eager hagiographers to fill in the gaps with ruminations on his unassuming genius. As far as the press were concerned, Tōgō was already the hero of the Russo-Japanese war; and if the man had failed to live up to the growing myth, the reporters of the foreign press were already in too far over their heads to say otherwise.

The war correspondent and shipyard emissary H C Seppings Wright, who wrote an account of his time with the Japanese fleet, described the Tōgō of the summer 1904 as a gentleman in his prime:

> He is a short, well-built man with rather a slight stoop, and just on the shady side of fifty. We all turned to look at the man whose name was on the lips of everyone in the world. His is a kindly face, but it was marked with lines of care, the result of the anxious watching and thought of the last six months. Although it might be the face of an ordinary, studious man, it indubitably impresses one. The eyes are brilliant and black, like those of all Japanese, and a slight pucker at the corner suggests humour. A small drooping nose shades a pursed up mouth with the under lip slightly protruding. He has a large head, which is a good shape and shows strongly defined bumps, and the hair is thin and worn very short. A slight beard fringes the face and it is whitening on the chin, and the moustache is thin and black. Like most great men, he can keep his own counsel. It is said that he can sit for weeks by himself without any companionship except his pipe, for like Bismarck, he is an inveterate smoker.[9]

On 26 June, the army had seized the heights of Wujiazi hill close to Port Arthur. Tōgō landed a naval brigade to help the soldiers, and the men had completed a gun battery by 7 July. The first the Russians knew of it was when a shell landed in the old quarter of Port

Arthur and started a fire. A similar artillery-based conflagration broke out the following day on the slopes of White Jade mountain. On 9 July, the gunners on Wujiazi scored a powerful propaganda victory by damaging the battleships *Tsetsarevich* and *Retvisan* at anchor in Port Arthur's harbour.

The pressure was on Vitgeft, not only from the new bombardment, but from Viceroy Alexeiev, who had sent him a new, strongly-worded message that arrived on a Chinese boat from Zhifu, ordering him to proceed with all haste to Vladivostok. Vitgeft's own captains pressed him with similar urgency – it had been bad enough for them in a state of siege, but they now felt like sitting ducks and would rather take their chances on the open water. It was all or nothing – in a state of war, the Pacific Fleet would find no fuel at any nearby ports. It was Vladivostok or bust.

Vitgeft made his move on 10 August. Thirty-two warships and an equal number of torpedo boats raised steam in Port Arthur harbour, creating a massive belch of black smoke behind the mountains. The news was telegraphed immediately to Tōgō from the watching Japanese scout ships, and the Japanese swung into action.

Presumably hoping to keep observers guessing for as long as possible, Vitgeft waited until he was out at sea before hoisting his signal. Although it is a simple statement of fact, for Vitgeft it carried a note of petulance, that he was acting contrary to his wishes as the local commander. 'The Tsar,' read his flags, 'has ordered our squadron to sail to Vladivostok.'[10]

Tōgō's fleet had been out to the south-east when Vitgeft's fleet was sighted. Although Vitgeft had left one ship behind, the clues were all there that he was not planning on returning to port. Specifically, Vitgeft's fleet included a hospital ship, the Red Cross plainly visible on her side – he was taking his wounded with him. Vitgeft was forced to limp along at the speed of his slowest ships; two of his battleships lacked engine parts, and although replacements were available in the Far East, they were far to the south in Shanghai and hence of no use.

Tōgō sighted the ships several miles away at half-past noon, and did nothing. If this was to be Vitgeft's showdown, Tōgō was determined to let his adversary get far enough out to sea that there was no longer any hope of running back for Port Arthur. Tōgō ran parallel to the Russian ships, keeping them tantalisingly out of range. When Vitgeft changed course by eight degrees to avoid phantom mines, so did Tōgō. But as the fleets shadowed each other through the sea, the Russians suddenly began to gain the advantage.

It was here that Tōgō took the decision that distinguished his naval genius from that of lesser commanders. Realising that the Russians were gaining, a lesser commander might have decided to swing his fleet right through the middle of the Russian lines. Anything in the Russian rear would probably be destroyed, although the foremost ships would probably get away. But Tōgō's mission was to stop the flight to Vladivostok at any cost, not merely to reduce its numbers. Instead, he gave the surprising order to break off the pursuit, setting a new course *away* from the Russians. But Tōgō was not truly breaking off. Instead, he was bringing his fleet up to full speed and heading away from the Russians in an ellipse designed to bring him back into their sights ahead of the foremost ships. The Russians would have to continue on a straight course, east-south-east. The Japanese intended to fade from view and then swing back in front of them.

The Russians kept on course for two hours, with Tōgō and his First Division matching them in a parallel course, watching the smoke on the horizon as the ships themselves slipped from view. As the minutes ticked past, Tōgō's lead ship gradually pulled ahead of Vitgeft's *Tsetsarevich*, and Tōgō allowed his helmsman to edge his course steadily nearer to that of the Russians' presumed location, ready to cross the 'T' and bottle the Russians up in the Yellow Sea between the Shandong Peninsula and a long wall of Japanese battleships stretching back to the horizon.

The drama, the tension, the heroism was not found above decks. There, the two fleets merely powered on their courses, gunners waiting at their posts, while officers peered through binoculars at their distant enemy. An occasional gunshot functioned as a rangefinder and was found wanting – neither fleet was capable of hitting the other at that distance. Only the growing noise of the engines and the tumultuous crashing of the waters gave any clue to the unknown struggle elsewhere. Below decks, in the engine rooms, the battle raged for seventy-five gruelling minutes, as stokers on both sides frantically piled on coal to keep the ships at full speed. They toiled in unbearable heat before raging red furnaces, feeding the warships' insatiable hunger for fuel. Speed alone would determine the battle. If Vitgeft pulled ahead, his fleet would reach open sea before Tōgō could catch up. If Tōgō pulled ahead, he would block Vitgeft's path entirely.

At 5:15 p.m., Tōgō's ellipse drew near and ahead of the Russian course. The sun was dropping low in the sky, and still the long-awaited Battle of the Yellow Sea had not taken place. At 5:45 p.m., after a long day of feverish pursuit, Tōgō gave the order to swing in towards the Russians. The Japanese fleet appeared *en masse* on the horizon, dispiritingly far ahead of the Russians. Even as Vitgeft registered that he had lost his advantage, the sea around his ship began to erupt in plumes of water. The Japanese attack had begun.

Tōgō's plan, all along, had been to 'cross the T' of his enemy, and thereby allow each of his ships in turn to fire towards the advancing column of enemy ships. Even with the ability of modern turrets to swivel, a broadside from a line of ships side-on could put significantly more shells in the air than an enemy that approached the same vessels head-on.[11]

While his crossed 'T' concentrated the Japanese fire on the lead ship of the Russian squadron, it also left the *Mikasa* herself exposed. Several shells slammed into the *Mikasa*, including a 12-inch round that smashed through the mainmast. The Russians seemed to be targeting the muzzle flashes from the *Mikasa* – if they weren't, then the next shot that hit a gun crew was lucky indeed, as was the next, which killed their newly-arrived replacements.

At 5:55 p.m., one of the *Mikasa*'s aft guns was hit, wounding eighteen officers and killing a sailor. This particular hit caused greater concern among the crew than many others, because the gun was being manned by a relative of the Emperor, Prince Fushimi Hiroyasu.[12] Torn between his duties to his captain and to his Prince, Fushimi's aide-de-camp abandoned his post at one of the forward guns and dashed astern. He discovered that the Prince had been wounded, but was well enough to be shouting at his fellow officers to attend to more severely injured personnel before wasting time on him. With great relief, the aide ran up to the bridge to tell Tōgō of this, although by that time, Tōgō had more pressing matters on his mind than the fate of one of his men, however noble-born. Amid the smoke and heat, the Russian flagship appeared to have gone crazy.

At 6:00 p.m., a shell splinter had killed Vitgeft aboard the *Tsetsarevich*. Thirty-seven minutes later, a direct hit on the bridge of the *Tsetsarevich* killed the captain and most of the surviving officers and jammed the damaged ship's helm hard to port that caused it to heel over by twelve degrees. The *Tsetsarevich* whirled around dangerously close to her own ships, while Russian vessels behind her made frantic course corrections to follow what they wrongly assumed to be some new tactic of the flagship. By the time the truth became clear – that the out-of-control *Tsetsarevich* was steering herself in a pointless, uncontrolled circle, the Russian ships were scattered in hopeless chaos, pointing in all directions and now concerned largely with not crashing into each other.

Tōgō wasted no time in forming a semicircle around the confused enemy, but his vital extra hours of summer light were fading, and twilight was upon him. Consequently, Tōgō ordered the capital ships to cease fire, leaving his destroyers and torpedo boats to search in the dark for enemy stragglers. While Tōgō remained calm and collected, it would seem that some of his men were hysterical. Surviving Japanese accounts of that vital hour aboard the *Mikasa* do not largely deal with Tōgō's cold, rational exploitation of the *Tsetsarevich*'s bad luck. Instead, they focus on the panicked to-ing and fro-ing of adjutants, checking after the health of Tōgō's princely gunner, and also after Tōgō himself.

Just before the *Tsetsarevich* lost control, another Russian shell had slammed into the forebridge of the *Mikasa*, where Tōgō habitually stood. Tōgō was unharmed, but eight officers were killed and the entire compartment was filled with a deathly pink mist. Tōgō, too, was drenched with blood, although none of it appeared to be his own. He stayed on the top deck, where he had the best view of the battle. Several of his officers begged him to head up to the conning tower, where they could reasonably expect him to be in less danger from flying pieces of his own ship; but Tōgō waved them away, claiming that there was too much smoke at the level of the conning tower for him to appreciate the disposition of his own forces and those of the enemy.

Admiral Tōgō's manservant, Hiwatashi, was wounded in the leg, but kept begging able-bodied passers-by in the sick bay to check after the health of the Admiral. He was witnessed pleading tearfully to an adjutant to ensure that the Admiral did not expose himself to danger – a bizarre concern in the middle of a firefight with a fleet of Russian battleships. Eventually, the adjutant did clamber up to Tōgō and pass on the message, to which Tōgō replied with a wry smile that Hiwatashi should not worry, and that he would soon come inside, out of harm's way.

The guns fell silent, and the Japanese were able to put out the worst of their onboard fires. Smoke clouds, the best way of seeing a distant foe, were now almost impossible to discern. Instead, but for the occasional searchlight, the Yellow Sea was dark. The Japanese had suffered 216 casualties, the Russians at least 300, although their figures were never really audited. The result had been a rout for the Russians. A handful of ships made it back to Port Arthur, where they would stay until the city eventually fell to the Japanese army. Of the others, the crew of the *Tsetsarevich* somehow regained control of her steering, and steamed with three destroyers for Jiaozhou Bay on the south side of the Shandong province. Other ships ran as far as they could, to Shanghai, Saigon and Zhifu, where they were captured or interned. Two ships ran aground in the aftermath – the cruiser *Bilni* on the coast of Shandong, and the *Novik*, after a tough race against Japanese pursuers, on the coast of Sakhalin Island. Only the *Novik* came even remotely close to obeying Vitgeft's final order to head for Vladivostok. With nowhere to refuel and no friendly harbours, the Pacific Fleet was soon as dead in the water as if Tōgō had sunk every ship. Despite this brilliant victory, there were still whispers below decks from the more fanatical Japanese that Tōgō had not taken enough of a risk.

'Some of our officers, chiefly the younger ones,' wrote one, 'also think it strange that Admiral Tōgō did not turn the last battle to better account, for he might have captured some of the enemy's ships.' But clearer heads prevailed – Tōgō had not merely neutralised the Russian threat, he had also preserved the naval strength of a Japanese fleet that was entirely without reserves, ready to continue the prolonged war against expected Russian reinforcements.[13] The rout of the Russian fleet would lure the trio of Russian cruisers in Vladivostok out of their harbour in what was presumably a search for stragglers and fugitives. The three ships ran into a Japanese patrol near Ulsan in Korea: one was sunk, and the other two beat a fast retreat for Vladivostok with heavy damage.

Tōgō's mission was largely accomplished. His fleet was still obliged to watch for a breakout from Port Arthur, and his patrols still accompanied transport ships in the area, but the threat from the Pacific Fleet was now removed. On 16 August, Tōgō was the joint signatory with General Nogi of a letter in which the two commanders asked the Russians within to surrender peacefully in the hope of avoiding a 'useless sacrifice on a large scale of lives and property'.[14]

General Stoessel, commander of Port Arthur, sent a brusque refusal, causing General Nogi to begin the first of several costly assaults on the town. While the siege dragged on, Nogi sent a message to Tōgō in recognition of the fact that Tōgō's role was, for the time being, now largely cosmetic, but that it was in his interests to prepare for new eventualities:

It may appear strange for an army man to express his views on naval matters, but tell the admiral that it is Nogi's hope, if it is possible, that one or two vessels at a time will be sent home for repairs so secretly that the enemy may not suspect it and so enable our squadrons to recover their full strength before the arrival of the enemy's reinforcement squadron.[15]

Nogi was referring to the Russian Baltic Fleet, so conspicuously earmarked for action in the Pacific, but not yet under sail. True enough, the Baltic Fleet would probably not arrive until 1905, but Nogi remained unable to put a date on when Port Arthur might fall. In fact, the land-based capture of Port Arthur would wear on for another four months.

Attrition still worked against the Japanese. On 18 September, the *Pingyuan* struck a mine and sank later in the day – once the pride of the Chinese fleet, the ship had served its new Japanese masters for a decade. Nogi made the remaining Russian ships in Port Arthur his top priority. From 19 September, he rained shells upon the surviving Russian ships until the heavily damaged vessels were forced to huddle even further out of sight. In early October, Tōgō wrote to Nogi asking if the ships were fully out of commission, but ten days later Nogi was obliged to inform him that the work was still continuing.

On 6 November, Nogi's men captured Erlingshan, a hill which offered them for the first time an entirely unrestricted view of the secluded Port Arthur harbour. There was literally nowhere left for the Russian ships to hide, as Tōgō's congratulatory note acknowledged:

> For the great victory in which with unyielding spirit you have captured the important ground which commands the fate of the enemy squadron, the Combined Squadron tenders its sincerest congratulations to your army and expresses its deep sympathy with its numerous dead and wounded officers and men.[16]

In only a few days after the taking of that vital hill, Nogi's artillery sank eight Russian warships at anchor, leaving only a single gunboat, a handful of destroyers, and the battleship *Sevastopol*. This latter vessel made a futile, desperate escape attempt on 9 November. There was nowhere for the *Sevastopol* to run, and Tōgō had no desire to risk any of his principal ships in her pursuit. Instead, the *Sevastopol* was hounded to her grave in a week of night attacks by swarms of Japanese torpedo boats. On 15 November, she was waylaid by nine separate flotillas of torpedo boats, but somehow survived until the following night, when she was finally sunk. It was a messy end to the fleet that had once been the late Admiral Makarov's pride. Nor did the loss of the last Russian ship put an end to Japanese casualties – three more Japanese ships struck mines before Christmas and suffered the same fate as the unlucky *Pingyuan*.

It was after the loss of the *Takasago*, which struck a mine on 12 December, that Nogi repeated his suggestion that Tōgō head for home. This time, he did so with the bold note that Tōgō should look to his own fleet before he worried about the troubles of the Third Army. Tōgō steered the *Mikasa* close to shore, all the better to get a look at the twisted wreck of the *Sevastopol*, before going ashore to see General Nogi. The two men shook hands for the first time in the conflict. Both were exhausted by their efforts; Tōgō had hardly set foot on dry land for months, while Nogi had been left wan and thin by running a hard-fought siege that had already claimed the lives of two of his own sons.

With Admiralty approval, Tōgō left his Third Squadron in charge of the blockade at Port Arthur, and returned to Japan, to Kure, and then by train to Tokyo to report in person to the Meiji Emperor. The Emperor's concern was the same as General Nogi's, that Tōgō and his fleet be ready for the inevitable arrival of the Baltic Fleet. 'When the enemy's reinforcement squadron comes,' said Tōgō, 'I swear I will set Your Majesty at ease by destroying it.'[17]

The Emperor's reply was directed not at Tōgō but at his navy minister. It was an order that Tōgō be kept in his post. Congratulated by his monarch, Tōgō then returned to his family home, where he steadfastly refused to talk of his recent activities, but listened intently to tales from his wife and children of the home front.

On New Year's Eve 1904, Tōgō called on Nogi's wife, where he received a reminder of samurai stoicism not unlike that of his own mother:

> When I called with Kamimura at General Nogi's during his absence, his wife brought a bottle of *sake* with cups on a stand and after persuading us to drink, congratulated us on our return after the victory. I expressed my condolence on the death in battle of her two sons … but our hostess replied quietly that [neither of] her children had … brought disgrace on the true name of a soldier and this gave her sufficient consolation. I was deeply impressed by her not showing any sign of sorrow and thought her an heroic woman of rare quality.[18]

The following day, General Nogi was able to arrange some happier news. The slow, costly advance of the Japanese at Port Arthur had now found them in control of several strategic hills, and on 1 January 1905, the all-important signal station.

General Stoessel still had ample food and ammunition to last many more weeks, but had lost the will to resist. Controversially, in a decision that would later see him imprisoned by the Tsar, Stoessel did not bother to consult with his officers, but unilaterally sent word to Nogi that he was prepared to surrender. The New Year's celebrations in Japan were not yet over when the news arrived from China that Port Arthur was in Japanese hands. The Japanese were now free to press north along the South Manchurian railway, up towards Mukden, where Russian forces had been digging in all winter to await the inevitable push. That, however, would not be Admiral Tōgō's problem. The land army would deal with the conflict in China and Manchuria. Tōgō's responsibility would be the Baltic Fleet, eleven battleships, eight cruisers and nine destroyers under Admiral Zinovy Petrovich Rozhestvensky, now underway from Europe. But as to where the Baltic Fleet was, how far away, and when it might arrive in Asian waters, nobody knew, not even the Tsar.

A torpedo boat carries the wounded Russian Admiral Rozhestvensky from the sinking battleship *Borodino* during the Battle of Tsushima 27 May 1905

12

Tsushima

The Baltic Fleet, unconvincingly renamed the 'Second Pacific Squadron' as opposed to the hapless 'First' that Tōgō had neutralised, finally got underway on 16 October 1904 from its home port of Libau, in what is now Latvia. In what was to prove to be an omen of many disasters to come, the flagship ran aground while trying to leave port, one of the cruisers lost her anchor chain, and the fleet lost its first vessel when a destroyer rammed another ship and had to put back to port for repairs.

The fleet was commanded by Admiral Zinovy Petrovich Rozhestvensky (1848–1909), a hot-tempered veteran of the Turkish War with a reputation for explosive anger and little patience. Although he was the same age as Tōgō, he was a radically different personality. Where Tōgō was possessed of legendary patience and composure, Rozhestvensky was better known for tantrums and shouting, and had infamously once hurled his binoculars overboard in a fit of pique. He had, however, every reason to be nervous, as he feared insurgency within his fleet, incompetence in the ranks, and the outrageous pressure of an 18,000-mile voyage into battle against Tōgō. Nor did he have much confidence in his deputies, referring to one as an 'Empty Space', and the other as a 'Sack of Shit'.

Rozhestvensky's fleet faced monstrous logistical problems, not the least the absence of any friendly ports along the route that could legitimately offer supplies to the ships. Russia was a land empire stretching from the Baltic to the Pacific and famously spanned by the Trans-Siberian Railway. It had never previously had any need to secure bases in distant ports on the Atlantic or Indian Oceans. Under the terms of the 1902 Anglo-Japanese Alliance, Great Britain would be obliged to step into the war if any other power came to the aid of the Russians, forcing all assistance to be underhand or indirect. Consequently, Rozhestvensky's fleet was tailed whenever possible by a swarm of sixty coal transports – German merchantmen that needed to keep up a constant cycle of deliveries merely to keep the fleet underway.

Unlike Tōgō's fleet, which had been training constantly for two years, the Baltic Fleet was ice-bound every winter, severely limiting the number of days that its sailors might practise even the simplest drills. Where Tōgō's navy was staffed by fanatics, former samurai from coastal regions such as Satsuma, career sailors and Imperial loyalists, many of the 'Russian' crews were under-motivated ethnic subjects of the Tsar – Poles, natives of the Baltic coast, Jews and Finns, who were all susceptible to revolutionary agitators. By virtue of Russian geography, any 'pure' Russians aboard the fleet were likely to have been born far inland, and hence lacking any long-term experience beyond the Baltic.

Similarly, where Tōgō's officers had been honed in active service in the very region where the conflict was sure to take place, fighting a war against China in the same waters only ten years previously, the Baltic Fleet had seen little action since the Crimean War in 1856. Its crews were either trained in hopelessly outmoded equipment and tactics, or theoretically tutored in the use of new inventions that had yet to be tested. Nor was such lack of experience limited merely to the men – many of the vessels were untried designs, whose ability to perform in battle conditions was as-yet unassessed. Many had been over-laden, which caused them to sit lower in the water than planned, submerging the extra 'belt' of anti-torpedo armour along their waterlines so that any torpedo would actually strike above it. The Russians must have known their ships were sitting too low, if only because many of the ships' lower guns were actually awash and impossible to fire. Many vessels were also top-heavy or suffered critical design flaws, which would only be revealed when it was too late – the 'ideal' battleship for early

20th century conditions, arguably HMS *Dreadnought* (1906), would not be established until *after* the Russo-Japanese War provided shipwrights and designers with data on how modern technology had altered traditional tactics. Hence, for several of the battleships in Rozhestvensky's fleet, including his own flagship, the French-designed *Suvorov*, the long journey to the Far East was not merely an arduous and unexpected dash to the rescue, but also the 'shake-down cruise' in which they were expected to test, refine and master their equipment.

The Japanese battle against the Baltic Fleet began before it even left port. Tōgō's greatest ally in his war against Rozhestvensky, an unsung hero of the Russo-Japanese War, was Akashi Motojirō, a Japanese naval attaché, who was regarded by the Japanese high command as a man worth ten divisions. Formerly based in St Petersburg, Akashi had been given a one-million-yen budget and instructed to set up a European espionage organisation. His mission was to cause as much trouble as possible for the Tsar, which he had duly commenced by funding seditious presses, running guns to would-be revolutionaries, and offering support to terrorists, anarchists and secessionists. By the time the Baltic Fleet put to sea in October 1904, Akashi believed he had outstayed his welcome in St Petersburg and ran for Helsinki, where he hoped to orchestrate a Finnish revolution. In the meantime, although there is no proof of his direct involvement in the misfortunes of the Baltic Fleet, at least some of his troublemaking fund appears to have been put to work in misdirecting and confusing Rozhestvensky's mission.[1]

Quite possibly Rozhestvensky was the architect of his own demise, running up a signal to repel torpedo boats as a drill, and not realising that some of his simpler crewmen might take it for an actual sighting of Japanese attackers. But Akashi's intrigues are a more likely explanation for a palpable fear among the crews of the Baltic Fleet that the Japanese might jump out at them at any time. In particular, we might point the finger of suspicion at certain crewmen aboard the auxiliary *Kamchatka*, a repair ship whose misleadingly 'mistaken' signals periodically brought the Baltic Fleet to the brink of disaster.

Even though Tōgō was half a world away, the Russians remained constantly watchful after rumours had spread among the fleet of the presence of 'Japanese torpedo boats' off the shore of Denmark. The source for this information, ironically, was Russian military intelligence, whose agent in Copenhagen had swallowed an entirely fictional account of Japanese saboteurs, and who had not realised that the sole aim of these 'saboteurs' was to feed Russian paranoia with such fictions. Entirely without evidence, talk arose among the crews of Japanese mines in the North Sea and threats of Japanese stealth attacks, so that Rozhestvensky himself ordered that no unidentified ships were to approach the fleet.[2] So, when a boat arrived bearing the news that Rozhestvensky had been promoted to Vice Admiral, his own sailors fired on it. Luckily for the crew of the target, if not for everyone's prospects against Tōgō, none of the Russians scored a hit. The Russians were similarly spooked by the sight of two balloons in the distance, whose origin and destination was never established, but whose aims were assumed to be those of Japanese spies. The *Kamchatka*, in the first of her many attempts to stir up trouble, then signalled that she was under attack by 'about eight' torpedo boats.

On 21 October in the North Sea, the Russians believed they had spotted a flotilla of Japanese torpedo boats. The fleet opened fire on the distant ships, with several panicked signals reaching Rozhestvensky that ships had been hit by 'Japanese' torpedoes. On one Russian ship, sword-wielding officers ran on deck to repel non-existent Japanese borders. It was an entirely false alarm; and the Baltic Fleet was found to have unleashed thousands of rounds against a surprised group of British trawlers, which had been innocently spreading their nets in the well-known fishing grounds of the Dogger Bank. In the fog, the Russians had sunk one fishing boat and damaged several others, killing three Britons. To Rozhestvensky's great rage and embarrassment, the Russians had also somehow managed to inflict damage on themselves, directing the bulk of their fire against two of their own ships.

The Dogger Bank Incident was a national outrage in Britain, regarded by many as an awful accident, but by the harder-line press and politicians as an act of war. While diplomats scurried to smoothe things over, Rozhestvensky discovered that he had gained a new escort, with battleships of the Royal Navy ominously shadowing him through the English Channel and across the Bay of Biscay. At Vigo on the north-west coast of Spain, Rozhestvensky dumped the officers responsible for the Dogger Bank Incident, although it is unclear whether he was ridding his fleet of the worst incompetents or the best Japanese agents.

The *Kamchatka* disappeared for several days in the Atlantic, where she diligently fired upon French, German and Swedish ships, claiming that each in turn was a Japanese attacker. Off the shores of Angola, she caused another scare, 'accidentally' mixing up the signals for 'All well' with 'Do you see torpedo boats?'. The Baltic Fleet steamed carefully down the African coast, the decks overladen with piles of coal from the latest delivery by the collier fleet. Coal dust created an unbearable fog of choking particles in the hot equatorial climate, while the fleet was tailed by a growing school of sharks, lunching on the offal and rotting meat dumped overboard from the malfunctioning refrigeration ship.

Eventually, Rozhestvensky rounded The Cape of Good Hope and put ashore at Madagascar on 9 January 1905, where he lingered for several weeks with a tropical sickness. His sailors busied themselves with their exotic acquisitions from the shore, which included the unwise purchase of a 'ship's crocodile', a giant poisonous snake that refused to unwrap itself from a warm gun, and a crate of 2,000 unexpectedly exotic cigarettes laced with opium. A resupply ship caught up with them in the heat of the Madagascan spring and proudly delivered a cargo of enough fur coats and winter boats to supply 12,000 men. It was, however, lacking the vital ammunition for which Rozhestvensky had been waiting. Eventually, after several stragglers had caught up with the main fleet, including some shallow-draft ships that had come through the Suez Canal, Rozhestvensky set out into the Indian Ocean with his fleet now numbering an impressive forty-five ships. And then, with nobody to observe his heading, he effectively disappeared.

With Rozhestvensky nothing more than a ghost somewhere between Madagascar and Malacca, Tōgō made preparations for the next phase of the war. His ships had been repaired to the best of their crews' abilities, and their location was now a closely-guarded secret. He sent Admiral Kamimura to lay mines outside the entrance to Vladivostok, all the better to keep the surviving two warships contained for the time being. He also briefed his commanders on his tactics for dealing with the Russian fleet when it eventually arrived. Among his admonitions to his commanders, he pressed upon them the need to imitate his cautious nature. Naval losses so far in the Russo-Japanese war had largely been caused not by Russian action, but by Japanese mistakes. Tōgō was only too aware that the numbers of the Japanese fleet were still at fighting strength solely because of the care he had taken to avoid risks – the surprise attack on Port Arthur, the blockade, and the refusal to commit his capital ships when the enemy might reasonably have a chance to sink them.

> In a battle, the most important thing is caution. We must not fear a great enemy nor make light of a small one. We must not be desiring that the enemy will not come; if there is anything we have long been waiting for, we must on no account be taken by surprise. It has often happened in the past that there have been matters for regret after a battle; that is due to our having a weak point which has been taken advantage of by the enemy. Lack of cautiousness is a great danger; and we must not even for a moment be off our guard in the slightest matters.[3]

Rozhestvensky's fleet remained invisible for several weeks, its location unknown and unreported. There was a sudden glimpse of the Baltic Fleet near Singapore on 8 April, news of which reached Tōgō by the following day. But after that, the forty-five ships vanished once again.

Meanwhile, the Russians made a half-hearted effort to match Japanese espionage. It was made widely known that the Russian ships interned in Shanghai after the Battle of the Yellow Sea were planning a breakout. This information seems to have been intended to lure Japanese ships down south, but Tōgō resolutely clung to his plans to meet the Russians closer to Japanese waters. As the days passed, there was no sign of the Baltic Fleet in Chinese waters, where the Japanese were sure to have plenty of agents to observe them. In fact, it was not merely the Japanese who were curious about the whereabouts of the Baltic Fleet. The world's press, too, was full of speculation as to where the great battle would take place.

The London *Daily Telegraph*, sensing a story in the offing, sent a telegram to its newly appointed Hong Kong correspondent, William Donald: 'RUSSIAN FLEET REPORTED LOST SINCE LEAVING RED SEA STOP MAY BE SOMEWHERE YOUR AREA STOP GO FIND IT.'[4] Donald booked passage in a steamer for Saigon, perhaps hoping to meet the fleet somewhere along the way. It certainly made sense to expect to see it somewhere in South East Asia, but Rozhestvensky's ships were a ghost fleet, invisible to the international community.

Donald got what he was looking for as his steamer passed the massive deepwater bay at Cam Ranh in Indochina. Donald plainly saw a forest of smoke-columns, belching coal fumes into the sky and creating a mist on the horizon. He asked the captain of his ship what the smoke was, and received the unlikely reply that it was 'from big industries'. From Saigon, Donald headed back north towards the suspicious 'industrial' phenomenon poking out of the jungle. He bribed the captain of another steamer to take him north to Nha Trang, only a few miles from the bay, discovering in the process that the mystery ships had been in Cam Ranh Bay since 14 April. Realising that if this was true, he had not only a scoop, but also an exposé, Donald knew that he needed to confirm the story with his own eyes. He emerged, sweating and dog-tired, from the jungle on 1 May, and found himself staring at the terrifying bulk of Rozhestvensky's flagship, the *Suvorov*, close to the shore. The rest of the Baltic Fleet stretched out in the bay behind them: everything from a hospital ship to coal transports, cruisers and torpedo boats. Far out to sea was the crucial element that turned Donald's story into journalistic gold – the French cruiser *Descartes* guarding the ocean approach.

Donald's story was cabled back to the *Telegraph*, where his editor saw its explosive potential. The Russian fleet was not permitted to stay in a 'neutral' port for longer than twenty-four hours. By looking the other way, the authorities in French Indochina were extending illegal assistance to the Russians; precisely the sort of assistance that was liable under the Anglo-Japanese Alliance to drag the British into the war. Amid strong protestations from the UK, the French went through the motions of shooing the Russians out of Cam Ranh Bay. At first, it was a daft charade, in which Rozhestvensky was asked to leave and then permitted to immediately return. Donald stirred up a second story, but found his access to telegraph transmission blocked by the locals, and only managed to smuggle his story out to the *Telegraph* and the *China Mail* with the collusion of the British consulate.

The Baltic Fleet was forced to get underway once more. To a certain extent, Rozhestvensky had got what he wanted, as he had been waiting for a 'Third' fleet to catch up with him. The extra ships, largely comprising antiquated vessels sent as an afterthought, arrived on 14 May, strengthening the Baltic Fleet for its forthcoming encounter with the famous Admiral Tōgō. Watching the fleet leave for the open sea, William Donald wrote a prescient assessment of the Russians' chances: 'These ships will be disgraced in their first engagement.'[5]

The amount of coal available to Rozhestvensky was not ideal. He resupplied near the Philippines and continued on his northward journey. Had he had better supplies, he might have been able to head around the east of Japan and take a safer route to Vladivostok. Instead, he decided to take the option that conserved more fuel but pointed him straight at Japan's main supply route to Korea. Rozhestvensky decided to risk running through the Korea Strait, past the island of Tsushima.

Rozhestvensky warned his men of the opponent they were sure to be facing, smartly noting that the Russians were facing an enemy with more experience, better drills and better equipment. So as not to present an entirely negative view, he urged his men to conserve ammunition by observing the effects of previous shots before firing off a new one, and also noted that while the Japanese had the Emperor, the Russians still had the Tsar:

> The loyalty of the Japanese to Throne and country is unbounded. They do not suffer dishonour and they die like heroes. But we have sworn before the Most High Throne. God has inspired us with courage. He has assisted us to overcome the unprecedented trials

of our voyage. He will bestow upon us His blessing so that we may carry out the will of our Sovereign and wash away with our blood the bitter shame brought upon our country.[6]

William Donald's scoop in Indochina was public knowledge by the following day – Tōgō now knew that Rozhestvensky was leaving Cam Ranh Bay. Unaware of Rozhestvensky's plans or coaling issues, the question remained for Tōgō whether the Baltic Fleet would come up through the Yellow Sea past Tsushima or seek to reach Vladivostok by sailing out behind Japan to the east. On 26 May, Tōgō heard that seven Russian auxiliary vessels had put into a harbour near Shanghai. It was all the confirmation that he needed – the Russians were coming through the Korean Strait.

Tōgō's plan for the Russians capitalised on Japanese access to safe harbours on both sides of the Korea Strait. While the Baltic Fleet would have no choice but to run the gauntlet, the Japanese could lie in wait, work in shifts, and return to friendly ports for recuperation and repair. Tōgō had plotted a four-day plan, in the course of which a Japanese squadron on patrol would spot the fleet as it approached the Strait and begin firing. The Russians would then have to contend with six further attacks as they worked their way past Tsushima and up the west coast of Japan towards Vladivostok. On each day, they would be attacked by squadrons of warships and cruisers. At night, while the big guns retired to safety, the Russians would be harried by constant probes from destroyers and torpedo boats. Moreover, the greater part of Tōgō's fleet, including the *Mikasa* herself, was stashed on the 'wrong' side of the Strait, in a large bay in south-west Korea. When the time came for Tōgō to deploy, his line of ships would wall off the Korean side of the Strait, presenting the Russians with a single exit route that took them *closer* to Japan and within range of squadrons of smaller ships based in Japanese ports.

Tōgō's plan was meticulous, brilliant, and seemed calculated to place the Russians in the maximum amount of danger, with the Japanese backed up at all times by overlapping spheres of interest or fields of fire. Luckily for Tōgō, the plan was also flexible – the Russians did not quite arrive in the way that he had expected, and the full-scale plan of attack was never implemented exactly as Tōgō had intended.

The alert was sounded at 4:45 a.m. on 27 May 1905. One of Tōgō's many patrol ships caught sight of unidentified vessels near the Gotō islands, at the north-western tip of Kyūshū. On Tōgō's map, the simple designation 'Square 203' told him precisely where the Russians had been sighted, but offered eavesdroppers no clue as to what the Japanese thought they knew. The news, conveyed by wireless, reached Tōgō ten minutes later. For once, noted other officers, even the quiet Admiral Tōgō seemed excited. The *Mikasa* was underway by 6:05 a.m., as was every other Japanese ship in the first interception area, steaming out of their Korean base and into the Sea of Japan.

Tōgō calculated that the Russians were on the Japanese side of Tsushima, heading straight down the Strait at full speed (for them, a rather slow nine knots, barely half the capabilities of the newer Japanese ships), and that consequently, the *Mikasa* would be in range of them somewhere near the island of Okinoshima at around 2:00 p.m. It was a decidedly *modern* calculation – thanks to the wireless telegraph transmissions from his scouts, Tōgō was able to steer a course for the middle of nowhere, sure that by the time he arrived at the appointed patch of sea, his guns would be facing the Russian fleet. This was particularly important in the light of the day's weather, as the dawn mist failed to dissipate as the sun rose. Visibility on the Strait was restricted to only five miles, allowing Tōgō to remain invisible to the Russians as late as 1:39 p.m., with the double column of the Russians chugging resolutely through the sea passage, a tantalising seven miles from Tōgō's waiting armada.

At 1:55 p.m., within five minutes of his calculated time of engagement, Tōgō raised a signal aboard the *Mikasa* that, as was his habit, he deliberately intended to recall the words of Nelson before Trafalgar: 'The rise or fall of the Empire depends on this battle. Let each man do his utmost.'

An officer suggested that Tōgō should get into the conning tower, which was considered less dangerous than the forward bridge. 'I am getting on for sixty,' answered the Admiral, 'and this old body of mine is not worth caring for; but you young men who still have a long future before you should take care of yourselves, for you must do your utmost for your country.'[7]

There is an element of knowing, almost wilful samurai fatalism in Tōgō's comment, as if he was almost hoping to be struck down in his hour of triumph. He ordered the course to be changed to south-southwest, so that, pending any other corrections, the two fleets were fated to pass each other in parallel lines, heading in opposite directions.

Tōgō remained on the port side of the *Mikasa*'s bridge, staring out to sea with his oversized marine binoculars. His left hand rested on the hilt of the sword at his side. His cheeks were puffed out – a sign that the Admiral was pondering a momentous decision.[8] Suddenly, Tōgō blew the air from his cheeks. He ordered the *Mikasa* to swing around to north-northeast, now heading in the same direction as the Russians, drifting inexorably closer. The Russians opened fire at 2:08 p.m., targeting the *Mikasa* and the *Shikishima* at the head of the Japanese line. The *Mikasa* suffered her first casualties, but Tōgō waited another three minutes before giving the order to return fire.

With Tōgō's flag prominent on her mast, the *Mikasa* attracted much of the Russian fire. The gunners who had proved so hapless in the North Sea had had many weeks to train and many of them were now far better shots. The *Mikasa*'s deck was so torn up as to be practically impassable, and her starboard side in particular suffered 40 direct hits. At 2:20 p.m., a 12-inch shell smashed into the starboard latrine, creating a deadly cloud of splinters that wounded fifteen men on the fore-bridge and four men on the conning tower, where Tōgō had recently refused to go. Tōgō himself was leaning over the ship's compass on another of the bridges, staring impassively at the dial, which had been transfixed by a huge splinter that had missed killing him by mere inches. It was just one of many hits on that long day – the *Mikasa* was by far the most heavily damaged ship on the Japanese side, and would eventually log 113 casualties, almost a quarter of the losses for the entire Japanese fleet.[9]

The Russians began a course correction to evade the oncoming Japanese attack, heading further to the east, but the bombardment was already on. The *Oslyabya* was pelted with shells and obscured by a cloud of smoke, already foundering in the water. Rozhestvensky in the *Suvorov* was forced to duck out of the line after a shell smashed the ship's steering gear. Much of the *Mikasa*'s task was accomplished in the first thirty minutes, as it was she who put the *Suvorov* out of action and threw the Russians into confusion. Dazed by a blow on the head, and bleeding from additional wounds on his heel and shoulder, Rozhestvensky was forced to hand command over to one of his subordinates as he was evacuated from the burning *Suvorov*. Rozhestvensky refused to admit that the *Suvorov* was done for and ordered that her flag should not be lowered. It was left to one of his officers to explain that the *Suvorov* was so badly damaged that there was nowhere left to hang the flag from. 'Hang it over the helm!' blurted Rozhestvensky, but his men wisely carried him off to a nearby destroyer.[10]

The *Suvorov* drifted as a floating wreck, her remaining crew members at the stern dutifully firing her single remaining gun into a new attacking wave of Japanese torpedo boats. Eventually, further damage caused her to capsize and sink, a mere thirteen miles from Okinoshima. After all the manoeuvres of the afternoon, she had drifted back practically to where she had started and she sank almost within sight of the island of Tsushima.

Realising that they would be unable to smash through the Japanese line without taking even heavier damage, the captain of the *Borodino* decided to head north around the Japanese. Tōgō, however, saw the Russians' change of course, and ordered an immediate course correction from his own ships. Admiral Kamimura, in charge of Tōgō's Second Division, kept to his original course, deliberately hoping to catch the Russians between the two Japanese lines. All the Russians could do was to turn back the way they had come, but with three autonomous flotillas of Japanese ships manoeuvring about them, it was easier said than done. After turning in a futile circle, the Russians were suddenly able to head south, disappearing back into the mists. There were enough Japanese ships on the water that this only gained them thirty minutes' respite. At 5:05 p.m., several of Tōgō's ships ran into part of the main squadron, successfully putting the *Borodino* out of action by incapacitating all her officers and causing critical damage to the *Orel*.

The Japanese fleet, both ahead and astern of the Russians, was able to put its superior speed and manouverability to good use. With each Japanese squadron functioning independently, the Russian fleet was forced to watch all sides and to answer repeated corrections in course, returns to previous courses, and new tacks. In some cases, particularly the lumbering support ships, the crews simply could not keep up with the darting Japanese. One by one, the Russian ships fell out of formation, strayed dangerously far from their protectors, or simply got lost.

Not every casualty was Russian. The flagship of Admiral Dewa's Third Division, the *Kasagi*, took a hit dangerously close to the waterline and was forced to disengage. Guarded closely by two ships he had ordered out of the line to watch his flank, Dewa steered his rapidly-sinking vessel in towards shore, and then transferred to the *Chitose* in order to re-enter the battle.

As the sun began to set, the remnants of the Russian fleet were heading to the north. The Japanese ships received a simple command from Tōgō that they were to reassemble at dawn near the Korean island of Ullong-do. The cruisers and battleships turned and disappeared back into the mist, leaving the Russian fleet to the very different night tactics of the torpedo boats. At dusk, the Baltic Fleet was already in tatters. Rozhestvensky's fleet had included five newly-built *Borodino*-class battleships, including the *Borodino* herself and his own flagship the *Suvorov*. Four of them had sunk, and the sole survivor was heavily damaged. Rozhestvensky had also lost a cruiser and an auxiliary ship, and both his hospital ships had been captured.

As Tōgō sat exhausted in his quarters, an aide brought him the text of the wireless transmission that was intended for the Admiralty. It bragged that 'at least' four Russian vessels had been sunk. Tōgō quietly ordered for the 'at least' to be deleted. The day had gone well enough without any attempts at spin. The Russians were, to be sure, equally exhausted, but had no chance of rest. Some forty-four Japanese torpedo boats and destroyers were now on the prowl, searchlights reaching into the gloom, gunners ready to unleash new attacks. While Tōgō rested his eyes, men implementing his careful plans sank one Russian ship, and damaged a battleship and two cruisers so severely that they were no longer able to steer.

The following morning, Tōgō was ready at dawn, as soon as he heard the first report of a sighting of enemy ships. The Russians had made it a little way further down the Strait and were now in the Sea of Japan itself – Japanese accounts often refer to the Battle of Tsushima as the Battle of the Sea of Japan, in acknowledgement of this later phase. The group comprised five Russian ships led by Rozhestvensky's second-in-command. At 10:34 a.m., the Japanese vessels opened fire. The Russians held their course for another ten minutes, before suddenly hoisting signal flags that announced their surrender.

Tōgō waited for several minutes before ordering a ceasefire – he wanted to be sure that the Russians really had stopped shooting back. By 1:37 p.m., a launch from the *Mikasa* had picked up the Russian Rear-Admiral Nikolai Nebogatoff and conveyed him to Tōgō's cabin, where the Admiral received his surrender. After agreeing standard terms, the handing over of the ships to the Japanese, and the prisoner-of-war status of the crews, the officers present drank a toast to the end of hostilities. Tōgō later revealed that this, too, had been a test. He had been watching the faces of the Russians to see how they took to this gentlemanly resolution, and saw only relief that their ordeal was over. It left him confident that the Russians would honour the terms of their own surrender, and that crews from Japanese vessels need not worry about sabotage or resistance as they took command of the captured Russian vessels.

Nebogatoff was even moved to discuss Tōgō's winning tactics with him, asking him how he had been so sure that the Baltic Fleet would come through the Korea Strait, instead of taking the safer route behind Japan and past Hokkaido or Sakhalin. Nebogatoff was curious: how could Tōgō have been so sure? 'I guessed,' lied Tōgō, before changing the subject.[11]

Elsewhere in the Sea of Japan, Tōgō's other squadrons were enjoying similar successes against surviving pockets of the shattered Baltic Fleet. Admiral Dewa sank a destroyer at dawn. Admiral Uryū ran into a cruiser and a destroyer 50 miles south of the dawn rendezvous, sinking the former and forcing the latter aground. The Fifth Destroyer Flotilla fought a long battle with the destroyer *Gromki* just off the coast of Korea, capturing her in such a state that she sank in the early afternoon. The Russian coastal defence vessel *Ushakov*, which certainly should never have been 18,000 miles from home in the first place, was spotted in the early afternoon, but refused to acknowledge signals telling her that the remnants of the fleet had surrendered. Her pursuers opened fire and pulled her crew from the water as she sank at sunset.

The battle was over in two days. By the evening of 28 May, some nineteen vessels of the Baltic Fleet had been sunk, and, including the two hospital ships, seven had been captured intact. Several others ran aground or sank on the run, still more fled for neutral ports and were interned, and only three made it to the intended destination of Vladivostok. Against Japanese casualties of 700 and the loss of three torpedo boats, the Russians lost more than 4,000 dead. The Japanese navy was left to process around 6,000 Russian prisoners of war, including wounded Admiral Rozhestvensky himself, who had been found aboard a destroyer captured in Korean waters late in the afternoon of 28 May.

On 3 June, Tōgō came ashore at Sasebo, and paid a visit to the bedside of Admiral Rozhestvensky. The Russian Admiral struggled to sit up in bed to shake Tōgō's hand, while Tōgō offered his thoughts through an interpreter:

Defeat is a common fate of a soldier and there is nothing to be ashamed of in it. The great point is whether we have performed our duty. I cannot but express admiration for the brave manner in which the officers and men of your vessels fought in the late battle for two days continuously. For you, especially, who fearlessly performed your great task until you were seriously wounded, I beg to express my sincerest respect and also my deepest regrets. I hope you will take care of yourself and recover as soon as possible.[12]

Japanese accounts of the aftermath emphasise gentlemanly deportment and courtesy, although Tōgō's visit to his fallen enemy seems to have been managed as much for his peace of mind as theirs. Once Tōgō, his fellow high-ranking Japanese officers and the foreign press had got their photo-call and their heart-warming anecdote, the Russians were left in the charge of junior Japanese officers who were not so welcoming. Rozhestvensky himself, scandalised at his poor food and dirty utensils, lodged a complaint with his captors, and 'told them quite plainly, that in Russia pigs were better treated than we had been in Japan'.[13]

Despite such rancour behind the scenes, Tōgō's victory was winning him plaudits far and wide. The ex-patriate British community in Yokohama wasted no time in publishing a commemorative commendation, comparing Tōgō to a famous English Admiral and concluding: 'Nelson, 1805. Tōgō, 1905.' As if that were not clear enough, the parchment included pictures of the two admirals side-by-side.

The crushing defeat of Russia secured many diplomatic victories for Japan. The British soon extended the terms of the Anglo-Japanese Alliance and recognised Japan's interest in Korea. In a secret communiqué of July 1905, so did the Americans. The Taft-Katsura memorandum outlined American interests in the Philippines, but also tentatively acknowledged the likelihood of Korea becoming a Japanese protectorate or even colony, as it would indeed become by 1910.

The American President Theodore Roosevelt stepped in to prevent any further fighting. The Russians might have lost their fleet, but the remnants of the land army were still in place north of Mukden; and fighting in Manchuria might be expected to stretch on for many more months. In fact, both Russia and Japan were at the limit of their powers. Already, back along the Trans-Siberian Railway, there were whispers of revolution against the Tsar. The Japanese, meanwhile, were already on the brink of bankruptcy after the expense of the two-year conflict.

Roosevelt helped both sides save face by inviting them to come to the negotiating table. Representatives of the countries met throughout August at Portsmouth, New Hampshire and eventually concluded the Treaty of Portsmouth, for which Roosevelt would win the Nobel Peace Prize in 1906. In it, the Russians agreed to pull out of Manchuria, leaving much of the southern Manchurian railway in Japanese hands, along with certain strategic points, including Port Arthur itself. Korea was essentially handed over to the Japanese. Russia also relinquished the lower half of Sakhalin Island, extending Japanese territory to the north by several hundred miles.

Neither the Russians nor the Japanese were pleased with the results. The Tsar suffered further damage to his standing with his people for giving up Russian territory and not keeping his original promise to continue the war on land. Among the Russians, there were further cavils over the wording in the document. Rozhestvensky, in particular, was astonished to discover that part of the settlement included the cost of accommodating many of the prisoners of war, which, by his estimate, overcharged the Russians by a factor of twenty, amounting to an extortionate indemnity charge, smuggled onto the books under a humanitarian cloak.[14]

If anything, Japanese public reaction was even more negative, with two days of rioting in Tokyo, Kobe and Yokohama, in which seventeen people died. The Japanese, it seemed, had expected *all* of Sakhalin, *all* of the Liaodong Peninsula (and not merely the railway), as well as a satisfactory indemnity from the Russians. Instead, at the end of the war, Japanese forces had been obliged to hand several captured places back to Russia, as if Japan were the defeated power, and not the unquestionable victor. In all these matters, there was little discussion of the feelings of the locals in Korea and Manchuria, who were citizens of neither Russia nor Japan, but in whose territory the war had been fought, and on whose heads the consequences would fall.[15]

Such arguments would cause many Japanese to harbour sour feelings towards many of their leaders, particularly the politicians who had carried them into the war with such hopeful promises. However, such a backlash did not extend to Admiral Tōgō, who remained the unimpeachable hero of the hour. When the dust of the Russo-Japanese war had settled, it was Tōgō's achievement at Tsushima that would be remembered as the purest, most uncorrupted, most resounding victory. It made him a national hero, and kept him in that role for the rest of his life.

Admiral Tōgō on a triumphant tour of the United States of America in 1911

13

Tōgō on Tour

Until 1905, discussion of Tōgō concentrated on his quiet demeanour, his unflappable expression and his incisive concentration. Tōgō was the man who slept in his uniform while on duty during the Taiwan campaign, who never once lost his temper over the reversals of Port Arthur, and who was nicknamed *Oni*, 'The Devil', by his officers.

While elements of those character traits remained in later life, accounts of Tōgō after the Russo-Japanese war took on a new tone. He was still portrayed as pathologically quiet, soft-spoken and dutiful, but also as a man somewhat out of sorts, awed by his own celebrity and much preferring a quiet retirement. The Tōgō of the 1910s and 1920s sometimes came across as an eccentric sea-dog, clinging keenly to his well-earned retirement, and lachrymose in his remembrances of war stories. Tōgō was getting old.

Tragedy marred Tōgō's triumphal return. Back in Sasebo, he received an Imperial Order to bring his ships north for a more photogenic 'homecoming' closer to the capital. In order to file a report swiftly, Tōgō left the *Mikasa* at Sasebo and headed north by train – a journey that may have saved his life. On the night of 11/12 September, an ammunition explosion ripped through the *Mikasa*, sinking her in six fathoms of water with the loss of 590 men. The ship had survived the entire Russo-Japanese war, only to sink at the dockside with a loss of life exceeding that of the actual Battle of Tsushima. Even the Russians thought it was a cruel twist of fate – from captivity, Rozhestvensky sent Tōgō a telegram of condolence.[1]

Consequently, it was the *Shikishima* that played the role of Tōgō's flagship at the celebrations. Tōgō's homeward journey largely proceeded by land, as he was called upon to give thanks at the Ise Shrine and then to ride by train from Yokohama to Tokyo. Flag-waving crowds flanked the streets as Tōgō rode silently in a richly garlanded carriage pulled by two white horses. All were familiar with the official portrait of the famous Admiral, and jockeyed for position to see him. When Tōgō climbed down from his carriage and took off his hat, a gasp rippled through the crowd. The Russo-Japanese war had turned his hair white. For Tōgō, who wore his hair cropped close to his skull and whose jet-black beard had been starkly apparent in his much-duplicated official portrait, the transformation appeared all the more sudden. In fact, as Seppings Wright had observed, the Admiral's hair was already streaked with flecks of grey in 1904, but the Japanese public had memorised his image from an old picture, and soon parleyed his rapid ageing into another folktale about his great loyalty to the Emperor.

Tōgō was mobbed as a conquering hero, much to his embarrassment – his sole expense amid the celebrations was a small outlay for the photographic negative of a picture of himself, taken by the court photographer. Even this was not vanity, but a concerted effort to stop the unscrupulous cameraman selling commemorative portraits. The British residents in Kobe were keen to claim him as one of their own, and entertained him at a banquet where he was honoured as an old cadet of the *Worcester* training college.[2]

Tōgō, however, remained quiet until the ceremony for the dead at Aoyama Cemetery, where he read an uncharacteristically lengthy speech. True to form, he saved his great moment and finest words for the heroic dead, whom he addressed directly:

> The war clouds have vanished from land and sea and the whole city now lives in peace. Such was the condition on the day when the officers and men who risked their lives together with you returned in triumph to the Imperial Headquarters. When, regardless of both heat and cold, you gallantly fought with the enemy, we were not yet in a position to know how the war would end; and whenever any of you passed away, we envied you the honour you won by your loyal

death and we fully expected to follow your example in showing our devotion to our country. But your hard and brave fighting had always been of such great effect that every battle of the Imperial forces ended in victory. The successive attacks on Port Arthur settled the trend of the war, and the Battle of the Japan Sea [i.e. Tsushima] decided by one engagement its issue, and thereafter not a single enemy vessel was to be seen at sea. This result, though it arose from the fathomless Imperial virtue, must also be attributed to the service you rendered regardless of your own lives. Now, when, the war having come to an end, we officers and men who have returned in triumph, behold scenes of jubilation on all sides, we are opposed by an unspeakable feeling resulting from joy being dashed with sorrow by the thought that you are unable to join with us in these rejoicings. But the way you died loyally and gallantly will long be the spirit of our Navy and will guard our Empire forever. With this commemorative service we hold a mass for your spirits and express our feelings towards you. We beseech you to gather on this place and hear us.[3]

Tōgō delivered the last line with a mighty bellow, silencing the birdsong of Aoyama. In the quiet that followed, a breeze blew up through the autumn leaves, whirling them in a magical confetti about the mourners. It was, assuredly, just the wind. But it was 'just the wind' that had defeated the medieval Mongol invasion and helped to fight off the British at Kagoshima. To the Japanese, whose native religion sees spirits in everything and divinity in the most mundane of objects, it was as if Tōgō's departed sailors had returned for one last roll-call. 'Those present at the ceremony,' noted one writer, 'say that it was the most dramatic moment in the history of the war.'[4]

The silence reigned for several minutes, as Tōgō was too overcome to speak and the audience too respectful to make a move. But soon, Tōgō beckoned the families of the dead to him and gave to each mourner a sacred Eurya branch as an offering. As the ceremony wound down, his fellow admirals waited by the gates to take their carriages back to headquarters, but Tōgō lingered among the crowds, helping widows and children into their waiting rickshaws.

The Combined Squadron was officially disbanded after a huge naval review off Yokohama, attended by the Emperor himself. With the *Mikasa* out of action, it was the *Shikishima* that flew Tōgō's farewell signal, an old samurai proverb that cautioned against complacency: 'At the moment of victory, tighten the strings of your helmet.'

Tōgō elaborated on this comment in a private address to his surviving men, in which he urged them to cultivate their spirit. Nor was this an idle gesture of numinous influence – Tōgō pressed home the belief that he had maintained throughout the months before the Russo-Japanese war: that preparation and training in peacetime was the only way to ensure victory when it counted. True to his training, Tōgō could not help but bring up the history of British sea power:

> [T]he English navy which had won the Battles of the Nile and Trafalgar at the beginning of the nineteenth century, not only put the country in perfect security, but fully maintained its military power even for later generations and, by keeping pace with the progress of the world, has been able to this day to protect its national interests and extend its national influence.[5]

Tōgō's days at sea were over, at least as a commander. He would be a passenger for the rest of his life, promoted to the level where he was largely kept on land. In December 1905, he was appointed as the new Chief of Staff for the Navy, succeeding his old commanding officer Itō Sukeyuki, who had been promoted to Fleet Admiral. One of his first duties was to attend the launch of the *Tsukuba*, a large armoured cruiser that was due to take to sea on Boxing Day 1905. Tōgō travelled down to the docks on the Imperial train, in the company of Yoshihito, the Japanese Crown Prince and future Taishō Emperor.

The Crown Prince had a reputation in court circles for strange behaviour, and this trip was no exception. As Tōgō passed down the train, the Crown Prince began tapping the shoulder of Tōgō's subordinate Ogasawara Naganari in a most unregal fashion. He urged Ogasawara to run ahead and check that Tōgō was all right, as the couplings between the carriages were hazardous. Ogasawara froze, paralysed by the etiquette that forbade him from pushing past a member of the Imperial family. Impatient, the Crown Prince practically pushed Ogasawara ahead of him, much to the latter's embarrassment. When Ogasawara reported this incident to Tōgō, the Admiral hung his head and wept 'with the tears rolling down his cheeks'. The Crown Prince of Japan himself, it seemed, rated Tōgō as a national treasure, but Tōgō's concern was less likely to be about himself than his Imperial fan – the Crown Prince's behaviour was becoming steadily more erratic, and it did not bode well for the Japanese monarchy.[6]

But it was Tōgō who captured the public imagination. Despite his efforts to suppress a personality cult in his name, his picture continued to adorn posters, biscuit tins and flags all over Japan. The Japanese public continued to endow him with divine status, and Tōgō continued to find it deeply embarrassing. He attempted to play the great statesman and began to compose obtuse, rather dull poems as befitted a great potentate, but the tales that linger of the elder Tōgō continue to emphasise his quiet, shy nature.[7]

Others were not above taking advantage of his fame. The signpost to the Tōgō household was forever being stolen by souvenir-hunters, not merely because of its subject, but because the simple wooden board was known to be an example of the great Admiral's calligraphy. As he grew older, Tōgō became increasingly less willing to dash off poems and autographs, which ironically only increased the incidences of people trying to cash in on his fame. On one occasion, Tōgō was aghast to discover that a boyhood friend was not quite the old pal he had thought. The man would regularly visit Tōgō and request samples of his calligraphy, but Tōgō grew suspicious when his old schoolmate became so keen that he even brought along the ink, paper and brushes, and began grinding the ink himself. Eventually, the old acquaintance admitted that he took the Admiral's calligraphy away to sell. When the original source of Tōgō memorabilia refused to play along, other individuals turned to forgery. Tōgō had never visited a police station before, but was invited to the West Kanda precinct to make a statement about the nature of fake Tōgō calligraphy, then in circulation.[8]

In 1906, Tōgō received a petulant piece of fan mail from a boy in Niigata, who had heard so many stories about Tōgō's divine prowess that he had found the sight of the man himself to be something of an anti-climax. The postcard read: 'I thought you were a god, but now I see you are a man. Can the Sea of Japan be protected by men?'[9] The child's blunt statement supposedly moved Tōgō to tears; but three years after his victory at Tsushima, his face was still plastered on tourist knick-knacks in harbour towns, and Japanese ladies still wore hairclips in the shape of battleships. Entirely without the owner's approval, Tōgō's name found its way onto uncountable products as an invincible brand, including Tōgō Crackers, Tōgō Dumplings and Tōgō Soap. The adoration was not limited to Japan; in Canada, when the small hamlet of Pelly Siding was upgraded to village status in 1906, the locals elected to change their home's name to Tōgō, Saskatchewan. In San Francisco, the comic artist Henry Kiyama lampooned the national hero by drawing a strip about a man who dreams he becomes rich by opening Tōgō Shoes, a store that sells shoes 'as strong as Admiral Tōgō'. Meanwhile, in Tokyo at a trade fair, the aging Admiral came face to face with a statue of himself made almost entirely of mushrooms and biscuits. 'The Admiral,' noted a colleague, 'could hardly control himself from smiling at the sight.'[10]

Tōgō was decorated again, with the Order of the Golden Kite and the Grand Cordon of the Chrysanthemum, and served on a medals committee that evaluated the deeds of others in the Russo-Japanese War. By 1906, he had taken matters into his own hands, collaborating with his army associate General Nogi on a monument to the 22,719 Japanese war dead. Their 281-foot Tower of Loyalty was built on top of Baiyu ('White Jade') hill at Port Arthur and completed in November 1909. Although regarded as a noble gesture in Japan, Tōgō's monument was deeply unwelcome to the Chinese – modern tourist brochures claim that the tower was built with the unwilling participation of some 20,000 Chinese labourers, many of whom died in its construction.[11]

Tōgō was released from his responsibilities as Chief of Staff a mere month after he attended the solemn dedication of the tower.

He was now made a member of the Council of Admirals and appointed to the High Military Council. But with no war to fight, his duties remained largely ceremonial. In 1911, he and General Nogi sailed on the *Kamo Maru* in the company of Prince Higashi-Fushimi, as part of the Japanese delegation to attend the coronation of the British King George V.

Passengers and crew expecting a performance from Tōgō were sorely disappointed. He kept to himself throughout the voyage, and spent most of the long trip playing Go in silence with General Nogi. Not even a party, given on the sixth anniversary of the Battle of Tsushima, could tempt Tōgō into making a grand speech. 'During the whole of the journey on the *Kamo Maru*,' sulked London's *Daily Express*, 'no passenger heard either the admiral or the general say anything more than a monsyllable.'

> Theirs was the silence of men whose worth is measured by great deeds. Sometimes a passenger who was acquainted with them would be so bold as to approach them with a passing remark on the weather. But both Admiral Tōgō and General Nogi only nodded or shook their heads.[12]

The sole comment heard from General Nogi for the whole trip was a single word of profane frustration, spat out involuntarily when he missed a putt at deck-golf. After fifty-seven quiet days, the *Kamo Maru* docked on the outer reaches of the Thames, where they were met by the Japanese ambassador.[13] From there, they took the train into London, arriving on 19 June.

It had been many years since Tōgō was in London, and the city was decked out for the festivities. To Tōgō's further embarrassment, he continued to attract relatively greater attention than the Prince. In an attempt to stay out of trouble, he went with the other minor members of the Japanese suite direct to Westminister Abbey on 22 June for the Coronation, leaving the Prince and Princess Higashi-Fushimi to wave at the crowds in the procession. He had less luck avoiding attention on his way out of the ceremony. While the Prince and Princess went on to Buckingham Palace, Tōgō tried to make his way with Nogi back to their London quarters at

Seaford House, only to face a shrieking crowd of well-wishers and handkerchief-wavers.

Not everyone in England was pleased to see Tōgō. An unnamed artist, commissioned to paint Tōgō's portrait, found the small, unassuming and silent man to have none of the military bearing appropriate for a celebrity portrait. He sent Tōgō away on nine occasions without explanation, until one of Tōgō's aides was moved to ask why the portrait was not yet done. 'It is no good today,' complained the artist. 'This Tōgō is not the world-renowned Tōgō. He lacks the spirit worthy of his name.' Tōgō himself, who had often expressed unease with his undesired status, was plainly within earshot of this scolding. 'His face,' noted his adjutant, 'buried in his white beard, flushed like a virgin maid.'[14]

The round of celebratory parties was over within a week, and the Japanese suite were relieved of their official duties and relocated from government accommodation to hotels. The British press, already disappointed at Tōgō's reticence when facing reporters, had all but given up trying to get any quotes out of him; and many press reports concluded almost apologetically, with the note that despite his limited responses, Tōgō was merely a shy man and not a rude one. Making the best out of his continued shyness, the press began to dub him the Silent Admiral, a sobriquet that the British public soon embraced with their customary cheekiness. It seems that nobody had taken the Japanese aside for a crash course in the British sense of humour. Many years after the trip to England, at the time of Tōgō's funeral, his travelling companion Taniguchi Naomi, by then an Admiral himself, remained utterly bemused by the 1911 London crowds, who persisted in chasing after Tōgō's motorcade and yelling: 'Speech! Speech!'[15]

It was left to an intrepid reporter from the *Times* to break the biggest story of the Silent Admiral. The day after the Coronation, Tōgō travelled back out along the Thames in order to pay a visit to his old training ship, the *Worcester*. Ever since the Russo-Japanese war, he had been the school's most famous alumnus. Correspondence between Tōgō and his old mentor, Captain Henderson-Smith, had only ceased with the latter's death, but plans to bring him back to the *Worcester* had been afoot for five years. Shortly after the

Russo-Japanese war, he had been invited to sail a Japanese battle-ship up the Thames in order to make the *Worcester's* prize-giving and graduation ceremony that year an occasion to remember. He had, unsurprisingly, declined the offer, but did so in a polite letter that kept channels of communication open in case he was ever in town. With his official duties out of the way, Tōgō was unable to resist, and dragged a group of Japanese officers on an impromptu trip along the Kent coast. He had very carefully timed it to ensure that he would be in town in time for the nautical college's anniversary celebrations, and the persistence of the *Times* reporter paid off when other journalists had given up. To an audience of assembled graduates of the *Worcester*, at a private function at Prince's Restaurant, the legendarily quiet man delivered a long and moving speech.

Tōgō, at the head of six Japanese naval officers and diplomats, had bowed in Japanese fashion on entering the dining room. Ready for this oriental gesture, the assembled sailors rose to their feet and bowed in return. That, it seemed, would be the summit of their interactions, until the closing stages of the meal, when the President, Captain A H F Young, proposed a toast to Tōgō's health. Much to everyone's surprise, Tōgō got to his feet, eyed the hushed crowd, and cleared his throat. After weeks of silence, Tōgō spoke, an act for which he would receive a standing ovation.

> Your Excellencies and Gentlemen, *Worcester* is a name very dear to me, and one which I have never for a moment forgotten during the last thirty years. It gives me the greatest pleasure to think that this, my second visit to England, has enabled me to satisfy my long cherished desire, which was to look once more on the dear old *Worcester*, and meet you all who are so dear to me.... You are all of different ages and different professions, and I, for instance, am of a different nationality, but there is one bond that joins us all here, and that bond is the *Worcester*. Seeing you here this evening, I feel as if I were meeting again the friends of my youth, and my mind goes back to the old days when as a young man aboard the *Worcester* I was taught with some of you how to make knots and splices. At the same time, my memory recalls to me the form and voice of my

old master, Captain Smith ... During our late war he often wrote to me kind letters, which were a source of great comfort and encouragement to me, coming as they did from far-off England, which to me is a second mother-country. The portraits of Captain and Mrs Smith adorn, together with a photograph of the *Worcester*, my study in my home at Tokyo, and are among my most valued treasures. While I rejoice that I have been able to visit dear old England, and to see once again Mrs Smith, I am filled with deepest regret to find that Captain Smith has left us without waiting for me to come to England, and thus deprived me of the opportunity of personally expressing my gratitude and thanking him for his kindness in the past. This *Worcester* Association, which is composed of old boys who studied maritime science under the superintendance of Captain Smith and his predecessors and successors, long may it flourish![16]

One 'old boy' elected not to attend. Thomas Galsworthy, former captain of the ill-fated *Kowshing*, was just as entitled to attend the *Worcester's* anniversary banquet as was Admiral Tōgō, but thought it improper to do so. 'The captain sent me a letter,' noted Tōgō, 'stating that he was privileged to welcome me at the dinner, but he thought it best to keep away on account of the *Kowshing* affair. Then I knew for the first time that the captain was an old ship-mate, and wondered at the strange affinity, and at the same time I was deeply impressed by this feature of the English character which made this man keep silent about this matter while he was on board my ship after the wreck of his own.'[17]

The news of Tōgō's uncharacteristic eloquence spread far and wide; by the following day, he was even teased about it by Lord Kitchener, who joked that he hoped Tōgō 'would not exchange his noted golden silence for silver speech'. Kitchener had arrived to escort Tōgō to Hyde Park to meet Robert Baden-Powell and inspect a troupe of Boy Scouts. Since Tōgō was staying at the Hyde Park Hotel, the party decided to walk there, along a promenade of passers-by who hissed excitedly to each other: 'Admiral Tōgō! Admiral Tōgō!'[18]

In the days that followed, there were several naval banquets and a visit to the fabled British Museum, where Tōgō faced another ghost from his past. As the Japanese party climbed the majestic steps at the front of the Museum, a towering old man with a huge white beard pushed forward and greeted Tōgō, offering his hand to shake. In the tense moments that followed, Tōgō asked his companion, Commander Taniguchi, who the pushy stranger was. Taniguchi, luckily, had a better memory for faces than Tōgō.

'This is Judge Dole, Admiral,' said Taniguchi, in what was hopefully Japanese impenetrable to any eavesdroppers. 'The President of Hawaii whom eighteen years ago you declined to salute.' It was indeed Sanford Dole, who had gone on to become the first US governor of the territory of Hawaii, before resigning to become a district court judge. Politely, if a little gingerly, Tōgō shook his old adversary's hand, before entering the Museum to look at more widely recognisable relics.[19]

Before long, the Japanese Prince and Princess had been waved off on the *Kamo Maru*, leaving Tōgō and Nogi free to carry out more mundane duties in Europe. Tōgō intended to drop in on several shipyards and then return home via America; Nogi wished to travel through Continental Europe on a goodwill trip. Tōgō tried to talk his old friend out of it, not the least because Nogi was determined to visit Russia, where Tōgō very much doubted that the conqueror of Port Arthur would be greeted with quite the same enthusiasm as they had found in Britain. Nogi, however, would have none of it, and set out on his trip through France, Germany and Austria, although he did not make good on his promise to visit the Russians.

For his part, Tōgō set out with Taniguchi for Scotland, where he intended to inspect the shipyards of the River Clyde. The ships in the slips were decked out in celebratory bunting, and in the company of the mayor and lord provost, Tōgō wandered the John Brown and Yarrow shipyards. He was invited to hammer a nail into the *Grenada* and the RMS *Aquitania*, both under construction, and entertained the crowds with reminiscences about the *Asahi*, built at John Brown & Co., and a surviving veteran of both Port Arthur, where she struck a mine, and Tsushima. But beyond such chats and merrymaking, Tōgō had other things on his mind.

The *Glasgow Herald*, unaware of Tōgō's habit of scouting potential adversaries before hostilities were declared, unwittingly recorded a more ominous development, noting: 'He seems to have taken great interest in watching the *Australia* ...'[20] This battle-cruiser, destined to be the flagship of the Australian navy, was the latest addition to the *Indefatigable* class, and hence afforded Tōgō a view not only of the inner designs of the Australian navy, but of the British ships from which the design had been taken.

Tōgō's homeward journey featured stopovers in Newcastle, where he was similarly feted by local dignitaries and praised the Armstrong shipyards. According to popular myth, he was also taken to see Newcastle United play a match at home, although the thoughts of the Silent Admiral on this display are not recorded. He finally took his leave at the dockside of Liverpool, where he delivered some final words of thanks:

> I feel sad and sorrowful in parting with you, but I feel gratified to think the bond of our friendship has been tied again by my second visit to England. Another fact that should never be forgotten is that the Anglo-Japanese Alliance was renewed during my stay in England. I most firmly believe that this will ensure the peace of the world and the eternal friendship between our two countries.[21]

The Anglo-Japanese Alliance was that strangely-worded treaty by which each signatory agreed to remain neutral if the other went to war with a single foe, and to come to his aid if there was more than one enemy. The threat of involving the British in an Asian war had been enough to keep all other powers out of the Russo-Japanese war, and left Japan free to seize Russian territory. It was now renewed for a further decade and would be in force in 1914 at the outbreak of the First World War, obligating Japan to pitch in on the side of the British, and to some extent, encouraging the British to look the other way while the Japanese snapped up former German possessions in China. But with the First World War away in the future, Tōgō made a peaceful voyage to New York aboard the *Lusitania*, arriving on 4 August.

The Americans were even more overwhelming in their reaction, leaving Tōgō taken aback at their enthusiasm and their energy. The pushy welcome began on the night that the *Lusitania* docked, when Tōgō found a midnight reception committee determined to whisk him onto land before dawn. Soon after, he faced a gesticulating, yelling wall of journalists and photographers from whom his American minders selected a lucky foursome to take his picture. Tōgō stood to attention and stared grumpily into the cameras, only to discover that the *paparazzi* wanted him in a multiplicity of poses and aspects. He seemed particularly galled by the constant strobing of camera flashes. One single image, it seemed, was not enough, and Tōgō suffered an excruciating fifteen minutes of manhandling and exhortations, until Chandler Hale, the Third Assistant Secretary of State, came to his rescue. 'I have been beaten by the zeal of those cameramen,' quipped Tōgō. 'It is rather easier to fight the world squadrons than meeting those men.'

It was not the last time that Tōgō would complain about the photographers. He wryly noted that more pictures were taken of him on that single day than in the combined years of the rest of his life. Not long after, he was beset by a second riot of newspapermen in Washington. Faced with his customary silence, the American press filled in the blanks for themselves with ruminations on the loneliness of command in the mysterious East or patronising conjecture about what Tōgō *might* have said had he been in a position to utter more than a few phrases. He was taken on a train to Washington by a welcoming committee that plainly assumed he had never seen a train before, and whose excited fishing for compliments on American railways he found rudely obtuse.

The *New York World* concentrated on Tōgō's encounter with local telephone exchange workers, whose place of work he visited on his way to the railway station. Dismissed as 'Hello Girls' in the early 20th century, switchboard operators were the subject of contemporary gossip – a woman on the other end of a phone line, ready, in a certain sense, to do one's bidding, and hence something of an erotic frisson. They were also habitually condescended to as bimbos, hence the *World*'s scoffing at the New York switchboard operators' failure to remember to greet Tōgō with the correct cheer, which, the reporter assured his readers, was *Banzai*: 'Ten

Thousand Years.' Other American crowds were soon educated by their press as to the expected form of address, and Tōgō was greeted with wild cries of *Banzai* everywhere he went. This verbal assault did not even escape him when riding in a government limousine, since on one occasion he found himself in an impromptu race with a car full of hysterical (and possibly drunken) flappers, who yelled *Banzai* at him and waved their handkerchiefs while the Admiral looked on in surprised amusement. At no point did Tōgō risk shaming his hosts by pointing out the unwelcome truth, which was that *Banzai* at the time was a military salute more appropriate to the gruff, tough army, whereas the more cultured navy tended to salute with calls of *Hōga*: 'Respectful Congratulations.'

The attention was clearly getting to Tōgō, as was the press's constant demand that he say something, no matter how ill-informed or unfelt. 'I have been frequently asked what I thought of America,' he said, with a rare scolding tone. 'But isn't it asking me too much? I have landed here only this morning, and I have nothing to tell.' Delving for serviceable soundbites, reporters urged Tōgō to give his thoughts on whether American women were educated to higher standards than women in Japan. In a pained answer, loaded with contradictory clauses, he mused that women's suffrage was best not extended to his home country. 'It is enough,' he frowned, 'if a woman is a good wife and a wise mother.'[22]

Despite such old-fashioned views, the American women seem to have been unable to get enough of Tōgō, whose sojourn in the United States was attended by crowds of excitable ladies keen to see the conquering naval hero. In Washington, the press took the hint and grilled him on more suitable matters for an admiral. He was asked for his predictions for the world's navies and replied that neither battleships nor naval guns had yet reached their maximum size. He was asked about the Arbitration Treaty, and expressed his hope that it would render international warfare unnecessary; regardless, however, he noted that a nation still required a strong navy, suggesting that he doubted the Arbitration Treaty would do its intended job. When the interrogation got to be too exacting, Tōgō noted that he was uncomfortable with the direction of the conversation, and questioning turned once more to trivial matters.

'He has a strange, soft voice like a woman's,' noted the *New York Truth* indelicately, 'and he smiles constantly. It makes one almost wonder if this is the hero who fought such brave battles, and whose fame stands high all over the world.'[23]

The *New York Evening Post* was more ready to believe the hype, recalling the incident before Port Arthur when Tōgō addressed his men around a bespoke suicide kit in case of failure. Lesser papers insisted on pushing the notion of a Tōgō fashion fad, urging their readers to snap up replicas of the innocuous sun hat worn by Tōgō when in civilian clothes.

Tōgō was back in uniform for Washington, where he was driven in a motorcade, with motorcycle outriders and a cavalry guard of honour, up to the White House to meet President William Howard Taft. He was back there the same evening for a state banquet, where Taft delivered stirring speeches in honour of the Emperor of Japan, and in honour of Tōgō himself. Taft's enthusiasm about the Anglo-Japanese Agreement was not something that Tōgō really wanted to address, and he limited his reply to taciturn thanks in Japanese, interpreted for him by Commander Taniguchi. Tōgō was then obliged to stand at the door at a 'Japanese-themed' reception in his honour – indistinguishable from any other reception, but for the presence of oriental lanterns throughout the halls. On 6 August, Tōgō paid his respects at the tomb of George Washington, before returning by the presidential yacht to Annapolis, where he visited the Naval Academy and was subjected to yet another banquet, this time from the Washington Press Club.

In Baltimore, he was introduced to a six-year-old boy, born on the day of the Battle of Tsushima, who had laboured throughout his life with the unfortunate name of Tōgō Matthews. Mrs Matthews, perhaps regarding the Admiral's visit as a vindication of her frivolous choice of name, pressed a bouquet of flowers into the Admiral's hand. By Baltimore, Tōgō had given up speaking English to the Americans, and preferred instead to communicate via an interpreter. But he made an exception for young Master Matthews, bending down to assure the unfortunate child that he would pray for his happiness.[24]

For Tōgō, at least, the highlight of his visit was a trip to see the former President Theodore Roosevelt, with whom Tōgō had enjoyed an occasional correspondence over the previous six years. In the wake of the Russo-Japanese war and the Treaty of Portsmouth, Tōgō had sent Roosevelt a revolver as a gift. Roosevelt, meanwhile, had been so taken by the speech that Tōgō delivered to the Combined Squadron on the day of its dissolution that he had quoted from it in one of his presidential orders, and sent a copy to Tōgō for his entertainment. Roosevelt had also invited Tōgō to visit him should he ever find himself in the United States; and it was in that capacity, several years on, that Tōgō arrived at Roosevelt's residence in Sagamore Hill, Oyster Bay, clutching a miniature set of samurai armour that the former President loudly proclaimed to be 'delightful'. 'Here at Sagamore Hill,' noted Roosevelt with obvious enthusiasm, 'we never received such a great man as you in the past; nor shall we in the future, perhaps.'[25]

Roosevelt proudly showed Tōgō a sword that had been presented to him by the Meiji Emperor, and Tōgō sternly pronounced that it had not been properly kept. While Roosevelt watched in rapt admiration, Tōgō cleaned the sword and oiled it in a manner suitable for display. Notably, Mrs Roosevelt observed when her husband was out of the room that it was uncharacteristic of Theodore not to boast to visitors of his military achievements. It was, she noted, a sign that Tōgō's own victories put Roosevelt's to shame. Returning to the room, Roosevelt caught the tail end of Tōgō's polite response, that he was sure that the former president was no less loyal than him in serving his country to the best of his ability. An embarrassed Roosevelt confirmed his wife's suspicions, by noting: 'Beside his great exploits, mine are not worth mentioning, and I should be ashamed to mention them before Admiral Tōgō.'[26]

Tōgō was, however, soon called away to race back to New York, where he was expected to entertain Japanese expatriates at Carnegie Hall, and a banquet at the Knickerbocker Hotel, where a scale model of the *Mikasa* was placed before him on the table, topped with a working wireless receiver that chattered throughout the meal with messages of goodwill from the townsfolk. On 14 August, Tōgō was stuffed once more, this time at a luncheon reception at the Astor, jointly hosted by the Japan Society and the

Peace Society. Tōgō had a prepared speech about the importance of peace and amity, playing in a punning fashion on the meanting of his own name – Tōgō Heihachirō, the 'peaceful man of the East [Village]'. However, he was taken aback by the over-enthusiastic reception, and one Japanese account goes so far as to suggest that the implacable Tōgō was 'somewhat annoyed'.[27] Many diners had arrived significantly ahead of the guest of honour; and the arriving Admiral was veritably mobbed by a scrum of shrieking womenfolk, elbowing each other aside for the pleasure of shaking his hand. Tōgō was clearly troubled by the display, and was rescued again by Chandler Hale. Later on in the day, the millionaire Andrew Carnegie put in an appearance by telegraph, wiring his good wishes to Tōgō from his Scottish castle.

In Boston, the rapid pace of Tōgō's tour finally caught up with him, and he was left feeling ill after yet another welcoming feast. True to form, the press dressed it up as a military exercise, and used it as an excuse to emphasise Tōgō's inscrutable Japanese nature:

> Tōgō was able to withstand the cannonballs of the Russians, but Boston codfish-balls and a few volleys of beans laid him low. The only criticism that the Admiral had to offer on America was a gentle suggestion that banquets belong to the age of the savage, and he was slightly surprised that we placed so much emphasis on our eating.[28]

For Tōgō, such a reply was strangely blunt, even rude, but his irascibility hid other concerns. It was in Boston that he first admitted to twinges and pains that were the first signs of gallstones – a condition that would plague him for the rest of his life, despite two operations. 'It was discovered afterwards,' recalled his colleague Taniguchi Naomi, 'that Admiral Tōgō had been bearing up the pain for some time.' From Boston, Tōgō and the Japanese headed to Niagara, and thence across the continent to the West Coast. Taniguchi, accompanying him, had vainly hoped that the Japanese might travel incognito, but the number of parties of Japanese naval officers in the area was predictably low and they were sure to be recognised. Taniguchi was forced to admit defeat:

One time we were at table in the dining room of a hotel, when a strange gentleman suddenly proposed Admiral Tōgō as a toast and the whole room rose to drink to his health. In such cases, my chief kept his quiet attitude, smiling his thanks; but it was myself that got flustered. I felt then that it was impossible for the Admiral to travel incognito.[29]

From the West Coast, Tōgō gained passage back to Japan on the *Tamba Maru*, arriving on 15 September 1911 after a long and gruelling circuit of the world. If possible, he left an America even more in love with him than when he arrived, fascinated by the achievements of such an unassuming man from such an distant culture against the Russian bear. At least part of the enthusiasm for Tōgō lay in the assumption that he represented a military order that could never be of direct interest to, or have direct impact on, the people of America. Few took heed of the warnings that Tōgō had uttered to the huddle of reporters, that the future would see nations and their fleets increasing in size, in power, and indeed in range, and hence in proximity to one other.

'It is fortunate,' gushed the *New York Tribune*, with what would prove to be awful irony, 'that our country is far away from this Japan. The distance makes us feel that war is impossible with a country in the eastern hemisphere.'[30]

Tōgō in old age, an international celebrity and Japanese nobleman

14

The Treasure of Japan

The Meiji Emperor passed away in 1912, throwing Tōgō into a round of funereal duties, praying at the Imperial shrine and following the coffin in its final procession to the funeral service in Aoyama and to Meiji's final resting place in Momoyama. Less than two weeks after the death of Meiji, Tōgō returned from the funeral to hear of another death. His old friend General Nogi had never forgiven himself for the thousands of lives lost in the taking of Port Arthur. He had previously asked for permission to take his own life in atonement, but had been refused by the Meiji Emperor. While Meiji lived, Nogi had obeyed the command not to punish himself for his supposed failures in the Russo-Japanese war. With Meiji now gone, Nogi and his wife had committed ritual suicide, leaving a note that listed Nogi's reasons. As well as his supposed disgrace at Port Arthur, Nogi also cited a long-forgotten incident in the Satsuma Rebellion, when a young Lieutenant Nogi had lost the regimental banner to the enemy – Tōgō's own kinsmen. The double suicide was a sharp shock to Japan and the Japanese, not the least to Tōgō, who was obliged to attend another funeral.

Tōgō and Mrs Tōgō were flung into each other's company for the first prolonged period in many years. All three of their surviving children had left home – the eldest, Hyo, was studying agriculture in England, their second son, Mitsuru, was at sea as a naval cadet, and their daughter, Yachiyo, had married a naval lieutenant. Tōgō busied himself with his bonsai trees and other garden plants, and began the slow recovery from a gallstone operation.

The new Emperor, son of Meiji, was given the reign title of Taishō. He was in his mid-thirties, but had never quite recovered from a childhood outbreak of cerebral meningitis.[1] This, or perhaps some other unspecified ailment, had caused the Imperial household to keep him out of the public eye as much as possible. He had been a sickly and feeble child, and his studies at the prestigious Gakushūin Academy had been cut short. He was mainly reared by private tutors, at least on those occasions when his spells of illness allowed.

It is difficult to say what was 'wrong' with the Taishō Emperor. As a young man, he did not seem to have had any trouble greeting foreign dignitaries; he had an avowed interest in other cultures and was even said to have irritated his Imperial father with his ability to drop French words into his conversations. Tōgō had accompanied him a decade earlier in an Imperial tour of Korea, after which the Prince had even began a truncated study of the Korean language. Whatever the reason, the Prince did not seem to have paid any attention to his lessons in court protocol. Tōgō had experienced the Taishō's weird behaviour first hand when travelling to the launch of the *Tsukuba*. Then a mere Crown Prince, Taishō had behaved in a manner befitting one of the pushy American women from whom Tōgō had fled in New York. But while such intimacy and boldness might seem perfectly normal outside Japan, to the Imperial family, they were the first signs of madness.

In 1913, at the state opening of the Japanese parliament, the new Emperor scandalised onlookers by rolling up his speech and staring through it as if it were a telescope. The next few years saw increasing incidents of strange behaviour, until he was carefully excluded from many Imperial duties. There is little discussion in Japanese sources of what the Imperial household made of all this, but he was gradually edged away from public functions throughout the second decade of the 20th century, until he was hardly seen at all after the end of the First World War. It is telling that Taishō's son, Prince Hirohito, would be made regent as soon as he reached the age of eighteen.

Admiral Tōgō, who had believed that his service to Japan was over, soon discovered that he was part of this programme of Imperial preservation. In 1914, when Hirohito was eleven years old, Tōgō was summoned to the palace to be given his new mission – he was to take charge of the education of Hirohito, in order to ensure that Japan's next Emperor was fully prepared for the job. He was informed of his new role by Prince Fushimi, who had clearly been assessing the Admiral's potential during their long days *en route* to England aboard the *Kamo Maru*. Unlike the brash, naive Taishō Emperor, Admiral Tōgō had somehow kept his reserve and demeanour aboard a crowded ocean liner for two whole months – here was an ideal man to put in charge of the education of Japan's Crown Prince.

Tōgō disagreed, thinking the task to be too much for him to handle. Prince Fushimi replied that he had been afraid that the Admiral might think so, and that was the reason that he had called this meeting. He wanted, he explained, to obtain the Admiral's informal consent, so that when the official command issued from the Taishō Emperor himself, everyone would know that Tōgō would say yes.

Tōgō, who had already said no, soon realised that he would have trouble disobeying a direct command, and so agreed to it. Aged sixty-eight, Admiral Tōgō became the chief tutor of the Crown Prince Hirohito, the superintendant of an entire squad of educators, charged with ensuring that Hirohito was ready to rule in record time. His appointment may have also masked some factional in-fighting at court. Even though fifty years had passed, the vestiges of Satsuma and Chōshū lived on in political parties and court factions. The old samurai domains may have been long gone, but many of their descendants continued to join forces along family lines. Tōgō, it was true, was a famous Satsuma man, but he was also a national icon, and his appointment seemed to please all parties equally.

'In general,' explained the *Chūō Kōron* newspaper, 'public men have their enemies, however perfect their characters may seem. Admiral Tōgō is an exception. He has no enemies, whether open or insidious, and few men are possessed of such an all-round personality as his ... True, we have a few admirals and generals who are great as such. But these men are either aspiring for power or wishing for fame; they cannot free themselves from such self-consciousness.[2] Not content with singing Tōgō's praises at the expense of other military men, the purple prose went on to compare him to radium, which looked like a humble metal, but glowed with uncanny, invisible power.

For the next six years, Tōgō oversaw Hirohito's education in subjects including the literature of China and Japan, French, fine art, physics, biology, geography, history, ethics, law, calligraphy and the four military necessities: horsemanship, drills, and army and navy affairs. Tōgō was also expected to travel with Hirohito on his study trips around old Japanese battlefields, usually by train, but occasionally by ship. The period of Hirohito's education coincided roughly with that of the First World War, in which the Anglo-Japanese Alliance obliged Japan to enter the conflict against Germany. It was thus a time of great expectations for the Japanese people, who regarded themselves as welcomed in the international community, equal partners of the Allies.

Hirohito came of age in a period when Japan was winning new victories in Asia, this time against Germany, whose colonies Japan seized in the name of the Allies, and expected to hold onto when the war was over. It was only afterwards, at the Paris Peace Conference of 1919, that Japan's position was questioned. The nation was edged out of many proceedings, deprived of the chance to put forward a bill for racial equality, and even forced to agree, however reluctantly, to pull out of the Shandong Peninsula.

Tōgō's last appointment came to an end in the spring of 1921, when Hirohito was packed off for a six-month tour of Europe.[3] With the Crown Prince's departure on his Grand Tour, Tōgō and the other tutors were officially relieved of their duties, and the Admiral, now in his seventies, returned home to play with his grandchildren.

Tōgō remained single-minded and self-sufficient, and as an old man, even arguably eccentric. The Tōgō residence eventually gained an extra wing, but the old Admiral refused to agree to remodelling the original house. He had, he complained, built it himself when he was young, and he did not want to see any changes. Tōgō pottered in his garden, played Go with friends and spoiled his grandchildren. Formerly a heavy *sake* drinker whenever the occasion allowed, he gave up alcohol on doctor's orders in 1914 – Hirohito's mentor was a born-again teetotaller, who occasionally railed against the idiocy of drink, despite a lifetime spent learning to appreciate it. He kept Imperial gifts and honours in pride of place, but one of his favourite possessions was an 'eight-stroke' clock, presented to him by an unnamed Englishman during his active service. The clock was designed for use aboard ship, keeping time not by hours and minutes, but by the eight 'bells' of a traditional ship's watch. Tōgō refused to part with the clock, and kept it by his side until his dying day.

After a lifetime at sea, he still insisted on sewing on his own buttons and darning his own socks, running his own baths, and was even occasionally caught doing his own laundry – washing his socks and handkerchiefs in the sink. His son Hyo recalled that the aging Admiral even once set about a basket of fruit given to him as a present by a well-wisher. The basket had been tarted up with a few pink ribbons, which Tōgō diligently snipped off with scissors and proceeded to sew onto some old cushions. When asked by a bemused Hyo what he was doing, Tōgō replied that he thought the ribbons would help outline the cushions more distinctly. Hyo then suggested that Tōgō might want to get the maid to do his embroidery, but 'he replied that he was used to doing the work himself in the Navy, and kept on sewing pink-coloured ribbons with his old hands'.[4] This may have been the bullish self-reliance of a career sailor, but it may also have helped to hide something else – as was only revealed by Tōgō's eldest son after his death, Mrs Tōgō had been in failing health for many years.

Tōgō was even found to be occasionally talkative, at least by his standards. In 1922, Joseph Joffre, Marshal of France, was entertained at a state banquet, presided over by two Japanese princes. Joffre's attitude suggests that he was mildly annoyed at being made to endure such an event, which was necessary in order to even out the protocols – the young Taishō Emperor had called on the French when he was a prince, and the sojourn required a return visit from the French of equal weight. Accordingly, when presented to Admiral Tōgō, also in attendance, Joffre limited his introduction to the merely factual. 'I am Joffre,' he said, 'the French envoy for returning courtesies.' However, Tōgō pounced on the military leader in an unusually outspoken way. 'I have heard of your name,' said Tōgō, 'and I have the great pleasure of meeting you for the first time. I want to thank you for your visit to this country, I am Count Heihachirō Tōgō, the admiral.'

Both men suddenly became very animated – Joffre with a desire to hear more about Tōgō's world-famous victory over the Russians, and Tōgō with an equally great wish to hear Joffre's personal recollections of the Battle of the Marne. It was only as the old warriors relaxed into their conversation, that both began to suspect that they had met before. Some twenty-eight years earlier, Joffre had been serving with the French navy during the Jilong campaign in northern Taiwan. Tōgō had been there as an observer. Eventually, Tōgō noted that an officer called Joffre had been his guide among the gun emplacements. In turn, Joffre recalled shepherding a short, quiet Japanese captain around the abandoned Chinese fortifications. 'That was you, sir?' exclaimed Joffre. 'That was *you*, sir!' Tōgō replied.[5]

Tōgō's air of authority returned at the time of the Great Kantō Earthquake. Striking at lunchtime on 1 September 1923, the earthquake caught the housewives of Tokyo at their cooking stoves. The damage from the tremors was greatly outweighed by the fires from wrecked kitchens, which soon created a firestorm among the wood and paper houses of the suburbs. Tōgō insisted first on checking on the safety of Hirohito, and only then returned to his home, which was threatened by a wall of flames. Although Mrs Tōgō and the family were dispatched to safety, Tōgō refused to leave his post, calmly directing firecrews in the defence of his burning home. Willing helpers clambered on the roof of his house, drenching the old building with pre-emptive buckets of water. Tōgō stood staring down the flames, which smouldered at the edges of his fence and engulfed his garage, but turned away before reaching the main building. Another catastrophe beset the Japanese the same year – 1923 was also the year in which the Anglo-Japanese Alliance officially came to an end, closing over twenty years of cooperation between the two great naval powers.[6]

Also in 1923, Tōgō the former samurai was brought face to face with a development of the new age – the motion picture. *La Bataille* (in America, *Danger Line*), directed by E E Violet, was the international star-studded epic of its day: the tale of the Japanese Marquis Yorisaka (Hayakawa Sessue) who suspects his wife of having an affair with the English captain Fergan (Felix Ford). The vengeful Yorisaka has Fergan transferred to his ship, and when wounded in action, orders the neutral Englishman to take charge of the ship. The film was an unabashed weepy, a refashioning of *Othello*, in which the wounded Marquis later discovers that his wife had been faithful to him and seeks a tearful reconciliation. However, when screened to an audience of Japanese dignitaries by the well-meaning Viscount Ogasawara, the film's scenes of naval combat had an unexpected effect on Admiral Tōgō. The sobbing Tōgō bolted from the theatre, confessing afterwards to Ogasawara: 'Many of the men around me died in just that way. Do you think I can keep myself from weeping when I see the sight? It does not matter if it is a moving picture.' It was a far cry from the unflappable, emotionless Admiral Tōgō of military renown.[7]

More in keeping with the Tōgō of old was his appearance as a slight, silent man, clad in an ill-fitting country suit and a flat cap, walking down the steps at Tokyo Shinbashi railway station. Tōgō's assistants were shocked to see the old man suddenly stop, draw himself up, and bow low towards the ground, heedless of the bustle and crowds of the station at rush-hour. While passers-by whirled out of the dawdler's way, Tōgō's aide asked him what he was doing. Tōgō calmly replied that he had seen an Imperial prince incognito in the crowd, and continued on his way.

In the aftermath of the Paris Peace Conference, Japan was plunged into a series of arms-limitations negotiations designed to prevent the kind of escalation that Tōgō had predicted in Washington. The result was the Washington Naval Treaty of 1922, the terms of which included a fixed ratio of shipping between the British Empire, the United States and Japan of 5:5:3. Many Japanese regarded this as a further insult from the international community, although the size of each navy's sphere of interest still gave the Japanese a huge fleet. Japan, after all, restricted its interests to the Pacific, whereas the US patrolled the Pacific and the Atlantic, and the British Empire had the same purview, but also additional interests in the Indian Ocean.

As part of the terms of the Washington Naval Treaty, several nations were obliged to reduce their naval strength. The *Australia*, which Tōgō had observed under construction in Scotland, was one of the victims within the British Empire, towed out to sea and scuttled in April 1924. It was not long before the news got out that a Japanese vessel was similarly scheduled for destruction – Tōgō's old flagship, the *Mikasa*.

Refloated after her tragic accident, the *Mikasa* had suffered the same gradual erosion of status as any warship. At the time of the Russo-Japanese war, she had been the most modern unit in Tōgō's fleet. She had been downgraded to a coast-defence ship, and in that capacity had run aground near Vladivostok. Refloated again but struck off the naval lists, she was regarded by naval accountants as an ideal candidate for destruction – a prominent vessel with impressive tonnage on paper, but no great loss to Japan's modern navy.

Tōgō and his flagship remained such celebrities, however, that a protest was inevitable. The *Mikasa* Preservation Society came into being in March 1924, formed as a concerted effort by several politicians, some enterprising newspaper reporters and several other interest groups. The Society printed pamphlets in Japanese and English, calling for the preservation of the *Mikasa* as a national monument and attempted to enlist the support of the British, American, Italian and French ambassadors. All four nations were Japan's co-signatories to the Washington Naval Treaty, and the decision to include ambassadorial weight shows an artful grasp of diplomacy. Several newspapers ran exposés on the parlous state of the *Mikasa*, which sat in a run-down condition at a non-descript Yokosuka dock.

In June 1925, Tōgō was officially invited to a Society lunch, in his capacity as the honorary president – he does not appear to have been actively involved before, but willingly gave his name as a figurehead for the real organisers. Tōgō was hence present when those present agreed that the best way to support the *Mikasa* was to raise the funds for her preservation by public subscription. Tōgō fished in his pocket and pulled out a 50-sen coin – half a yen. 'I second the motion,' he said. 'I will constitute myself the first man to subscribe to the fund.'

With that, he flung his money on the table, where it was soon joined by a clatter of identical coins. Also present was the Navy Minister, Admiral Takarabe Takeshi, who as a young lieutenant in 1900 had nearly killed Tōgō by slapping his horse in Tianjin during the Boxer Uprising. Takarabe dove for Tōgō's coin and snatched it up, making it possible for the first donation to be preserved as a museum exhibit in its own right. The *Mikasa* was later officially inaugurated as a floating museum at a ceremony attended by Tōgō and the Prince Regent, his former pupil Hirohito.[8]

Times had changed. Once regarded as the plucky 'British of the East', the Japanese were now seen as a race possessed by dangerously martial fervour. Tōgō's victory over the Russians had been the last time that Japanese militarism met with wide approval among other powers. In the generation that followed, Japanese expansion had taken on a sinister pall among her allies, and many victories were won in spite of or against the objections of her fellow nations. Korea had become a full-fledged Japanese colony in 1910 and the Japanese had seized German Pacific possessions in 1914–18. The Shandong Peninsula, too, was a spoil of war, and one which Japan was forced to secede with great reluctance and agonising slowness. Shandong, like Port Arthur, had been Chinese territory under foreign occupation, and the Japanese had rather hoped to keep it for themselves after throwing out the Germans. The Chinese, however, were also inconveniently on the Allied side and preferred that the land was returned to them.[9]

The Japanese were reprimanded in the Siberian Intervention of the early 1920s, when Allied action in support of the White Russians risked turning into a new Japanese conquest on mainland Asia. By the 1930s, changes in policies and constitution had turned the military from the servants of the Japanese government into its masters. With the power of veto and the ability to topple Cabinets, the ministries of the Army and Navy began to drive foreign policy. And if that failed, they looked the other way while younger, lower-ranking officers took unilateral action in the Emperor's name, daring their superiors to chastise them for 'loyalty'.

Tōgō paid close attention to the newspapers, but never allowed the discussion of political matters in his house. He remained true to the ideal of the dutiful sailor – in Tōgō's world, the navy followed orders, it did not give them. Pointedly, he never made any show of seeking the post of Navy Minister, nor did he entertain any thoughts about running for office, despite his ever-popular status. 'I am a military man,' he protested to his son, 'and know nothing about politics.'[10]

This, too, singled Tōgō out as an anachronism, in an age when Japanese military men *were* politicians and came to dominate every issue of the day. In Tōgō's last years, Japan was falling into what later historians would call the 'Dark Valley', a spiral into militarism that turned the entire country into an engine of conquest and would end in the cataclysms of Pearl Harbor, the Pacific War and Japanese defeat. The old Admiral had been one of the standard-bearers of the Meiji Restoration and the modern navy, fighting to assert the Emperor's rule, and spearheading many of Japan's early conquests. Tōgō had been instrumental in winning Taiwan for Japan; the fruits of his victories included the handover of Port Arthur, southern Sakhalin and, to a certain extent, Korea. Two years before Tōgō's death, his successors manufactured a crisis in Manchuria and marched to its 'aid' from bases in Korea and strongholds along the railway. Whether or not Tōgō approved of the new Japanese puppet state of Manchu-kuo, it was built on foundations that he himself had laid.

On 23 December 1933, Japan gained a new Crown Prince – Hirohito's son Akihito, destined to be the future Heisei Emperor. As was his wont, Tōgō celebrated the occasion with a dash of calligraphy, muttering happily 'How splendid!' His son recalled that Tōgō's brush daubed out two impressive characters, but whereas a younger Tōgō might have plumped for a respectful naval *Hōga*, the spirit of the times had got to him, too. He wrote *Banzai*, the same word that was on the lips of Japanese everywhere, at every celebration, at every homecoming, and every dispatch of troops to new postings.

Tōgō's gallstones continued to trouble him, and he had had a second operation in 1927. In August 1933, he complained of a constant ache in his throat, which was found to be cancer. This news was largely kept from the public, but became impossible to keep secret after 27 May 1934, when Tōgō failed to make his customary appearance at the anniversary celebrations of the Battle of Tsushima. His eldest son, Hyo, instead sent his father's apologies, giving in the process a stark view of the 88-year-old Admiral's decline:

> He has been suffering from stones in the bladder since the latter days of Meiji. The pain was intermittent, and he used to suffer at intervals of a few months. When the pain begins, he is not able either to lie down or lean against anything. The best way seems to be standing up. He sometimes has to spend the whole night in that posture.[11]

Hyo noted that Tōgō had suffered three stone-related attacks that year, but also revealed that Tōgō had been complaining of a 'pain in the throat' since contracting a cold the preceding summer. An onset of neuralgia had also kept the Admiral confined to bed for the past two months, attended constantly by a nurse, refusing visitors and somewhat hurt by the continued barrage of requests for him to mail strangers an autograph or sample of his calligraphy. Tōgō no longer kept his false teeth in, and had subsisted on a diet of soup and gruel for several months. However, even that news was somewhat out of date – the press release that same evening noted that Tōgō was coughing so much that he was unable to swallow his food, and that he was being kept alive by glucose injections.

A rushed palace meeting on 28 May conferred a final honour on the Admiral, promoting him to the rank of Marquis. Tōgō's son was given the news the following day, and returned to his father's bedside to announce the Imperial edict. True to courtly etiquette, the dying Admiral insisted on first putting on ceremonial dress before hearing his son's report of the words of the Emperor. 'I desire only to rest until the end,' Tōgō replied. 'My thoughts turn to my Emperor.' Tōgō let out a long sigh. 'And to roses,' he added, never to speak again.[12] By 11 p.m. that night, Tōgō's doctor reported a 'mind not clear'. He died in the small hours of the morning, and his passing was officially reported to the Emperor at 7 a.m. on 30 May 1934.

Tōgō was awarded a state funeral. His body was kept at his home in a humble coffin until 3 June, when amid 'rain as fine as smoke', state representatives delivered a more ornate coffin suitable for Imperial honours. Condolences arrived from foreign powers and foreign navies, and an honour guard of British, American, French and Italian marines marched in Tōgō's funeral procession.

The poet Doi Bansui sent a seven-stanza *Song of Condolence*, with the traditional Japanese metre struggling to encompass foreign nouns. But such a hybrid form was necessary for Doi's aims of drawing, one final time, the parallels between Tōgō and Nelson, with the words 'greater than the hero of Trafalgar':

> You are the treasure of Japan
> The glory of the world
> The embodiment of *bushidō*
> And the flower of the Far East.[13]

True to the prevailing martial nature of the times, Doi's elegy pondered the report that the spirit of Tōgō might offer in Heaven to the Meiji Emperor, now that the Far East faced a 'pressing peril'. In a more playful homage, Doi also reversed the traditional sobriquet applied to the Admiral, noting that Tōgō, 'the Nelson of Japan', had lived a long and fruitful life, dying at eighty-eight years of age, whereas Nelson, 'the Tōgō of England', had died aboard his flagship.

Tōgō's final journey began with a tour of his home – Mrs Tōgō was herself bedridden, and could barely raise herself up enough to offer a final gesture of farewell. Tōgō's coffin was placed on a gun carriage and taken through the silent streets, past crowds that mirrored in silence the enthusiastic welcome of his 1905 homecoming. His procession included his relatives, surviving former adjutants, veterans of the *Mikasa* and a scattering of politicians. The foreign dignitaries present comprised many ambassadors, but also an ominous reminder of the uses to which Tōgō's victories had been put.

Korea, where Tōgō had fought in two wars, was now a Japanese colony, and members of the Korean royal family walked in the procession. The rightful ruler of Korea, King Gojong's son Uimin, instead marched in the procession as an officer in the Japanese military. The Last Emperor of China, Puyi, was now the ruler of a Japanese puppet state in Manchuria, unrecognised by most other countries. Puyi did not attend in person, but sent a 'sacred tree' as a gift of condolence.

On the radio that night, in a long reminiscence about Tōgō, Admiral Kobayashi Seizō noted that there was another presence in the procession that he was proud to see. From the dockside at Greenhithe, the boys of the *Worcester* had sent a memorial wreath.[14]

The breathless excitement of Tōgō's era, caught up with the idea of Japan as an Asian Britain, served to mask many intimations of trouble to come. Even Tōgō's own life contains ominous presentiments of the Japan of the 1930s and 1940s. His monument to the fallen of Port Arthur, which still stands on White Jade Hill overlooking the harbour, is now thought to have been built with forced labour. The disguised young Prince Takeda, to whom Tōgō bowed devoutly at a crowded Shinbashi station, was probably Takeda Tsunayoshi, who was later accused of supervising germ-warfare experiments in wartime Manchuria. Hirohito himself, the figurehead of the Japanese in the Second World War, was the product of the old Tōgō's mentoring, although who is to say whether his actions, whatever they may have been, were taken in spite of his tutor, or because of him?

Changes in attitude and fortune present tantalising *what-ifs*, not concerning historical events, but their reception. In 1904, Tōgō's attack on Port Arthur met with widespread British acclaim. 'The Japanese navy,' wrote the London *Times*, 'has opened the war by an act of daring which is destined to take a place of honour in naval annals.' The same tactics, executed some thirty-seven years later at Pearl Harbor, were decried by the United States of

America on a 'date which will live in infamy'. And yet, were they even Tōgō's tactics? The Japanese of the time certainly thought so, although Tōgō's own actions in 1904 suggest that it was *he* who was surprised by the lack of Russian preparation – the grumbles of his own underlings, that he had failed to truly make good on the incredible advantage of surprise, have been silenced only in hindsight. The Tōgō myth – that he was infallible, unstoppable – has been allowed, even among the Japanese, to obscure the more prosaic reality, that Tōgō prevailed by diligence, practice and preparation. A large part of his achievement in the Russo-Japanese war lay in conserving his resources, eking out his available ships, bottling the overwhelming Russian tonnage in places where its full firepower could not be brought to bear, despite the urgings of his junior officers to take greater risks. Tsushima might have been Tōgō's crowning glory, but it is his plodding ascent to that height that makes him so compelling.

One is tempted to ask, if 'crossing the T' is such a devastating manoeuvre, concentrating broadside fire on an enemy head-on, why did it not happen more often in the days before telegraphy and turrets? This is because the crosser is invariably dangerously exposed on his approach. Tōgō, like Nelson before him, was able to risk the manoeuvre because he had the strongest possible confidence in the accuracy of his own gunners and in the poorer aim of his opponents. Gunnery practice does not make for heroic narratives or stirring stories, but like many of Tōgō's other great successes, the groundwork for wartime success was laid in peacetime efforts. Readers of naval history usually focus on the guns and the torpedoes, the epic conflicts and derring-do, but many of Tōgō's victories were won on paper, or with flags and signals. The Silent Admiral was already fighting the Chinese when he was clambering over a Taiwanese fort as an observer. He was already fighting the Russians when he was surveying Japanese coastal waters. He was a man who was able to look at laundry on a washing line and extrapolate it into the way a crew would behave under fire.

It surprises me, even now, that many Japanese still do not realise that *no enemy ships were sunk* during the famous Battle of the Yellow Sea. Tōgō did not have to sink them; he merely needed to stop them reaching Vladivostok, a mission in which he was entirely succesful. Although it is the tales of suicidal valour that endure among the Japanese, their heroic Admiral Tōgō largely reined in the trigger-happy young lieutenants and captains, preventing them from squandering their resources in the kind of attack that today we would call *kamikaze*. After the Battle of the Yellow Sea, Tōgō's work was done for him by German port officials at Jiaozhou, French customs men in Indochina, and dockside police in Shanghai, who impounded Vitgeft's vessels when they had fled as far as their fuel would carry them. Such mundane details contributed to Tsushima, leaving Tōgō with the manpower and preparations to fight the Baltic Fleet and win.

Tōgō's funeral was accompanied by speech after speech by admirals and ministers, many of whom struggled for something to say after they had remembered his service at Tsushima. Few, it seems, knew him well. Most comments about Tōgō were bland statements of approval or praise, while others meekly recounted his shyness and introversion, and left it at that. Only one, Admiral Nawa Matahachirō, offered a glimpse of Tōgō that alluded to his dual position as both a quiet, unassuming man and an invincible admiral:

> The personality of Admiral Tōgō is like the great sky. It is an inch in size if looked at through an inch-wide tube. It appears as large as one foot, if you peep through a one-foot tube. If you go out into the ocean and look at it, it will be an illimitable expanse.[15]

Notes

Introduction

1. *Hansard*, HC Deb 15 October 1996 vol 282 cc669.
2. 'Sea Noon', *Time* (8 November 1926).

1: The Last Samurai

1. Tōgō was born on the 22nd day of the 12th lunar month, which many sources have misread as 22 December 1847. In fact, his birthday was 27 January 1848, eight days before what we would now call Chinese New Year.
2. G Blond, *Admiral Tōgō* (Jarrolds, London: 1961) p 20.
3. N Ogasawara, *Life of Admiral Togo* (Seito Shorin Press, Tokyo: 1934) pp 13–14.
4. Blond, *Admiral Tōgō*, p 24.
5. Tōgō Gensui Hensankai, *Admiral Tōgō: A Memoir* (Tōgō Gensui Hensankai, Tokyo: 1934) p 58, hereafter *ATAM*. See also E Satow, *A Diplomat in Japan* (Stone Bridge Press, San Francisco: 2006) p 41; *Hansard*, HC Deb 15 June 1863 vol 171 cc897–8.
6. *ATAM*, p 54, although *ATAM* claims they were seven 'warships', when one, the *Havoc*, was merely a gunboat. Blond, *Admiral Tōgō*, p 39, claims that there were ten ships all-told, but presumably means the seven ships previously mentioned, plus the *Sir George Grey*, the *Contest* and the *England*, three merchant ships seized by Lieutenant Colonel Neale as collateral pending the payment of Satsuma's indemnities. These

can hardly be called part of the British forces, as they were stolen from the Japanese and then set on fire! Satow, *A Diplomat in Japan*, pp 79–90, is an eyewitness account – Satow was aboard the *Argus*.

7. *Illustrated London News*, 7 November 1863, has a detailed account of the incident, with a chart.

8. *ATAM*, p 53, prefers 'Don't come back beaten, my sons'. But I have translated the far blunter farewell recorded in Japanese in M Okada, *Tōgō Heihachirō: Kindai Nihon o Okoshita Meiji no Kigai [TH: The Revival of Meiji Spirit in Modern Japan]* (Tendensha, Tokyo: 1997) p 28.

9. According to Ogasawara, *Life of Admiral Tōgō*, p 19, the mines would have wrought havoc among the British had the British ships not taken evasive manoeuvres to avoid a salvo of cannon fire from the shoreline, which ironically took them out of harm's way.

10. Blond, *Admiral Tōgō*, pp 41–2.

11. The tale of Masuko under fire is a staple of Tōgō lore and appears in all accounts. Blond, *Admiral Tōgō*, p 44, doubts this story is true, but repeats it anyway, as do I. The same story appears in *ATAM*, p 56. *ATAM* describes Satsuma-jiru as a 'bean soup', but this seems to be a translation error that confuses the *miso* (bean) soup base with the contents.

12. Although the Japanese were suitably cowed, there was also significant embarrassment back in London about the Kagoshima action. There were questions in Parliament about the validity of a bombardment of a civilian target and a call to admonish Admiral Kuper for over-stepping the boundaries of his mission. Whereas Neale merrily reported 'In respect of the Prince of Satsuma, after long forbearance, his capital is in ashes', there was a shocked reaction in some quarters that civilian Kagoshima should have been a target at all, particularly in Holland and in America, where one observer noted: 'When an outcry is made by England about the inhumanity of other nations, we must stop her mouth by the one word "Kagoshima". *Hansard*, HC Deb 9 February 1864 vol 173 c335–6. After almost a hundred pages of lengthy debate, a

proposal to express Parliament's regret for the treatment of Kagoshima was rejected.

13. H Jentschura *et al.*, *Warships of the Imperial Japanese Navy, 1869–1945* (Arms and Armour Press, London: 1977) p 89. Ogasawara, *Life of Admiral Tōgō*, p 27, notes that the *Shoho* and the *Kaiten* had already exchanged fire sometime earlier, with the *Shoho* struck ten times and only warding off the *Kaiten* by attempting to ram her. Until 1905, there was no official naming standard for Japanese vessels. After that date, the practise was generally that battleships were named after ancient Japanese provinces (e.g., *Yamato*), battlecruisers after mountains, 1st and 2nd class cruisers after rivers, gunboats after popular sightseeing spots, torpedo boats after birds, escorts after islands, destroyers after weather phenomena, and so on. For a full list, see Nishida, *Imperial Japanese Navy*, http://homepage2.nifty.com/nishidah/e/index.htm.

14. *ATAM*, p 60. Enomoto's rank in the Tokugawa navy at the time was *Kaigun Fukusōsai* – roughly equivalent to Vice Admiral.

15. *ATAM*, p 61, does not specify who fired first, but Jentschura does not list the *Kasuga* as having a gun larger than a 30-pounder. If a 100-pound ball was fired, it must surely have come from the *Kaiyō*. Some of the more enthusiastic Japanese accounts claim that Tōgō brought down the *Kaiyō*'s mast, but the more trustworthy translation in Ogasawara's *Life of Admiral Tōgō*, p 32, suggests that he merely shot away a yardarm. Satow, *A Diplomat in Japan*, p 335, describes an encounter a week earlier between the *Kaiten* (which he calls by its former name, the *Eagle*) and a Satsuma steamer, which appears to have been the *Shoho* on her way to Hyogo. Ogasawara similarly reports that the *Shoho* tried to ram the *Kaiten* on her way to Hyōgo – could this have cost the *Kaiten* her prominent foreyard? Satow agrees that the *Kaiten* lost her 'foreyard' in that encounter, as observed by sailors aboard HMS *Rodney*. It is possible that both stories are true, but it would be remarkable that two Shōgunate ships with easily

confused names should both reportedly lose a yardarm in the same week.

2: The Republic of Ezo

1. *ATAM*, p 35.
2. Jentschura *et al.*, *Warships of the Imperial Japanese Navy*, p 113.
3. Jentschura *et al.*, *Warships of the Imperial Japanese Navy*, p 12, listed under her post-1871 name of *Azuma*.
4. E Collache, 'Une Aventure au Japon', in *Le Tour du Monde: Nouveau Journal des Voyages*, no. 77 (1874) p 51.
5. Collache, 'Une Aventure au Japon', p 51. Collache wrote his account some time afterwards, but there were clearly still sensitivities about the behaviour of the Frenchmen in 'deserting' their commissions to serve the Republic of Ezo. Consequently, Collache only uses his friends' initials in his account. I have restored their full names.
6. Collache's account is at odds with what is generally believed in modern Japan. Ogasawara, *Life of Admiral Tōgō*, p 39, credits Admiral Enomoto with the idea for the entire operation and does not mention the French at all.
7. R Hillsborough, *Shinsengumi: The Shōgun's Last Samurai Corps* (Tuttle Publishing, Tokyo: 2005) p 172. E and J Barnes (eds), *Naval Surgeon: Revolt in Japan 1868–1869, The Diary of Dr. Samuel Pellman Boyer* (Indiana University Press, Bloomington: 1963) p 270, repeats the assertion of an observer at the time that the *Kōtetsu* may have been 'under the management of Englishmen, several of whom are reported to be in the service of the Mikado and in this expedition'. However, these mystery Britons are even more obscure in the record than their French adversaries – Japanese accounts concentrate largely on the Japanese and have edged foreign participants out of history.
8. Collache, 'Une Aventure au Japon', p 54.
9. Collache, 'Une Aventure au Japon', p 55. This was a particular irritation to Collache, as neither he nor his men had eaten

for 20 hours, and now knew that they would not eat again for some time. Collache surrendered several days later and was sentenced to death, but was reunited with his fellow Frenchmen after the fall of Hakodate and returned to France. Like the other Frenchmen, he was judged to be a 'deserter' by a military tribunal, but punished so lightly that he was back in French service by the time of the Franco-Prussian War. At least two of the French stayed behind in Japan and one, the non-commissioned officer Clateau, opened Japan's first French restaurant.

10. Andō Tarō, quoted in Ogasawara, *Life of Admiral Tōgō*, pp 42–3.
11. R Bodley, *Admiral Tōgō: The Authorized Life of Admiral of the Fleet, Marquis Heihachirō Tōgō, O.M.* (Jarrolds, London: 1935) p 54.
12. *ATAM*, p 65, misdates this with the lunar calendar as 24 April.
13. Ogasawara, *Life of Admiral Tōgō*, p 44.
14. Jentschura *et al.*, *Warships of the Imperial Japanese Navy*, p 115. Ogasawara, *Life of Admiral Tōgō*, p 48, rates Matsuoka Bankichi, the commander of the *Banryū*, alongside the late Captain Kōga of the *Kaiten*, killed in the Battle of Miyako Bay, as 'unequalled for bravery in the feudal government's navy'. The *Banryū* had a long afterlife. She was salvaged by the Americans and returned to the Imperial navy after a refit as the *Raiden*. In 1888, she was struck off the naval lists and sold as a whaler, in which capacity she served for a further eleven years.

3: Johnny Chinaman

1. *ATAM*, p 66. Other sources give the name as Wagman, but Charles Wirgman is the most likely candidate among the foreigners then in Japan.
2. Ogasawara, *Life of Admiral Tōgō*, p 54.
3. Jentschura *et al.*, *Warships of the Imperial Japanese Navy*, p 12.

4. A Capel, 'Admiral Haihachi [sic] Tōgō as a youth', in *The Strand Magazine*, April 1905 issue, pp 474–5. The article is illustrated by Tōgō's signature in his own hand, demonstrating that 'Haihachi' was how he chose to romanise his name in his student days. Most sources claim that Tōgō was lodged with the Capels *after* his naval studies, but this seems unlikely. Not only does Capel himself state the opposite, but his account of Tōgō's linguistic ability is that of a faltering newcomer to the language, not the fluent sailor of Henderson-Smith's memories of Tōgō on the *Worcester*. Furthermore, the Imperial Japanese Troupe, featuring the famous 'All Right', toured England in 1868. If Tōgō did not arrive until 1874, surely young Master Capel would have been *too* young to have remembered a visit by Japanese acrobats some six or seven years earlier. Tōgō may have stayed with the Capels both before and after his service on the *Worcester*, which would help explain the discrepancies, although it would still not explain why Capel would think that a young Tōgō, believing himself to be going blind, would volunteer for active nautical training. One final explanation, rooted in Japanese etiquette, may be that Tōgō was not as happy with the Capel family as they believed and that his removal from their care 'for medical reasons' was a discreet brush-off.

5. *ATAM*, p 66, says Tōgō was sent to Portsmouth. Blond, *Admiral Tōgō*, p 54, says Plymouth. Both, however, claim that Tōgō regularly went down to the docks to see Nelson's flagship, HMS *Victory*, which makes Portsmouth a far more likely location. F Stafford, *The History of the 'Worcester': The Official Account of the Thames Nautical Training College, HMS Worcester 1862–1929* (Frederick Warne, London: 1929) p 160, settles the argument by noting that Tōgō signed up at Greenhithe with the claim that his 'former school' had been the Royal Naval Academy at Gosport (i.e. close to Portsmouth). However, this does not explain how Tōgō could think he had attended a school that his biographers universally agree was closed to him at the time.

6. E Falk, *Tōgō and the Rise of Japanese Sea Power* (Longmans, Green and Co., New York: 1936) p 92.

7. *ATAM*, p 244.

8. Falk, *Tōgō and the Rise of Japanese Sea Power*, p 91; *ATAM*, p 67. The *ATAM* version seems to have been lifted from a Japanese source, possibly Ogasawara, and retranslated back into English, hence the slight differences between the two texts.

9. Stafford, *The History of the Worcester*, p 160.

10. Stafford, *The History of the Worcester*, pp 160–1.

11. Ogasawara, *Life of Admiral Tōgō*, p 56.

12. *ATAM*, p 67.

13. Ernest Vanderstegen, letter to the *Times*, quoted in Ogasawara, *Life of Admiral Tōgō*, p 470. Vanderstegen, a resident of Reading, appears to be the same man who patented a device for 'assembling or dismantling the pistons of engine cylinders' in 1924.

14. D Keene, *Emperor of Japan: Meiji and His World 1852–1912* (Columbia University Press, New York: 2002) p 247. See also R Eskildsen, *Foreign Adventurers and the Aborigines of Southern Taiwan, 1867–1874: Western Sources Related to Japan's 1874 Expedition to Taiwan* (Academica Sinica, Taipei: 2005) p 238. Ironically, the imposition of Japanese rule, not only on the Ryūkyū Islands, but on Taiwan itself after 1895, was no guarantee of peaceable behaviour from the natives. In an embarrassing incident in 1904, a number of American sailors were murdered on an island off the coast of Taiwan. What had been a *casus belli* for the Japanese when the Chinese were in charge was left by the Americans for the new Japanese rulers to police. See H Toiviainen, *Search for Security: United States Citizens in the Far East, 1890–1906. A comparative study of problems related to safeguarding Americans in China and Japan* (Studia Historia Jyväskyläensia 33, Jyväskylä: 1986) p 348.

15. J Rawlinson, *China's Struggle for Naval Development 1839–1895* (Harvard University Press, Cambridge, MA: 1967) pp 61–2.

16. The shipyard is no longer there, but it is now the Samuda Estate.
17. *ATAM*, p 36.

4: Delicate Diplomacies

1. Bodley, *Admiral Tōgō*, p 74. An inferior translation of the same passage is in *ATAM*, pp 74–5.
2. *Jingei*: 'Fast Whale'. Jentschura *et al.*, *Warships of the Imperial Japanese Navy*, p 88.
3. Falk, *Tōgō and the Rise of Japanese Sea Power*, p 108.
4. *ATAM*, p 69, with which most other sources agree. Bodley, *Admiral Tōgō*, p 67, claims February *1882*.
5. Falk, *Tōgō and the Rise of Japanese Sea Power*, p 110. Some foreign sources call her Tetsuko, but Japanese sources agree on Tetsu. The *–ko* suffix is common in Japanese girls' names, but seems to have been absent in this case.
6. *Amagi*: 'Celestial Fortress', named for a mountain in Shizuoka. Jentschura *et al.*, *Warships of the Imperial Japanese Navy*, p 90.
7. Or so claims Lloyd, *Admiral Tōgō* (Kinkōdō, Tokyo: 1905), p 52.
8. Blond, *Admiral Tōgō*, p 71.
9. Falk, *Tōgō and the Rise of Japanese Sea Power*, p 113; *ATAM*, p 71. Nire commanded the *Kongō*, Hanabusa was aboard the two-masted *Meiji*; the other ships were the *Amagi*, *Nisshin*, *Seiki*, *Hiei*, *Moshun*, *Iwaki* and Tōgō's former ship, the imperial yacht *Jingei*. Falk claims there were eight *warships*, but appears to have discounted the *Meiji*, a schooner that is also not included in Jentschura *et al.*
10. Bodley, *Admiral Tōgō*, p 69, suggests that the idea *came* from Tōgō, an assertion not repeated elsewhere, although Bodley does claim that his biography is 'authorised'. Falk, *Tōgō and the Rise of Japanese Sea Power*, p 114, claims that the idea was Nire's. Blond, *Admiral Tōgō*, p 73, claims that the vessel they tracked was 'local', and that the Chinese warships arrived afterwards. Keene, *Emperor of Japan*, p 376, claims that

the Chinese arrived first, saw the *Kongō*, which had arrived shortly ahead of the others, thought better of it and went away. The Chinese ships then returned shortly afterwards, hence technically arriving 'after' the Japanese although they had been in the vicinity for twenty-four hours.

11. Keene, *Emperor of Japan*, pp 376–7.

12. Bodley, *Admiral Tōgō*, p 69.

13. Falk, *Tōgō and the Rise of Japanese Sea Power*, p 116. Ogasa-wara, *Life of Admiral Tōgō*, p 71, notes that Tōgō fired a salute appropriate for a commodore, but that the captain demanded a salute fit for a 'commander' (*sic*) – presumably Ogasawara means that Tōgō had kindly upgraded the captain to a com-modore because he was commanding a flotilla of several ships, but the captain insisted that he warranted an admiral's salute.

14. *Daini Teibō*: the name appears to be a reference to a famous date in the Chinese calendar (1636), when Abahai, the Manchu father of the first Qing emperor, invaded Korea. Jentschura *et al.*, *Warships of the Imperial Japanese Navy*, p 113.

15. Blond, *Admiral Tōgō*, p 82.

16. R Wright, *The Chinese Steam Navy 1862–1945* (Chatham Publishing, London: 2000) p 62, claims that Courbet *did* notify the Chinese of his intentions to attack, but that the missive was lost in the confusion of local bureaucracy and not truly understood until it was too late. R Johnson, *Far China Station: The US Navy in Asian Waters 1800–1898* (Naval Institute Press, Annapolis: 1979) p 210, notes that the Chinese commanders had wanted to initiate hostilities against the French, but had been prevented from doing so by their own superiors, because the Chinese thought it was improper behaviour to begin without an official declaration of war and had assumed that the French would act with similar discretion. See also Rawlinson, *China's Struggle for Naval Development*, p 119.

17. Blond, *Admiral Tōgō*, p 82.

18. Falk, *Tōgō and the Rise of Japanese Sea Power*, p 123.

5: Princes and Prisoners

1. *Yamato*: a classically poetic name for Japan. Jentschura *et al.*, *Warships of the Imperial Japanese Navy*, p 91.

2. A daughter, Yachiyo, born 13 October 1891. She was the only Tōgō girl to survive, two elder sisters having died in infancy. *ATAM*, p 76.

3. Jentschura *et al.*, *Warships of the Imperial Japanese Navy*, p 14. She appears in a Japanese naval list because she would eventually fall into Japanese hands in 1895, as would the *Pingyuan*, listed on the same page.

4. Rawlinson, *China's Struggle for Naval Development*, p 92, notes that Ding's homeward journey was a disaster. The *Chaoyong* was briefly stuck on a shoal while under Ding's command, and the *Yangwei* unforgivably ran out of coal partway across the Mediterranean and drifted helplessly for two days. With such problems in mind, we can readily understand Tōgō's refusal to be impressed.

5. Keene, *Emperor of Japan*, p 460.

6. *Times*, 24 July 1883, quoted in Wright, *The Chinese Steam Navy*, p 54. For 'practically invincible', ibid, p 50.

7. *ATAM*, p 76. W Tyler, *Pulling Strings in China* (Constable, London: 1929) p 47, also notes Lin's habitual reticence. Scandalously, neither Ding Ruchang nor Lin Taizeng (nor, less surprisingly, Liu Buchan) are included among the biographies in A Hummel's landmark *Eminent Chinese of the Ch'ing Period (1614–1912)* (US Government Printing Office, Washington: 1943), despite their service to their Emperor.

8. Blond, *Admiral Tōgō*, p 87.

9. *ATAM*, p 76. Tōgō's superiors were sufficiently spooked by the *Dingyuan* and *Zhenyuan* that they ordered the construction of a ship in France with guns specifically designed to take them out. The resulting vessel, the top-heavy *Unebi*, was completed in 1886 but disappeared without a trace on the long journey to Japan, presumed sunk by her own unseaworthiness. Jentschura *et al.*, *Ships of the Imperial Japanese Navy*, p 96; Wright, *The Chinese Steam Navy*, p 80. Rawlinson, *China's Struggle for Naval Development*, p 152, reports a

similar 'courtesy call' made by three Japanese warships on the Fuzhou dockyard in 1894. The local authorities vainly suggested that the Chinese reciprocate by sending six ships of their own to shame the Japanese, seemingly unaware that the Japanese were only answering a previous Chinese challenge.

10. Keene, *Emperor of Japan*, p 349.
11. Keene, *Emperor of Japan*, p 792 n.14.
12. *Naniwa*: a poetic name for the Osaka area. Jentschura *et al.*, *Warships of the Imperial Japanese Navy*, pp 95–6.
13. J Morgan, *Senate Report 227*, a.k.a. *The Morgan Report* (Washington: US Government, 53rd Congress, 2nd Session, 1894), pp 1106–7. Online version at http://morganreport. org. Accessed 21st July 2009. Consul Fuji's obfuscating reply was crafted in a single unwieldy sentence and included in the US Senate Report 227 of the 53rd Congress as a 'letter of recognition', although it was nothing of the sort. Whereas, for example, the consuls of most other nations clearly and immediately acknowledged the Provisional Government, Fuji's reply seems deliberately verbose and unclear: 'The receipt of your communication, dated the 17th instant, inclosing a copy of proclamation issued on the same day, informing me that for reasons set forth in said proclamation the Hawaiian monarchy has been abrogated and a Provisional Government established, which is now in possession of the Government departmental buildings, the archives, and the treasury, and requesting me on behalf of [His Imperial Japanese Majesty's] Government to recognize said Provisional Government as the *de facto* Government of the Hawaiian Islands, pending the receipt of instructions from H. I. J. M.'s Government, to whom advices of your action and of the position which I have taken in relation thereto have been despatched.'
14. *ATAM*, p 79.
15. *Daily Bulletin*, 21 March 1893, quoted in Falk, *Tōgō and the Rise of Japanese Sea Power*, p 141.
16. The usually reliable Falk, *Tōgō and the Rise of Japanese Sea Power*, p 141, scoffs at the suggestion that a prince was aboard, although his rebuttal suggests that he has confused

the young Prince Yamashina with his elder half-brother, Komatsu Akihito (1846–1903), who had a similar title but was demonstrably not the youthful nobleman described in the newspaper. In fact, the *Daily Bulletin* article, long derided, seems to have hit the nail on the head. *ATAM*, p 79, openly states that a 'Prince Yamashina' was aboard the *Naniwa* at the time. The presence of Prince Yamashina aboard the *Naniwa* in Hawaii is also clearly indicated in his naval record of service in Nishida's *Imperial Japanese Navy*.

17. Falk, *Tōgō and the Rise of Japanese Sea Power*, p 143; *ATAM*, p 79.
18. Falk, *Tōgō and the Rise of Japanese Sea Power*, p 145.
19. *Daily Pacific Commercial Advertiser*, 17 March 1893, quoted in Falk, *Tōgō and the Rise of Japanese Sea Power*, pp 145–6.
20. Keene, *Emperor of Japan*, p 347. In fact, the promised revocation of extraterritoriality took until 1898 to implement, but it was the thought that counted.
21. Falk, *Tōgō and the Rise of Japanese Sea Power*, p 146.
22. Falk, *Tōgō and the Rise of Japanese Sea Power*, pp 148–9, cites the *Philadelphia*'s log as his source.

6: Sink the Kowshing

1. *ATAM*, p 81. Falk, *Tōgō and the Rise of Japanese Sea Power*, p 157, claims that the larger of the two vessels was the *Dingyuan*, not the *Zhenyuan*, but *ATAM* seems to be correct here. *ATAM* adds a comment from Lin Taizeng, expressing his surprise that Tōgō's men had manned their guns, although Tōgō's own account implies that the Chinese had done likewise. There seem to have been similar tensions wherever the Chinese and Japanese were in sight of each other. 'Vladimir' [Zenone Volpicelli], *The China-Japan War: Compiled from Japanese, Chinese and Foreign Sources* (Sampson Low, Marston and Company, London: 1896) p 115 and pp 375–9, notes a grisly incident in Shanghai, where a witchhunt for Japanese 'spies' led to the arrest, torture and execution of two Japanese men. They were controversially handed over to the

Chinese without trial by the American consul, shortly after the Chinese had tried to similarly apprehend a 'Japanese spy' who turned out to be an Arab stoker on a French steamer.

2. Strictly speaking, the Mandarin romanisation should be *Gaosheng*, but the ship's name appears variously as *Kaosheng*, *Kowhsing* and *Kowshing* in contemporary accounts, indicating perhaps the southern accents of her crew, many of who appear to have been Cantonese or Hokkienese speakers. Rawlinson, *China's Struggle for Naval Development*, p 92, notes an unlikely accusation from Chinese sources that Tōgō did not merely stumble across the *Kowshing*, but had been tipped off as to her course by spies within the Chinese arsenal at Tianjin.

3. 'Vladimir', *The China-Japan War*, p 96; Wright, *The Chinese Steam Navy*, p 86.

4. *ATAM*, p 84. See also Lloyd, *Admiral Tōgō*, pp 67–70, for an extensive appraisal.

5. Testimony of Thomas Galsworthy, in 'Vladimir', *The China-Japan War*, p 367. Notably, the translation in *ATAM*, p 85, adds an additional comment from Galsworthy, that he was left 'speechless' at the 'foolish words' of the Chinese. Albeit wholly justified, this comment is not recorded in 'Vladimir's' transcripts, and is presumed to be an invention of the Japanese.

6. Falk, *Tōgō and the Rise of Japanese Sea Power*, p 167.

7. Von Hanneken, testimony on the *Kowshing* incident, in 'Vladimir', *The China-Japan War*, p 357. Von Hanneken was the only person who seemed to believe that the damage was done by the torpedo – all other accounts hold that the torpedo missed and that the ship was sent to the bottom solely by the *Naniwa*'s guns.

8. S Suzuki (ed), *Nisshin Sensō Emaki [Pictures from the Sino-Japanese War]* (Shunyōdō, Tokyo: 1904) vol 2 'The Asan Sea', p 28, makes the ridiculous claim that it was von Hanneken who ordered the Chinese to fire at the foreigners in the water.

9. Testimony of Lewes Henry Tamplin, quoted in Falk, *Tōgō and the Rise of Japanese Sea Power*, pp 171–2. Falk leans heavily on

'Vladimir', *The China-Japan War*, pp 349–69, which includes
several contradictory testimonials of the last moments of
the *Kowshing*, including one claim (Galsworthy's) that the
Japanese did not fire at the Chinese, another (from Von
Hanneken) that admitted that men on the *Kowshing* had been
firing at their own lifeboats, and another (from the stoker
Tung Ha-shin) that the Japanese deliberately turned their
ship-mounted machine guns on the Chinese in the water.
It should be noted, however, as does Blond, *Admiral Tōgō*,
p 104, that Tung's testimony was extremely confused. He was
convinced that the Japanese had somehow carried Gatling
guns up to the tops of the *Naniwa*'s masts – an unlikely feat.
The case of the *Kowshing* would drag on for many years, and
crops up in the *Hansard* record of Parliamentary business on
several occasions after 1894. Five years on, there were questions in the British Parliament about the status of reparations
to the families of the dead (HC Deb 26 October 1899 vol 77
cc732–3), which were delayed indefinitely, first by wrangles
over responsibility and then by a suspicious two-year 'illness'
on the part of the Chinese ambassador. The question was last
raised in 1900 (HC Deb 08 August 1900 vol 87 cc979–80),
during a House of Commons debate wherein Joseph Walton
MP recounted a recent trip to the Far East, where he had
talked about the fate of the Kowshing with a steamer captain
who had been Galsworthy's first mate (presumably Tamplin).
Walton noted that: 'The *Kowshing* was sunk not in a moment,
but gradually, from the firing of guns from the Japanese
cruiser. She would not have been sunk at all had it not been
that the British commander and the officers, after they had
been summoned and were willing to surrender to the Japanese cruiser, were forcibly prevented from surrendering by
the Chinese soldiers on the *Kowshing*... . The three Europeans
who escaped did so only by diving into the sea and swimming
to the Japanese cruiser, being repeatedly fired upon by the
Chinese soldiers, who believed that their capture was due
to the bribery of the British commander by the Japanese.'
The sinking of the *Kowshing* is last mentioned in *Hansard* in

1902, where John Denny MP suggests that the commission heading to China to arrange an indemnity accruing from the Boxer Uprising should also attach *Kowshing* reparations to its agenda.

10. *ATAM*, pp 85–6.
11. Ogasawara, *Life of Admiral Tōgō*, p 162.
12. *ATAM*, p 86; see also T Holland, *Letters to The Times Upon War and Neutrality (1881–1920)* (The Echo Library, Teddington: 2006) pp 43–6.
13. See, for example, Tyler, *Pulling Strings in China*, p 39; and Falk, *Tōgō and the Rise of Japanese Sea Power*, p 171. The *Kowshing* was not the last foreign transport ship in the zone of conflict. J Allan, *Under the Dragon Flag: My Experiences in the Chino-Japanese War* (Frederick A Stokes, New York: 1898) [Dodo Press POD reprint, not dated] pp 6–12, arrived in the area in late August, aboard an American-registered blockade runner – long and slender, with an impressive top speed of 20 knots that could outrun most warships and boilers burning virtually smokeless anthracite as fuel. In late August, Allan's ship was smuggling ammunition on the Yellow Sea when she was boarded by a party from a Japanese cruiser. The smugglers escaped by bodily throwing the inspecting lieutenant overboard and running for Tianjin, counting on their souped-up engines to outrun the cruiser – which they did, with the loss of five lives aboard due to Japanese gunfire. The same ship subsequently served as one of the troop transports taking men to the Yalu, and hence was on her way home, the Stars and Stripes boldly proclaiming her new-found neutrality, when she ran into the Battle of the Yalu. Unable to resist, Allan put ashore to watch the fight and hence was able to supply the eyewitness account upon which I draw in the next chapter. During the later Russo-Japanese War, Tōgō was famously lenient in his treatment of blockade-runners. As implied in 'H Tikovara', *Before Port Arthur in a Destroyer: The Personal Diary of a Japanese Naval Officer* (John Murray, London: 1907) pp 198–9 and 205, Tōgō may have been soft on blockade-runners because such behaviour

made other smugglers less likely to put up a deadly fight –
perhaps a result of his *Kowshing* experience.

14. *ATAM*, p 18.
15. Keene, *Emperor of Japan*, p 483.

7: The Angry Dragons

1. Tyler, *Pulling Strings in China*, p 44. Tyler has some remarkably negative things to say, even about Chinese officers who
   were regarded by the Japanese as noble opponents. Long after
   McGiffin's suicide, one of his relatives compiled his extant
   papers into L McGiffin, *Yankee of the Yalu: Philo Norton
   McGiffin, American Captain in the Chinese Navy 1885–1895*
   (Dutton, New York: 1968), which presents an understandably
   different account to Tyler's. Blond, *Admiral Tōgō*, p 109,
   mistakenly asserts that McGiffin was the *captain* of the
   Zhenyuan.
2. Falk, *Tōgō and the Rise of Japanese Sea Power*, p 180, has the
   Japanese spotting the Chinese at 11:20 a.m. Meanwhile, on
   the *Dingyuan*, Tyler, *Pulling Strings in China*, p 49, recalls
   that 'eight bells had struck' (i.e., it was past noon) and that
   he was just about to tuck into a roast pigeon when the news
   arrived.
3. *ATAM*, p 88.
4. Tyler, *Pulling Strings in China*, pp 49–50. Tyler was convinced that there was a wooden splinter embedded in his eye
   and even tried to strangle a Chinese surgeon who claimed
   otherwise. But the stabbing pain turned out to be simply the
   effect of the concussion.
5. Rawlinson, *China's Struggle for Naval Development*, p 168.
   The *Yoshino* had managed a spectacular 23 knots on her sea
   trials and was using barely 60 per cent of her engine capacity
   by leading the Japanese fleet into battle at a sedate 14 knots.
   She was the fastest warship afloat in 1894.
6. Allan, *Under the Dragon Flag*, p 16.
7. Allan, *Under the Dragon Flag*, p 17. G Ballard, *The Influence
   of the Sea on the Political History of Japan* (John Murray,

London: 1921), p 146, claims that the *Saikyō*'s course was not a foolhardy endeavour, but a simple attempt to catch up with the faster ships by taking a short cut. This short cut, unfortunately, turned out to be right through the enemy battle line.

8. Falk, *Tōgō and the Rise of Japanese Sea Power*, pp 191–2. *Saikyō* ('Western Capital') does not appear in Jentschura *et al.*, as she was not technically a naval vessel. Her captain, 'John Wilson' (a.k.a. Frederick Walgren, 1851–99) was one of the few Europeans remaining in Japanese service by that time. The Swedish-born, British-trained Wilson was later decorated by the Meiji Emperor for his actions, although notably, in Japanese war prints of the *Saikyō*'s moment of glory, Wilson has his back to the artist, in order to give the impression that the ship had an all-Japanese crew. For the defective ammunition in use on both sides, see Rawlinson, *China's Struggle for Naval Development*, pp 184–5.

9. Allan, *Under the Dragon Flag*, pp 16–17.

10. Tyler, *Pulling Strings in China*, p 54.

11. Falk, *Tōgō and the Rise of Japanese Sea Power*, p 193, claims it was the *Dingyuan* that did this damage to the *Matsushima*. *ATAM*, p 89, is adamant that it was the *Zhenyuan* in her heroic defence of the *Dingyuan* later in the day.

12. Allan, *Under the Dragon Flag*, pp 17–18.

13. Tyler, *Pulling Strings in China*, p 57, notes that the *Qiyuan*'s captain, Fang Boqian, was beheaded for 'this and for a previous act of cowardice'. But Rawlinson, *China's Struggle for Naval Development*, p 177, notes McGiffin's accusation that the Chinese fleet contained 'traitors, even drawing monthly salaries from the enemy'. Can we be sure that the blame for the sabotage truly lies with the unfortunate Captain Fang? For discussion of possible enemies of Fang within the Chinese fleet, see Rawlinson, *China's Struggle for Naval Development*, pp 193–4. Notably, 'Vladimir', *The China-Japan War*, p 97, not only argues that Fang (in his text, Fong) was a scapegoat whose execution was ordered by ignorant Beijing bureaucrats and unsuccessfully opposed by Admiral Ding, but also that the Japanese themselves were impressed by his

conduct at the Battle of the Yellow Sea and expressed surprise on hearing that he had been executed.

14. McGiffin, *Yankee of the Yalu*, p 140.

15. One dissenting voice in this story is McGiffin, *Yankee of the Yalu*, p 140, who claims that Lin spent most of the battle cowering on the floor and howling in anguish every time he heard a loud bang. McGiffin claims that the *Zhenyuan* was effectively under the command of another officer, Yang Yongling, for much of the battle; and hence that it was he, and not Lin, who came to the rescue of the *Dingyuan*. However, McGiffin's testimony, already called into question by Tyler, above, would rather require him to be in a dozen places at once; and we might reasonably discount it here.

16. P McGiffin, 'The Battle of the Yalu', in *Century Magazine*, no.50 (August 1895) p 601.

17. N Chaïkin, *The Sino-Japanese War* (Nathan Chaïkin, Martigny: 1983) pp 150–1. The same tale recounts the appearance of two doves before the battle, cited as yet another omen, albeit one of unknown meaning. One almost gets the impression that the sailors in the Japanese fleet had never seen a bird before.

18. Bodley, *Admiral Tōgō*, pp 99–101 contains the complete text of Tōgō's matter-of-fact report on the Battle of the Yalu, more properly called the Battle of the Yellow Sea (in Japan, but thereby confusing it with his later encounter with Vitgeft in the Russo-Japanese War) or the Battle of Haiyang [Island] in some sources. Tōgō reports breaking off action at '6:30 p.m.', whereas Tyler, *Pulling Strings in China*, p 51, records the time as 'about half past five' with 'about another hour of daylight.' In modern parlance, the Japanese were fighting in their home time zone, which they share with Korea, whereas the Chinese were an hour behind.

19. Falk, *Tōgō and the Rise of Japanese Sea Power*, p 200. Falk calls the boat the *Kwang-Kai*, possibly a misreading of *Kwang-chia* (i.e., *Guangjia*), a gunboat run aground in the Battle of the Yalu; see Rawlinson, *China's Struggle for Naval Development*, p 254.

20. Tyler, *Pulling Strings in China*, p 92.
21. Rawlinson, *China's Struggle for Naval Development*, p 190.
22. Wright, *The Chinese Steam Navy*, p 95. Although Lin took the blame, he may have struck a charted hazard in a desperate attempt to avoid some of his own navy's mines, which had been laid near his ship without warning.

8: Though Your Swords Be Broken

1. 'Vladimir', *The China-Japan War*, p 270.
2. Letter of Itō Sukeyuki to Ding Ruchang, 25 January 1895, quoted in Bodley, *Admiral Tōgō*, pp 105–7. The full correspondence is preserved in 'Vladimir', *The China-Japan War*, pp 380–6.
3. Tyler, *Pulling Strings in China*, p 78.
4. Bodley, *Admiral Tōgō*, p 114.
5. Tyler, *Pulling Strings in China*, p 74.
6. Tyler, *Pulling Strings in China*, p 79.
7. Falk, *Tōgō and the Rise of Japanese Sea Power*, p 217.
8. *ATAM*, p 92. Tyler, *Pulling Strings in China*, p 85, claimed that Ding killed himself before his 'reply' was written, and hence that the famous letter was actually a forgery, frantically assembled by the surviving foreign and Chinese officers in the late Admiral's name. However, this seems unlikely as both replies are in Ding's personal style, and there is no reason to suspect that he would take his own life *without* first making sure that the safety of his subordinates was guaranteed by Admiral Itō. There is a less exacting translation in Bodley, *Admiral Tōgō*, pp 114–15.
9. Bodley, *Admiral Tōgō*, pp 115–16. 'Vladimir', *The China-Japan War*, p 297, suggests that Ding could not accept any gift from the Japanese because, as with the case of the *Kowshing*, any form of cordiality would be read by the Chinese as a sign of bribery.
10. Rawlinson, *China's Struggle for Naval Development*, p 190.
11. McGiffin, *Yankee of the Yalu*, p 140.

12. Falk, *Tōgō and the Rise of Japanese Sea Power*, marks Tōgō's promotion as 26 February 1895. Nishida, *Imperial Japanese Navy*, in Tōgō's online naval record, dates the promotion ten days earlier.

13. Even in Chinese, Taiwan was sometimes referred to as *Dai Liuqiu* (Great Ryūkyū), although such terminology is uncommon today. To imply that Taiwan is one of the Ryūkyū islands is to suggest that it should remain part of Japan. Hence, while one might hear the term Great Ryūkyū from Japanese right-wing organisations, it is rare indeed to hear it from the Chinese. Taiwan remained part of Japan from Tōgō's expedition until 1945, when the island was restored to China, although arguments then ensued about *which* China, the Republic or the People's Republic, should take control. See J Clements, *Wellington Koo* (Haus Publishing, London: 2008) pp 151–2.

14. Falk, *Tōgō and the Rise of Japanese Sea Power*, p 225, names a governor-designate who was a retired Rear Admiral called Tanaka (presumably Tanaka Tsunatsune, 1842–1903).

15. Falk, *Tōgō and the Rise of Japanese Sea Power*, p 225, asserts that Tōgō took a course along the east coast of Taiwan. This is strangely at odds with accounts elsewhere but shows true cunning.

16. Ogasawara, *Life of Admiral Tōgō*, pp 153–4. 'Vladimir', *The China-Japan War*, p 320, similarly notes a two-phase battle, with the majority of the Chinese fleeing 'like frightened sheep' while a handful of brave soldiers remained at their posts to surprise the Japanese landing force.

9: Republicans and Rebels

1. J Clements, *Pirate King: Coxinga and the Fall of the Ming Dynasty* (Sutton Publishing, Stroud: 2004) p 229; R Croizier, *Koxinga and Chinese Nationalism: History, Myth, and the Hero* (Harvard University Press, Cambridge, MA: 1977) p 60.

2. Ogasawara, *Life of Admiral Tōgō*, p 162.

3. Ogasawara, *Life of Admiral Tōgō*, p 166. *ATAM*, pp 262–6, includes the complete course outline under Tōgō's stewardship.

4. Ogasawara, *Life of Admiral Tōgō*, pp 166–7.

5. Falk, *Tōgō and the Rise of Japanese Sea Power*, p 241, claims that Tōgō represented the navy at the funeral of 'the Mikado's mother' during this period, but she did not die until 1907. The confusion originates with the fact the Meiji's birth mother was an imperial concubine and that he was adopted by his father's chief wife, the Empress Dowager.

6. J Clements, *Prince Saionji* (Haus Publishing, London: 2008) pp 82–3.

7. I Nish, *The Russo-Japanese War, 1904–5: A Collection of Eight Volumes* (Global Oriental, Folkestone: 2003) [8 vols] pp 31–2.

8. Clements, *Wellington Koo*, p 21.

9. *Atago*: named after a Tokyo district; Jentschura *et al.*, *Warships of the Imperial Japanese Navy*, p 115.

10. *ATAM*, pp 95–6.

11. *ATAM*, p 96.

12. *ATAM*, p 96.

13. *ATAM*, pp 305–6. The errant officer later became *Admiral* Takarabe.

10: Port Arthur

1. Ogasawara, *Life of Admiral Tōgō*, p 182.

2. Falk, *Tōgō and the Rise of Japanese Sea Power*, p 281.

3. Ogasawara, *Life of Admiral Tōgō*, p 194.

4. Tikovara, *Before Port Arthur in a Destroyer*, p 217: 'The Marconi wireless-telegraphy … was installed on all our ships three months before mobilisation began …', so presumably November-December 1903. Tikovara (Chikawara?) was purportedly the captain of a Japanese ship in the campaign, whose memoirs were translated first into Spanish and then into English. Published very soon after the events they describe, they contain rare moments of criticism and com-

plaint about Admiral Tōgō, whose reputation was otherwise unassailable by 1907.

5. Falk, *Tōgō and the Rise of Japanese Sea Power*, p 291. It is Falk who times the meeting to the 'mid-watch', i.e., between midnight and 4 a.m. in the early hours of 6 February. Falk calls the article on the tray a short sword; but *Time* magazine, recounting the incident some years later, persuasively identifies the display as 'a lacquer tray containing the instruments used in committing *hara-kiri*'. In other words, not a *wakizashi* short sword but a *tantō* dagger. *Time*, 'Sea Noon', 8 November 1926.

6. *New York Evening Post*, 4 August 1911, quoted in *ATAM*, p 253. Further to the above note, the *Evening Post* article precisely measures the blade as 'three inches and a half' – hardly a 'sword'.

7. Ogasawara, *Life of Admiral Tōgō*, pp 195–6.

8. Tikovara, *Before Port Arthur in a Destroyer*, p 15.

9. Keene, *Emperor of Japan*, pp 606–7.

10. *ATAM*, p 110. The text says 'christening day of St Maria', which is presumably Our Lady of Lourdes (11 February in the Gregorian calendar).

11. Falk, *Tōgō and the Rise of Japanese Sea Power*, p 294–5.

12. *ATAM*, p 111.

13. Falk, *Tōgō and the Rise of Japanese Sea Power*, p 297. Ogasawara, *Life of Admiral Tōgō*, p 210, prefers: 'You will do your utmost.'

14. Bubnoff, quoted in Ogasawara, *Life of Admiral Tōgō*, p 214.

15. There is a strange coda to the story of the *Variag*, in that the reaction of the Japanese public to Uryū's initial failure to sink her led to crowds throwing stones at the absent Admiral's house. To appease the mob, Mrs Uryū conspicuously went to pray at a local Buddhist temple, whose priests then claimed the credit for the *Variag*'s subsequent demise. Tōgō accompanied other admirals to the temple, the Myōhōji, to give thanks after the war, and would later sponsor a campaign by the temple's sect to have its medieval founder, Nichiren, conferred with the honorary title of *Daishi*. Tōgō would later

admit to being a follower of Nichiren, perhaps understandably, given that the Nichiren sect was also associated with the original *kamikaze* storm that destroyed the fleet of Mongol invaders in the 13th century. The calligraphy on a statue of Nichiren near Senzoku Pond, Meguro, Tokyo, was based on that of Tōgō himself. Inouye Tetsujiro, 'Fleet-Admiral Tōgō from a Spiritual Point of View,' in *ATAM*, p 7.

16. Tikovara, *Before Port Arthur in a Destroyer*, p 83. In the light of later successes and Tōgō's ultimate victory over the Russians, early criticism such as Tikovara's has been largely swamped or forgotten by posterity.

17. Ogasawara, *Life of Admiral Tōgō*, p 223; *ATAM*, p 199.

18. Ogasawara, *Life of Admiral Tōgō*, p 231. Falk, *Tōgō and the Rise of Japanese Sea Power*, p 307.

19. Ogasawara, *Life of Admiral Tōgō*, pp 235–6, recounts the demise of the Russian destroyer *Steresgutchi*, although he does not mention any resistance on board. Falk, *Tōgō and the Rise of Japanese Sea Power*, p 309, recounts the resistance and scuttling, but does not name the ship.

20. *ATAM*, p 117.

21. *ATAM*, p 118.

22. Jentschura *et al.*, *Warships of the Imperial Japanese Navy*, p 204. Tikovara, *Before Port Arthur in a Destroyer*, p 119, notes that the navy had been waiting for the *Koryo* for weeks. 'At last,' he writes, 'we possess a craft which we ought to have had since the beginning of the war.'

23. *ATAM*, p 120.

24. Ogasawara, *Life of Admiral Tōgō*, p 277. Characteristically, it was another five months before the Baltic Fleet got underway. Had it left for the Far East in May and not October 1904, it might have conceivably reached the Yellow Sea before the fall of Port Arthur.

25. Ogasawara, *Life of Admiral Tōgō*, p 270.

11: The Battle of the Yellow Sea

1. *ATAM*, p 124.

2. Ogasawara, *Life of Admiral Tōgō*, p 274.
3. F Unger, *The Authentic History of the War Between Russia and Japan* (Bible Publishing House, Philadelphia: 1905) pp 312–13.
4. C G E Mannerheim, *Päiväkirja Japanin Sodasta 1904–1905 sekä Rintamakirjeitä Omaisille [Diary from the Japanese War 1904–1905 with Letters to His Family]* (Otava, Helsinki: 1982) pp 38–9. Ying Kou was the original home of Miss Maud's Complete Nursing, a brothel chain that soon franchised itself all along the Siberian railways.
5. Ogasawara, *Life of Admiral Tōgō*, p 288.
6. F Villiers, *Port Arthur: Three Months with the Besiegers, a Diurnal of Occurrents* (Longmans, Green and Co., London: 1905) p 66.
7. Villiers, *Port Arthur: Three Months with the Besiegers*, p 67.
8. Villiers, *Port Arthur: Three Months with the Besiegers*, p 68.
9. H Wright, *With Tōgō: The Story of Seven Months Active Service Under His Command* (Hurst and Blackett, London: 1905) p 57.
10. Ogasawara, *Life of Admiral Tōgō*, p 290.
11. Many years later, Tōgō would comment to an interviewer that his 'crossed T' had not quite gone according to plan. He was determined to try it again before he retired and this desire would find its final fruition at Tsushima in 1905. *ATAM*, p 13.
12. Ogasawara, *Life of Admiral Tōgō*, p 297; for Prince Fushimi's account of his wounds, see *ATAM*, p 132.
13. Tikovara, *Before Port Arthur in a Destroyer*, p 180.
14. Ogasawara, *Life of Admiral Tōgō*, p 303.
15. Ogasawara, *Life of Admiral Tōgō*, p 307.
16. Ogasawara, *Life of Admiral Tōgō*, p 311.
17. Ogasawara, *Life of Admiral Tōgō*, p 322.
18. Ogasawara, *Life of Admiral Tōgō*, p 317.

12: Tsushima

1. R Deacon, *History of the Japanese Secret Service* (Frederick Muller Limited, London: 1982) p 55.

2. G Regan, *Great Naval Blunders* (Carlton, London: 2001) pp 1–3.
3. Ogasawara, *Life of Admiral Tōgō*, p 326.
4. E Selle, *Donald of China* (Harper and Brothers, New York: 1948) p 24. The phrase 'Go find it' seems curiously American for the *Daily Telegraph*, but perhaps brevity won out.
5. Selle, *Donald of China*, p 29.
6. Ogasawara, *Life of Admiral Tōgō*, pp 328–9.
7. Ogasawara, *Life of Admiral Tōgō*, p 337.
8. Testimony of the *Mikasa*'s chief gunnery officer, *ATAM*, p 178.
9. Ogasawara, *Life of Admiral Tōgō*, p 349.
10. Ogasawara, *Life of Admiral Tōgō*, p 345.
11. Ogasawara, *Life of Admiral Tōgō*, p 362. Tokutomi Iichiro, 'Admiral Tōgō from a Historical Point of View', in *ATAM* pp 9–16, suggests that Tōgō had another reason, which was that he was all too aware of the seasonal rough seas at the Tsugaru and La Pérouse straits, and hence thought that any reasonable commander would take Tsushima as the safest route. But such an explanation appears to credit the Russians with considerably better knowledge of Japanese waters than they may have had.
12. Ogasawara, *Life of Admiral Tōgō*, p 385.
13. Vladimir Semenov, Russian prisoner of war, quoted in D Wells (ed), *Russian Views of Japan 1792–1913: An Anthology of Travel Writing* (Routledge/Curzon, London: 2004) p 188.
14. Wells, *Russian Views of Japan*, p 200.
15. Clements, *Prince Saionji*, p 90.

13: Tōgō on Tour

1. Vladimir Semenov offers greater detail: 'A fire broke out on the *Mikasa*, and ... this fine cruiser [*sic*] had been blown up and sunk.' Wells, *Russian Views of Japan*, p 194.
2. Stafford, *History of the Worcester*, p 206.
3. Ogasawara, *Life of Admiral Tōgō*, pp 398–9.
4. Bodley, *Admiral Tōgō*, pp 222–3.

5. Ogasawara, *Life of Admiral Tōgō*, p 401.
6. *ATAM*, p 231.
7. *ATAM*, p 279, includes several examples of Tōgō's well-meaning but charmless versifications, which seem to have been more useful to him as a hook on which to hang his more accomplished calligraphy. The best he could manage at his homecoming after Tsushima, for example, was the leaden: *Even by sinking the vessels attacking us / Let us set forth Imperial virtues / Oh, sons of the Empire.*
8. *ATAM*, p 297.
9. *ATAM*, p 293.
10. *ATAM*, p 272. H Kiyama, *The Four Immigrants Manga: A Japanese Experience in San Francisco, 1904–1924* (Stone Bridge Press, San Francisco: 1999) pp 66–7.
11. Ogasawara, *Life of Admiral Tōgō*, p 404. Now in Chinese hands, the monument was officially renamed the Baiyushan Tower in 1985. Although it is entirely possible that the Japanese used forced labour in the construction of the tower, the alleged number of Chinese *deaths* seems curiously close to the number of Japanese *dead* commemorated on the tower itself.
12. *Daily Express*, quoted in Ogasawara, *Life of Admiral Tōgō*, p 413.
13. Or so claims *ATAM*, p 153. Ogasawara, *Life of Admiral Tōgō*, p 418, thinks that Tōgō and the rest of the party arrived at Victoria Station, which implies that they landed not at Tilbury on the north side of the Thames, but at Gravesend on the south. *ATAM*, however, has Tōgō arriving in London at St Pancras, a remarkably roundabout route for someone supposedly arriving from the Thames Estuary. Both authorities, however, seem to confuse several 'arrivals' in London by Tōgō – he would have arrived back at Victoria from the naval review at Spithead and would have left from St Pancras for his trip to Newcastle. One part of *ATAM* puts Tōgō at Claridge's Hotel after the Coronation, but elsewhere, p 335, Admiral Taniguchi Naomi remembered it as the Hyde Park Hotel.

14. *ATAM*, p 295.
15. *ATAM*, p 335.
16. *Times*, 1 July 1911, quoted in *ATAM*, p 244; and in Ogasawara, *Life of Admiral Tōgō*, pp 424–5. Tōgō's letter refusing the first invitation, dated 13 February 1906, is included in Stafford, *History of the Worcester*, p 41. Reading between the lines, many had expected Tōgō to accompany the earlier tour of Britain by the Japanese Prince Fushimi in 1907, hence the initial invitation and Tōgō's heartfelt demurral. Tōgō's use of the term 'Captain Smith' to refer to Captain *Henderson*-Smith seems to have been commonplace – the index in the *Worcester*'s school history files him under S.
17. Ogasawara, *Life of Admiral Tōgō*, pp 103–4.
18. Testimony of Taniguchi Naomi, in *ATAM*, p 335; ATAM, p 157, replaces 'silver' with 'iron'.
19. Falk, *Tōgō and the Rise of Japanese Sea Power*, p 144.
20. *Glasgow Herald*, 13 July 1911, quoted in *ATAM*, p 246. The *Aquitania*, launched in 1913, subsequently became the only liner to serve in both world wars, before being scrapped in 1950.
21. *Liverpool Post*, 31 July 1911, quoted in *ATAM*, p 249.
22. *New York World*, 5 August 1911, quoted in *ATAM*, p 258.
23. *New York Truth*, 5 August 1911, quoted in *ATAM*, p 250.
24. *ATAM*, p 260.
25. *ATAM*, p 337.
26. *ATAM*, pp 167–8.
27. *ATAM*, p 169.
28. E Hubbard, *The Elect: Elbert Hubbard's Selected Writings, Part 5* (Roycrofters, East Aurora, NY: 1928) p 114.
29. *ATAM*, p 337.
30. *New York Tribune*, 4 August 1911, quoted in *ATAM*, p 252.

14: The Treasure of Japan

1. Keene, *Emperor of Japan*, p 320.
2. *Chūō Kōron*, 2 November 1916, quoted in *ATAM*, p 172.
3. See Clements, *Prince Saionji*, p 151.

4. *ATAM*, pp 193, 303.

5. *ATAM*, pp 228–9.

6. *ATAM*, p 278.

7. *ATAM*, p 305.

8. *ATAM*, p 274. The *Mikasa* herself continued to suffer bad luck. During the Second World War, she looked as much like a battleship from above as any other and was hit several times by Allied air raids. After the Japanese defeat, the Soviet ambassador demanded that this symbol of Russian humiliation be taken out to sea and sunk, but was talked round by the Americans by being shown the sorry state of the hulk of the *Mikasa* at the dockside. The ship was eventually repaired once more in the 1960s.

9. Clements, *Prince Saionji*, pp 137–44.

10. *ATAM*, p 195.

11. *ATAM*, p 177.

12. Blond, *Admiral Tōgō*, p 252.

13. *Song of Condolence*, in *ATAM*, p 187.

14. Radio broadcast of Kobayashi Seizō, 5 June 1934, in *ATAM*, p 346.

15. *ATAM*, p 277.

Sources and Further Reading

Tōgō is a difficult subject. The famously Silent Admiral made little effort to help his biographers place him in events that are otherwise only broadly described in naval reports. Non-Japanese writers persist in padding their accounts of Tōgō with little bits of incidental mariners' business, ascribing orders or actions to Tōgō that actually issued from his superiors or subordinates. Meanwhile, Japanese authors eternally flail in search of numinous portent or Imperial approval, or tiptoe around contentious issues – one modern account manages to whisk through the period 1878–93 in less than a page, thereby avoiding all mention of Japan's predatory behaviour towards Korea.

Tōgō's finest hour was in 1904–5, when he achieved international renown and the cover of the *London Illustrated News*, although a decade too late for the edification of his former English teacher, the paper's former Japan correspondent Charles Wirgman (1832–91). Nevertheless, even without Wirgman's help, the British press seemed keen to regard Tōgō as an honorary Englishman. Tōgō received considerable coverage in the foreign press at the time, and became the subject of a hastily written book by Arthur Lloyd. Detailed appraisal of Tōgō's career did not appear in English until after his death. In 1934, the Tōgō Society published a large-format book called *Admiral Tōgō: A Memoir* (listed as *ATAM* in my references; only the cover adds the subtitle *Hero of the World*), which collates a series of articles, reminiscences, poems and other *Tōgōbilia*, including Tōgō's own military dispatches from the Russo-Japanese war (pp 196–228) and some pointless paintings of mountains and trees by well-meaning admirers. *ATAM* is a wonderful source for Japanese local colour, but haphazardly translated and an unreliable source when it comes to many facts, often confusing foreign names and places. Like a surprising number of modern history books in Japan, it also fails to take into account the use of the lunar calendar during the early Meiji period, and consequently misdates every event that occurred before Japan adopted the Western calendar in 1873, including Tōgō's date of birth.

The prime source for both *ATAM* and all subsequent accounts is Vice Admiral Ogasawara Naganari's *Life of Admiral Tōgō*, a hefty 1920s biography that was itself translated (and translated well) into English in 1934. Ogasawara not only knew Tōgō personally, but was at his side on many occasions. It is, therefore, something of a surprise that with these publications preceding him, Ronald Bodley would begin his 1935 'authorised' biography with the words 'I was faced with the problem of writing the story of a man about whom nothing had been written before.' One is tempted to assume that Bodley arrived back in England from a four-year sojourn in the Far East, clutching a freshly-published copy of Ogasawara and hoping to rush his own derivation into print before any others reached Europe. Although Bodley possesses a few bonus insights on naval matters, he is easily surpassed by Edwin Falk's superb 1936 *Tōgō and the Rise of Japanese Sea Power*, which is packed with detail and meticulously referenced.

Although Tōgō was the subject of many hagiographies in the early 20th century, from a European establishment that regarded the Japanese as the plucky underdogs in a war against the Russian bear, his reputation suffered in later years as the status of Japan itself plummeted before and during the Second World War. Although he was dead before the outbreak of the war, he was often assumed to have been directly involved in it, either for being the 'tutor' of Hirohito or through the simple confusion of many members of the public, some of whom still assume that he and the executed war criminal Tōjō Hideki are the same person.

By the mid-1930s, the world was already concerned with how the Japanese military would behave *after* Tōgō, and discussion of him disappears from the English language for a generation bracketing the Second World War. George Blond's readable *Admiral Tōgō* (1961) summarises much of Ogasawara and presents a good run-through of Tōgō's glory days, but concentrates on reports of naval battles in which Tōgō fought *outside* Japan. Hence, Blond's account leaps from Tōgō joining the Satsuma navy in 1866 to his arrival in Europe in 1871, neglecting the entire Boshin War. Strangely, Blond ignores the Battles of Awa, Miyako Bay and Hakodate, despite the presence of great detail in Ogasawara and even a French eyewitness account: Collache's 'Aventure au Japon.'

There are other glimpses of important events in Tōgō's life in the accounts of others. A young Ernest Satow was present at the bombardment of Kagoshima and gave a detailed account in his memoirs. The Reverend Capel, whose son once mistook Tōgō for a juggler, wrote a priceless portrait of his former lodger for *The Strand Magazine*, which remains one of the most human accounts of this famous military man. James Allan, a sailor smuggling arms to the Chinese, left a detailed eyewitness account of the Battle of the Yalu in *Under the Dragon Flag*. Last but not least, Nishida Hiroshi's *Imperial Japanese Navy* website contains detailed career breakdowns of the ships and leading officers who served during the Meiji period, and has proved invaluable in solving old questions and scotching old myths.

Akashi, M, *Rakka Ryūsui: Colonel Akashi's Report on His Secret Cooperation with the Russian Revolutionary Parties during the Russo-Japanese War* (Studia Historica 3, Helsinki: 1988)

Allan, J, *Under the Dragon Flag: My Experiences in the Chino-Japanese War* (Frederick A Stokes, New York: 1898) [Dodo Press POD reprint, not dated]

Allen, H, *The Betrayal of Liliuokalani: Last Queen of Hawaii 1838–1917* (Mutual Publishing, Honolulu: 1982)

[Anonymous], 'Sea Noon', in *Time* magazine, 8 November 1926

_____, 'London Greets Fushimi – He Visits King Edward, Wants to Hear "The Mikado"' in *New York Times*, 7 May 1907

Armstrong, W, *Around the World with a King* (Charles Tuttle, Rutland, VT: 1977)

Ballard, G, *The Influence of the Sea on the Political History of Japan* (John Murray, London: 1921)

Barnes, E, and James Barnes (eds), *Naval Surgeon: Revolt in Japan 1868–1869, The Diary of Dr. Samuel Pellman Boyer* (Indiana University Press, Bloomington: 1963)

Beasley, W, *The Meiji Restoration* (Stanford University Press, Stanford: 1973)

____, *Japanese Imperialism 1894–1945* (Clarendon Press, Oxford: 1987)

Berger, G (ed), *Kenkenroku: A Diplomatic Record of the Sino-Japanese War 1894–1895* (Princeton University Press, Princeton, NJ: 1982)

Blond, G, *Admiral Tōgō* (Jarrolds, London: 1961)

Bodley, R, *Admiral Tōgō: The Authorized Life of Admiral of the Fleet, Marquis Heihachirō Tōgō, O.M.* (Jarrolds, London: 1935)

Capel, A, 'Admiral Haihachi [sic] Togo as a Youth,' in *The Strand Magazine*, no.172 (April 1905) pp 474–5

Chaïkin, N, *The Sino-Japanese War* (Nathan Chaïkin, Martigny: 1983)

Chuang, F, *et al.* (eds), *Historical Sites of the First Rank in Taiwan and Kinmen* (Council for Cultural Planning and Development, Executive Yuan, Taipei: 1987)

Clements, J, *Pirate King: Coxinga and the Fall of the Ming Dynasty* (Sutton Publishing, Stroud: 2004)

____, *Prince Saionji* (Haus Publishing, London: 2008)

____, *Wellington Koo* (Haus Publishing, London: 2008)

____, *Mannerheim: President, Soldier, Spy* (Haus Publishing, London: 2009)

Cobbing, A, *The Satsuma Students in Britain: Japan's Early Search for the 'Essence of the West'* (Japan Library, Richmond: 2000)

Collache, E, 'Une Aventure au Japon,' in *Le Tour du Monde: Nouveau Journal des Voyages*, no. 77 (1874) pp 49–64

Connaughton, R, *The War of the Rising Sun and Tumbling Bear: A Military History of the Russo-Japanese War 1904–5* (Routledge, London: 1988)

Cortazzi, H, *Victorians in Japan in and around the Treaty Ports* (Athlone Press, London: 1987)

Croizier, R, *Koxinga and Chinese Nationalism: History, Myth, and the Hero* (Harvard University Press, Cambridge, MA: 1977)

Deacon, R, *A History of the Japanese Secret Service* (Frederick Muller Limited, London: 1982)

Dodd, J, *Journal of a Blockaded Resident in North Formosa During the Franco-Chinese War 1884–5* (Daily Press Office, Hong Kong: 1888)

Duus, P, *The Abacus and the Sword: The Japanese Penetration of Korea 1895–1910* (University of California Press, Berkeley: 1995)

Eastlake, F, and Yamada Yoshiaki, *Heroic Japan: A History of the War Between China & Japan* (Kelly & Walsh, Yokohama: 1896)

Eskildsen, R, *Foreign Adventurers and the Aborigines of Southern Taiwan, 1867–1874: Western Sources Related to Japan's 1874 Expedition to Taiwan* (Academica Sinica, Taipei: 2005)

Falk, E, *Tōgō and the Rise of Japanese Sea Power* (Longmans, Green and Co., New York: 1936)

Hillsborough, R, *Shinsengumi: The Shōgun's Last Samurai Corps* (Tuttle Publishing, Tokyo: 2005)

Holland, T, *Letters to The Times Upon War and Neutrality (1881–1920)* (The Echo Library, Teddington: 2006)

Hough, R, *The Fleet That Had to Die* (New English Library, London: 1958)

Hubbard, E, *The Elect: Elbert Hubbard's Selected Writings, Part 5* (Roycrofters, East Aurora, NY: 1928)

Hummel, A (ed), *Eminent Chinese of the Ch'ing Period (1644–1912)* (US Government Printing Office, Washington: 1943)

Jentschura, H, *et al.*, *Warships of the Imperial Japanese Navy, 1869–1945* (Arms and Armour Press, London: 1977)

Johnson, R, *Far China Station: The US Navy in Asian Waters 1800–1898* (Naval Institute Press, Annapolis: 1979)

Johnston, R, *Lion and Dragon in Northern China* (John Murray, London: 1910)

Katō, T, *Boshin Sensō Tōhoku Kikō [Travels among North Honshū Sites of the Boshin War]* (Mumyōsha, Akita: 1999)

Keene, D, *Emperor of Japan: Meiji and His World 1852–1912* (Columbia University Press, New York: 2002)

Kiyama, H, *The Four Immigrants Manga: A Japanese Experience in San Francisco, 1904–1924*. Translated by Frederik L Schodt (Stone Bridge Press, San Francisco: 1999)

Kōda, I, *Taikun no Katana: Brunet ga Mochikaetta Nippon Katana no Nazo [Sword of the Tycoon: The Mystery of the Japanese Sword Brought Home by Brunet]* (Hokkaidō Shinbun, Sapporo: 2007)

Kowner, R (ed), *The Impact of the Russo-Japanese War* (Routledge, London: 2007)

Kurobane, S, *Nichi-Ro Sensō to Akashi kosaku [The Russo-Japanese War and the Deeds of Akashi]* (Nanso-sha, Tokyo: 1976)

Lloyd, A, *Admiral Tōgō* (Kinkōdō, Tokyo: 1905)

Mannerheim, G, *Päiväkirja Japanin Sodasta 1904–1905 sekä Rintamakirjeitä Omaisille [Diary From the Japanese War 1904–1905 with Letters to his Family]* (Otava, Helsinki: 1982)

Matten, M, 'The Japanizing of a Chinese hero: the role of Koxinga in the Japanese colonial discourse', in Peter Lutum (ed), *Japanizing: the Structure of Culture and Thinking in Japan* (Münster, Piscataway, NJ: 2006) pp 158–95

McAleavy, H, *Black Flags in Vietnam: The Story of a Chinese Intervention* (George Allen and Unwin, London: 1968)

McGiffin, L, *Yankee of the Yalu: Philo Norton McGiffin, American Captain in the Chinese Navy 1885–1895* (Dutton, New York: 1968)

McGiffin, P, 'The Battle of the Yalu', in *Century Magazine*, no.50 (August 1895) pp 585–602

McKay, A, *Scottish Samurai: Thomas Blake Glover 1838–1911* (Canongate, Edinburgh: 1993)

McKenzie, F, *From Tokyo to Tiflis: Uncensored Letters From the War* (Hurst and Blackett, London: 1905)

Medzini, M, *French Policy in Japan During the Closing Years of the Tokugawa Regime* (Harvard University Press, Cambridge, MA: 1971)

Morgan, J, *Senate Report 227*, a.k.a. *The Morgan Report* (Washington: US Government, 53rd Congress, 2nd Session, 1894). Online version at http://morganreport.org . Accessed 21st July 2009.

Murano, M, *Shimazu Nariakira no Subete [All About Shimazu Nariakira]* (Shinjin Buraisha, Tokyo: 2007)

Nish, I, *The Russo-Japanese War, 1904–5: A Collection of Eight Volumes* (Global Oriental, Folkestone: 2003) [8 vols]

Nishida H, *Imperial Japanese Navy*: http://homepage2.nifty.com/nishidah/e/index.htm

Ogasawara, N, *Life of Admiral Togo* (Seito Shorin Press, Tokyo: 1934)

Okada, M, *Tōgō Heihachirō: Kindai Nihon o Okoshita Meiji no Kigai [TH: The Revival of Meiji Spirit in Modern Japan]* (Tendensha, Tokyo: 1997)

Paine, S, *The Sino-Japanese War of 1894–1895: Perceptions, Power and Primacy* (Cambridge University Press, New York: 2003)

Polak, C, *Soie et Lumières: L'âge d'or des échanges franco-japonais (des origins aux années 1950) [Silk and Lights: The Golden Age of Franco-Japanese Exchanges (from the beginning until the 1950s)]* (Hachette Fujigaho, Tokyo: 2002)

Rawlinson, J, *China's Struggle for Naval Development 1839–1895* (Harvard University Press, Cambridge, MA: 1967)

Regan, G, *Book of Naval Blunders* (Carlton, London: 2001)

Satow, E, *A Diplomat in Japan* (Stone Bridge Press, San Francisco: 2006)

Schencking, J, *Making Waves: Politics, Propaganda, and the Emergence of the Imperial Japanese Navy 1868–1922* (Stanford University Press, Stanford: 2005)

Selle, E, *Donald of China* (Harper and Brothers, New York: 1948)

Sharf, F, *et al.*, *A Much Recorded War: The Russo-Japanese War in History and Imagery* (Museum of Fine Arts, Boston: 2005)

Stafford, F, *The History of the 'Worcester': The Official Account of the Thames Nautical Training College, HMS Worcester 1862–1929* (Frederick Warne, London: 1929)

Suzuki, S (ed), *Nisshin Sensō Emaki [Pictures from the Sino-Japanese War]* (Shunyōdō, Tokyo: 1904)

'Tikovara, H', *Before Port Arthur in a Destroyer: The Personal Diary of a Japanese Naval Officer* (John Murray, London: 1907)

[Tōgō Gensui Hensankai], *Admiral Tōgō: A Memoir* (Tōgō Gensui Hensankai, Tokyo: 1934)

Toiviainen, H, *Search for Security: United States Citizens in the Far East, 1890–1906. A Comparative Study of Problems Related to Safeguarding Americans in China and Japan* (Studia Historia Jyväskyläensia 33, Jyväskylä: 1986)

Tyler, W, *Pulling Strings in China* (Constable, London: 1929)

Unger, F, *The Authentic History of the War Between Russia and Japan* (World Bible House, Philadelphia: 1905)

Villiers, F, *Port Arthur: Three Months with the Besiegers, a Diurnal of Occurrents* (Longmans, Green and Co., London: 1905)

'Vladimir' [Zenone Volpicelli], *The China-Japan War: Compiled from Japanese, Chinese and Foreign Sources* (Sampson Low, Marston and Company, London: 1896)

Walker, B, *The Conquest of Ainu Lands: Ecology and Culture in Japanese Expansion 1590–1800* (University of California Press, Berkeley: 2001)

Wells, D (ed), *Russian Views of Japan 1792–1913: An Anthology of Travel Writing* (Routledge/Curzon, London: 2004)

White, Colin, 'The Long Arm of Seapower: The Anglo-Japanese War of 1863–64' in Peter Hore (ed), *Seapower Ashore: 200 Years of Royal Navy Operations on Land* (Chatham Publishing, London: 2001)

Wright, H, *With Tōgō: The Story of Seven Months' Active Service Under His Command* (Hurst and Blackett, London: 1905)

Wright, R, *The Chinese Steam Navy 1862–1945* (Chatham Publishing, London: 2000)

Xie, Z, *Beiyang Haijun Ziliao Huibian [North China Sea Naval Data Collection]* (China National Library, Beijing: 1994)

Zhu, T, *Mazu to Chūgoku Minkan Shinkō [Mazu and Chinese Popular Religion]* (Hirakawa Shuppansha, Tokyo: 1996)

Acknowledgements

My wife, Kati Clements, has patiently lugged her camera across Japan, from Hakodate to Sendai to Yokosuka, in search of Tōgō relics. Lee Brimmicombe-Wood happily discussed old boilers and the logistics of 'raising steam', Frederik L Schodt pointed me at Henry Kiyama's 1904 recollections of Tōgō-mania, Matt Thorn took the trouble to send me wartime propaganda about Tōgō from the magazine *Housewife's Friend*, and Ellis Tinios dug up the Asan Sea episodes from *Nisshin Sensō Emaki*. The library of London's School of Oriental and African Studies has faithfully preserved many rare first-hand accounts of the Russo-Japanese War. I am also grateful to all at Haus Publishing, particularly Barbara Schwepcke, who bought this book, and Stephen Chumbley, who kept maritime matters ship-shape. Any remaining mistakes, of course, are mine.

Index

Picture Sources

The author and publishers wish to express their thanks to the following sources of illustrative material.

Akg-images, London. p: 148 ; Corbis. pp: 206, 226; Mary Evans Picture Library, pp: 170, 188; Topham Picturepoint. pp: 6, 24, 38, 54, 72, 90, 104, 118, 134.